C++ Core Guidelines Explained

Explained

C++ Core Guidelines Explained

Best Practices for Modern C++

Rainer Grimm

◆◆ Addison-Wesley

Boston • Columbus • New York • San Francisco • Amsterdam • Cape Town
Dubai • London • Madrid • Milan • Munich • Paris • Montreal • Toronto • Delhi • Mexico City
São Paulo • Sydney • Hong Kong • Seoul • Singapore • Taipei • Tokyo

Cover image: SVPanteon/Shutterstock
Author photo on page xxix: © Karin Ruider
Cippi illustrations on pages 3, 7, 15, 27, 53, 131, 139, 165, 213, 231, 279, 293, 301, 375, 383, 397: © Beatrix Jaud-Grimm
Figure 5.2: © Howard Hinnant
Figure 9.7: © Matt Godbolt
Figures 4.2, 4.3, 8.11, 9.11, 10.13, 10.16, 12.1, 16.9, A.1-A.4: © Microsoft Corporation 2021
Figures 3.1, 4.3-4.8, 5.2-5.20, 6.1, 7.1-7.4, 7.6, 7.7, 8.1-8.9, 8.11-8.14, 9.1-9.5, 10.5-10.11, 10.13, 10.14, 10.16, 10.17, 13.1-13.11,
    13.13-13.17, 13.24-13.27, 14.1-14.4, 15.1-15.4, 16.1-16.8, 18.1, 18.2, A.5, A.6: Screenshot of Konsole © KDE
Figures 10.2, 10.3: Screenshot of ThreadSanitizer © Google LLC

For information about buying this title in bulk quantities, or for special sales opportunities (which may include electronic versions; custom cover designs; and content particular to your business, training goals, marketing focus, or branding interests), please contact our corporate sales department at corpsales@pearsoned.com or (800) 382-3419.

For government sales inquiries, please contact governmentsales@pearsoned.com.

For questions about sales outside the U.S., please contact intlcs@pearson.com.

Visit us on the Web: informit.com

Library of Congress Control Number: 2022930162

ISBN-13: 978-0-13-687567-3
ISBN-10: 0-13-687567-X

1 2022

Contents

List of selected C++ Core Guidelines

List of figures

List of tables

Foreword

C++ is a very rich, very expressive language with lots of features. It has to be because a successful general-purpose programming language must have more facilities than any one developer needs, and a living and evolving language will accumulate alternative idioms for expressing an idea. That can lead to choice overload. So, what does a developer choose for programming style and mastery? How does a developer avoid getting stuck with outdated and ineffective techniques and programming styles?

The C++ Core Guidelines (https://github.com/isocpp/CppCoreGuidelines/blob/master/CppCoreGuidelines.md) are an ongoing open-source project to address such issues by gathering widely recognized modern C++ best practices together in one place. The Core Guidelines rely on decades of experience and earlier sets of coding rules. They share a conceptual framework with C++ itself, with a focus on type safety, resource safety, and the elimination of avoidable complexities and inefficiencies. The Core Guidelines are organized to address known problem areas and partly phrased to enable enforcement by a static analyzer.

The Core Guidelines are organized as a reference work to make it easy to look up and share specific topics, not as a tutorial to be read sequentially to learn themes for using modern C++ well. We are therefore very pleased to see Rainer Grimm applying his teaching skills and industrial background to tackle the hard and necessary task of making the rules accessible to more people. We hope that you find learning the Core Guidelines stimulating and, especially, that applying them to your real-world problems will make your work significantly more effective and more enjoyable.

Bjarne Stroustrup

Herb Sutter

Preface

This preface serves one purpose: to give you, dear reader, the necessary background to get the most out of this book. This background includes technical details about me, my writing style, my motivation for writing this book, and the challenges of writing such a book. If you want to skip this section, fine, but at least read the Acknowledgments section.

Conventions

I promise, only a few conventions.

Rules versus guidelines

The authors of the C++ Core Guidelines often refer to them as rules. So do I. In the context of this book, I use both terms interchangeably.

Special fonts

Bold	Sometimes I use bold font to emphasize important terms.
Italic	Italics designate hyperlinks (eBook only).
`Monospace`	Code, instructions, keywords, names of types, variables, functions, and classes are displayed in monospace font.

Boxes

I use boxes with a bullet list for the information concluding each chapter.

Related rules

Often rules are related to other rules. I provide this valuable information at the end of the chapter if necessary.

Distilled

Important

Get the essential information at the end of each chapter.

Source code

I dislike using directives and declarations because they hide the origin of the library functions. Due to the limited length of a page, I have to use them from time to time. I use them in such a way that the origin can always be deduced from the using directive (`using namespace std;`) or the using declaration (`using std::cout;`). Not all headers are displayed in the code snippets. Boolean values are displayed with `true` or `false`. The necessary I/O manipulator `std::boolalpha` is mostly not part of the code snippets.

Three dots (...) in the code snippets stand for missing code.

When I present a complete program as a code example, you will find the name of the source file in the first line of the code. I assume that you use a C++14 compiler. If the example needs C++17 or C++20 support, I mention the required C++ standard after the name.

I often use markers such as `// (1)` in the source file to ease my explanations. If possible, I write the marker in the cited line or, if not, one line before. The markers are not part of the more than 100 source files that are part of the book (available from https://github.com/RainerGrimm/CppCoreGuidelines). For layout reasons, I often adjusted the source code in this book.

When I use examples from the C++ Core Guidelines, I often rewrite them for readability by adding `namespace std` if it is missing, or unify the layout.

Why guidelines?

This subjective observation is mainly based on my more than 15 years of experience as a trainer for C++, Python, and software development in general. In the last few years, I was responsible for the team and the software deployed on defibrillators. My responsibility included regulatory affairs for our devices. Writing software for a defibrillator is extremely challenging because they can cause death or serious injury for the patient and the operator.

I have a question in mind that we should answer as a C++ community. This question is: Why do we need guidelines for modern C++? Here are my thoughts, which consist for simplicity reasons of three observations.

Complex for novices

C++ is, in particular for beginners, an inherently complex language. This is mainly because the problems we want to solve are inherently complicated and often complex as well. When you teach C++, you should provide a set of rules that work for your participants in at least 95% of all use cases. I think about rules such as

- Let the compiler deduce your types.
- Initialize with curly braces.
- Prefer tasks over threads.
- Use smart pointers instead of raw pointers.

I teach rules such as the ones mentioned in my seminars. We need a canon of best practices or rules in C++. These rules should be formulated positively and not negatively. They should declare how you should write code and not what should be avoided.

Challenging for professionals

I'm not worried about the sheer amount of new features that we get with each new C++ standard every three years. I'm worried about the new ideas that modern C++ supports. Think about event-driven programming with coroutines, lazy evaluation, infinite data streams, or function composition with the ranges library. Think about concepts, which introduce semantic categories to template parameters. It can be quite challenging to teach C programmers object-oriented ideas. When you shift, therefore, to these new paradigms, you have to rethink and presumably change the way you solve your programming challenges. I assume that this plethora of new ideas will, in particular, overwhelm professional programmers. They are the ones who are used to solving the problems with their classical techniques. With high probability, they fall into the *hammer-nail trap*.

Used in safety-critical software

In the end, I have a strong concern. In safety-critical software development, you often have to stick to guidelines. The most prominent are MISRA C++. The current MISRA C++:2008 guidelines were published by the *Motor Industry Software Reliability Association*. They are based on the *MISRA C guidelines* from the year 1998. Initially designed for the automotive industry, they became the de facto standard for the implementation of safety-critical software in the aviation, military, and medical sectors. As MISRA C, MISRA C++ describes guidelines for a safe subset of C++. But there is a conceptual problem. MISRA C++ is not state of the art for modern software development in C++. It's four standards behind! Here is an example: MISRA C++ doesn't allow operator overloading. I teach in my seminars that you should use user-defined literals to implement type-safe arithmetic: `auto constexpr dist = 4 * 5_m + 10_cm - 3_dm`. To implement such type-safe arithmetic, you have to overload the arithmetic operators and the literal operators for the suffixes. To be honest, I don't believe that MISRA C++ will ever evolve in lockstep with the current C++ standard. Only community-driven guidelines such as the C++ Core Guidelines can face this challenge.

MISRA C++ integrates AUTOSAR C++14

However, there is hope. MISRA C++ integrates AUTOSAR *C++14*. *AUTOSAR C++14* is based on C++14 and should become an extension of the MISRA C++ standard. I'm highly skeptical that organization-driven guidelines can keep in lockstep with the dynamics of modern C++.

My challenge

Let me share the essential lines of my e-mail discussion in May 2019 with Bjarne Stroustrup and Herb Sutter telling them that I wanted to write a book about the C++ Core Guidelines: "I'm an absolute fan of the value which is inside the C++ Core Guidelines because my strong belief is that we need guidelines for the correct/safe usage of modern C++. I often use examples or ideas from the C++ Core Guidelines in my C++ classes. The format reminds me of the MISRA C++ or AUTOSAR C++14 rules which is presumably intentional, but this is not the ideal format for a big audience. I think that more people would read and reason about the guidelines if we had a second document which describes the general ideas of the guidelines."

I want to add a few remarks to these previous conversations. In the last few years, I wrote on my German and English blogs more than a hundred posts about the C++ Core Guidelines. Additionally, I write for the German *Linux-Magazin* a series on the C++ Core Guidelines. I do this for two reasons: First, the C++ Core Guidelines should become better known, and second, I want to present them in a readable form, extended with background information if necessary.

Here is my challenge: The C++ Core Guidelines consist of over five hundred guidelines, most of the time just called rules. These rules are designed with static analysis in mind. Many of the rules are lifesaving for a professional C++ software developer, but also many of the rules are quite special, often incomplete or redundant, and sometimes the rules even contradict. My challenge is to boil these valuable rules down to a readable, even entertaining, story, removing the esoteric stuff and filling the gaps if necessary. In the end, the book should contain the rules that are mandatory for a professional software developer in C++.

Panta rhei

Panta rhei, or "everything flows," from the Greek philosopher *Heraclitus* stands for the challenge I'm faced with while writing this book. The C++ Core Guidelines are a *GitHub-hosted* project with more than 200 contributors. While I was writing this book, the source I was basing my writing on may have changed.

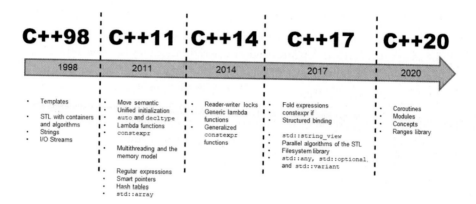

The guidelines already include C++ features, which may become part of an upcoming standard, such as contracts in C++23. To reflect this challenge, I made a few decisions.

1. I provide links in the electronic version of this book to the mentioned C++ Core Guidelines so you can quite easily refer to their origins.

2. My focus is on the C++17 standard. If appropriate, I include guidelines targeting the C++20 standard, such as concepts.

3. The C++ Core Guidelines evolve constantly, in particular as new C++ standards are published. So will this book. My plan is to update this book accordingly.

How to read this book

The structure of this book represents the structure of the C++ Core Guidelines. It has the corresponding major sections and parts of the supporting sections. In addition to the C++ Core Guidelines, I included appendixes, which provide concise overviews of missing topics, including C++20 or even C++23 features.

I still have not answered one question: how to read this book. Of course, you should start with the major sections, best from top to toe. The supporting sections provide additional information and introduce, in particular, the Guidelines Support Library. Use the appendixes as a kind of reference to get the necessary background information to understand the major sections. Without this additional information, this book would not be complete.

Register your copy of *C++ Core Guidelines Explained* on the InformIT site for convenient access to updates and/or corrections as they become available. To start the registration process, go to informit.com/register and log in or create an account. Enter the product ISBN (9780136875673) and click Submit. Look on the Registered Products tab for an Access Bonus Content link next to this product, and follow that link to access any available bonus materials. If you would like to be notified of exclusive offers on new editions and updates, please check the box to receive email from us.

Acknowledgments

First of all, I have to thank all contributors to the C++ Core Guidelines. The Core Guidelines are the work of about 250 contributors; the most prolific so far have been Herb Sutter, Bjarne Stroustrup, Gabriel Dos Reis, Sergey Zubkov, Jonathan Wakely, and Neil MacIntosh (Guidelines Support Library). If you want to know all other contributors, go to https://github.com/isocpp/CppCoreGuidelines/graphs/contributors.

Second, I want to thank my proofreaders very much. Without their help, the book would not have the quality it has now. Here are their names in alphabetic order: Yaser Afshar, Nicola Bombace, Sylvain Dupont, Fabio Fracassi, Juliette Grimm, Michael Möllney, Mateusz Nowak, Arthur O'Dwyer, and Moritz Strübe.

Third, many thanks to my wife, Beatrix Jaud-Grimm, for drawing the illustrations for this book.

About the author

I have worked as a software architect, team lead, and instructor since 1999. In 2002, I created a continuing education program at my company. I have given seminars since 2002. My first seminars were about proprietary management software, but seminars for Python and C++ followed immediately. In my spare time, I like to write articles about C++, Python, and Haskell. I also like to speak at conferences. I publish weekly in English and German on my blog *Modernes Cpp*, hosted by *Heise Developer*.

Since 2016, I have been an independent instructor giving seminars about modern C++ and Python. I have published several books in various languages about modern C++ and concurrency, in particular. Due to my profession, I always search for the best way to teach modern C++.

PART I

The Guidelines

Chapter 1

Introduction

Cippi learns the basics.

Before I dive into the details of the C++ Core Guidelines in the next chapters, I want to provide a short introduction.

Target readership

The target readership for the C++ Core Guidelines is all C++ programmers, including programmers who might consider C.

Aim

The rules of the guidelines promote modern C++ and aim to achieve a more uniform style. Of course, not all rules can be applied to legacy code in particular. This means you should apply these rules to new code but also to legacy code that is broken or has to be refactored. The focus is on type safety and resource safety. The rules are not just about "don't do that"; they are prescriptive and often checkable. Their design allows gradual adoption.

Non-aims

Now we know what the aim of the rules is. The non-aims are also interesting. The guidelines are not meant to be read serially or be a replacement for a tutorial. Additionally, they provide no recipes to convert old C++ to modern C++, nor are they so precise that you can follow them blindly, nor are they a safe subset of C++.

Enforcement

Without enforcement, the guidelines are not manageable in large code bases. For this reason, each rule has an enforcement section. The enforcement can be a code review, dynamic or static code analysis. Related rules are grouped into profiles. The C++ Core Guidelines define profiles to protect from type violations, bounds violations, and lifetime violations.

Structure

The rules follow a typical structure:

- **Reason:** rationale for the rule
- **Example:** code snippet, which shows good or bad code regarding the rule
- **Alternative:** alternative for a "don't do this" rule
- **Exception:** reasons to not apply the rule
- **Enforcement:** how the rule can be checked
- **See also:** references to other rules
- **Note:** additional notes to a rule
- **Discussion:** references to additional rationales or examples

Major sections

The C++ Core Guidelines consist of 16 major sections. I listed them for a short overview.

- Introduction
- Philosophy
- Interfaces
- Functions
- Classes and class hierarchies
- Enumerations
- Resource management
- Expressions and statements
- Performance
- Concurrency
- Error handling
- Constants and immutability
- Templates and generic programming
- C-style programming
- Source files
- The Standard Library

Distilled

Important

- The target readership is all C++ programmers.
- The aim of the C++ Core Guidelines is to adopt more modern C++ and to achieve a universal style.
- The rules are neither a tutorial nor precise enough to follow them blindly.
- Each rule has an enforcement section.

Chapter 2

Philosophy

Cippi thinks deeply.

The *philosophical rules* have a general focus and are, therefore, not checkable. The philosophical rules provide the rationale for the following concrete rules. Due to the fact that there are only 13 philosophical rules, I can cover all of them in this chapter.

Express ideas directly in code

A programmer should express their ideas directly in code because code can be checked by compilers and tools. The two following methods make this rule obvious.

```
class Date {
    // ...
public:
    Month month() const;  // do
    int month();          // don't
    // ...
};
```

The second member function `month()` expresses neither that it is constant nor that it returns a month. The same argument typically holds for loops such as `for` or `while` compared to the algorithms of the Standard Template Library (STL). The next code snippet makes my point.

```
int index = -1;                          // bad
for (int i = 0; i < v.size(); ++i) {
    if (v[i] == val) {
        index = i;
        break;
    }
}
```

```
auto it = std::find(begin(v), end(v), val); // better
```

A professional C++ developer should know the *algorithms of the STL*. By using them, you avoid the usage of explicit loops, and your code becomes easier to understand, easier to maintain, and therefore, less error prone. There is a proverb in modern C++: "When you use explicit loops, you don't know the algorithms of the STL."

P.2   Write in ISO Standard C++

Okay, this rule is a no-brainer. To get a portable C++ program, the rule is quite easy to understand. Use a current C++ standard without compiler extension. Additionally, be aware of undefined or implementation-defined behavior.

- **Undefined behavior:** All bets are off. Your program can produce the correct result or the wrong result, crashes during run time, or may not even compile. That behavior might change when porting to a new platform, when upgrading to a new compiler, or as a result of an unrelated code change.
- **Implementation-defined behavior:** The behavior of your program may vary between various implementations. The implementation must document each behavior.

When you have to use extensions that are not written in ISO Standard, encapsulate them in a stable interface.

Catch-fire semantics

There is a proverb in the C++ community describing undefined behavior. When your program has undefined behavior, your program has catch-fire semantics. This means your computer can catch fire.

P.3   Express intent

What intent can you derive from the following implicit and explicit loops?

```
for (const auto& v: vec) { ... }                        // (1)

for (auto& v: vec) { ... }                              // (2)

std::for_each(std::execution::par, vec, [](auto v) { ... }); // (3)
```

Loop (1) does not modify the elements of the container vec. This does not hold for the range-based for loop (2). The algorithm `std::for_each` (3) performs its job in parallel (`std::execution::par`). This means that we don't care in which order the elements are processed.

Expressing intent is also an important guideline for good documentation of your code. Documentation should state what should be done and not how it should be done.

P.4	Ideally, a program should be statically type safe

C++ is a statically typed language. Statically typed means that the type of the data is known to the compiler. Statically type safe additionally states that the compiler detects type errors. Due to existing problematic areas, this goal cannot always be achieved, but there is a cure for unions, casts, array decays, range errors, or narrowing conversions:

* With C++17, you can use *std::variant* as a type-safe replacement for a union.

* Generic code based on templates reduces the need for casting and, therefore, for type errors.

* Array decay happens when you invoke a function with a C-array. The function takes the array via a pointer to its first element and its length. This means you start with a type-rich data structure C-array and end with a type-poor pointer to its first element. The cure is part of C++20: *std::span*. *std::span* automatically deduces the size of a C-array and also protects you from range errors. If you don't have C++20, use the implementation provided by the Guidelines Support Library.

* Narrowing conversion is an implicit conversion of arithmetic values including a loss of accuracy.

  ```
  int i1(3.14);

  int i2 = 3.14;
  ```

  The compiler detects narrowing conversion if you use the { }-initializer syntax.

  ```
  int i1{3.14};

  int i2 = {3.14};
  ```

P.5	Prefer compile-time checking to run-time checking

What can be checked at compile time should be checked at compile time. This is idiomatic for C++. Since C++11, the language has supported static_assert. Thanks to static_assert, the compiler evaluates an expression such as static_assert(size(int) >= 4) and produces, eventually, a compiler error. Additionally, the type-traits library allows you to formulate powerful conditions: static_assert(std::is_integral<T>::value). When the expression in the static_assert call evaluates to false, the compiler writes a human-readable error message.

P.6	What cannot be checked at compile-time should be checkable at run-time

Thanks to the `dynamic_cast`, you can safely convert pointers and references to classes up, down, and sideways along the inheritance hierarchy. If the casting fails, you get back a `nullptr` in case of a pointer and a `std::bad_cast` exception in case of a reference. Read more details in the section `dynamic_cast` in Chapter 5.

P.7	Catch run-time errors early

Many countermeasures can be taken to get rid of run-time errors. As a programmer, you should take care of pointers and C-arrays by checking their range. Of course, the same holds for conversions, which should be avoided if possible, and of course, for narrowing conversions. Checking input also falls into this category.

P.8	Don't leak any resources

Resource leaks are, in particular, critical for long-running programs. A resource may be memory but also file handles or sockets. The idiomatic way to deal with resources is RAII. RAII stands for Resource Acquisition Is Initialization and means, essentially, that you acquire the resource in the constructor and release the resource in the destructor of a user-defined type. By making the object a scoped object, the C++ run time automatically takes care of the lifetime of the resource. C++ uses RAII heavily: Locks take care of mutexes, smart pointers take care of raw memory, or containers of the STL take care of the underlying elements.

P.9	Don't waste time or space

Saving time or space is a virtue. The reasoning is quite concise: This is C++. Do you spot the issues in the following loop?

```
void lower(std::string s) {
    for (unsigned int i = 0; i <= std::strlen(s.data()); ++i) {
        s[i] = std::tolower(s[i]);
    }
}
```

Using the algorithm `std::transform` from the STL makes a one-liner out of the previous function.

```
std::transform(s.begin(), s.end(), s.begin(),
               [](char c) { return std::tolower(c); });
```

In contrast to the function `lower`, the algorithm `std::transform` automatically determines the size of its string. Consequently, you don't have to specify the length of the string using `std::strlen`.

Here is another typical example, often found in production code. Declaring copy semantics (copy constructor and copy-assignment operator) for a user-defined data type suppresses the automatically defined move semantics (move constructor and move-assignment operator). Ultimately, the compiler can never use cheap move semantics if applicable but always relies on expensive copy semantics.

```
struct S {
    std::string s_;
    S(std::string s): s_(s) {}
    S(const S& rhs): s_(rhs.s_) {}
    S& operator = (const S& rhs) { s_ = rhs.s_; return *this; }
};

S s1;
S s2 = std::move(s1); // makes a copy instead of moving from s1.s_
```

If these examples scare you, read more in the section Default Operations in Chapter 5.

P.10	Prefer immutable data to mutable data

There are many reasons to use immutable data. First, it is easier to verify your code when you use constants. Constants also have higher optimization potential. But first and foremost, constants provide a big advantage in concurrent programs. Constant data is data-race free by design because mutation is a necessary condition for a data race.

P.11	Encapsulate messy constructs, rather than spreading through the code

Messy code is often low-level code, which hides bugs and is, therefore, error prone. If possible, replace your messy code with a high-level construct from the STL such as a container or algorithms of the STL. If this is not possible, encapsulate the messy code in a user-defined type or a function.

P.12	Use supporting tools as appropriate

Computers are better than humans at doing boring and repetitive tasks. That means that you should use static analysis tools, concurrency tools, and testing tools to automate these verifying steps. Compiling your code with more than one C++ compiler is often the easiest way to verify your code. An undefined behavior that may not be detected by one compiler may cause another compiler to emit a warning or produce an error.

P.13	Use support libraries as appropriate

That is quite easy to explain. You should go for well-designed, well-documented, and well-supported libraries. You will get a well-tested and nearly error-free library and highly optimized algorithms from the domain experts. Outstanding examples are the C++ standard library, the Guidelines Support Library, and the *Boost* libraries.

Distilled

Important

- The philosophical rules (or meta-rules) provide rationales for the concrete rules. Ideally, the concrete rules can be derived from the philosophical rules.
- Express intent and ideas directly in code.
- Write in ISO Standard C++ and use support libraries and supporting tools.
- A program should be statically type safe and should, therefore, be checkable at compile time. When this is not possible, catch run-time errors early.
- Don't waste resources such as space or time.
- Encapsulate messy constructs behind a stable interface.

Chapter 3

Interfaces

Cippi assembles components.

An interface is a contract between a service provider and a service user. *Interfaces* are, according to the C++ Core Guidelines, "probably the most important single aspect of code organization." The section on interfaces has about twenty rules. Four of the rules are related to contracts, which didn't make it into the C++20 standard.

A few rules related to interfaces involve contracts, which may be part of C++23. A contract specifies preconditions, postconditions, and invariants for functions that can be checked at run time. Due to the uncertainty of the future, I ignore these rules. The appendix provides a short introduction to contracts.

Let me end this introduction with my favorite quote from Scott Meyers:

Make interfaces easy to use correctly and hard to use incorrectly.

I.2 Avoid non-const global variables

Of course, you should avoid non-const global variables. But why? Why is a global variable, in particular when it is non-constant, bad? A global injects a hidden dependency into the function, which is not part of the interface. The following code snippet makes my point:

```
int glob{2011};

int multiply(int fac) {
    glob *= glob;
    return glob * fac;
}
```

The execution of the function `multiply` changes, as a side effect, the value of the global variable `glob`. Therefore, you cannot test the function or reason about the function in isolation. When more threads use `multiply` concurrently, you have to protect the variable `glob`. There are more drawbacks to non-const global variables. If the function `multiply` had no side effects, you could have stored the previous result and reused the cached value for performance reasons.

The curse of non-**const** global variables

Using non-const globals has many drawbacks. First and foremost, non-const globals break encapsulation. This breaking of encapsulation makes it impossible to think about your functions/classes (entities) in isolation. The following bullet points enumerate the main drawbacks of non-const global variables.

- **Testability:** You cannot test your entities in isolation. There are no units, and therefore, there is no unit testing. You can only perform system testing. The effect of your entities depends on the state of the entire system.

- **Refactoring:** It is quite challenging to refactor your code because you cannot reason about your code in isolation.

- **Optimization:** You cannot easily rearrange the function invocations or perform the function invocations on different threads because there may be hidden dependencies. It's also extremely dangerous to cache previous results of function calls.

- **Concurrency:** The necessary condition for having a data race is a shared, mutable state. Non-const global variables are shared and mutable.

I.3   Avoid singletons

Sometimes, global variables are very well disguised.

```cpp
// singleton.cpp

class MySingleton {

public:
    MySingleton(const MySingleton&)= delete;
    MySingleton& operator = (const MySingleton&)= delete;

    static MySingleton* getInstance() {
      if ( !instance ){
        instance= new MySingleton();
      }
      return instance;
    }

private:
    static MySingleton* instance;
    MySingleton()= default;
    ~MySingleton()= default;
};

MySingleton* MySingleton::instance= nullptr;


int main() {

  std::cout << MySingleton::getInstance() << "\n";
```

```
    std::cout << MySingleton::getInstance() << "\n";

}
```

A singleton is just a global, and you should, therefore, *avoid singletons*, if possible. A singleton gives the straightforward guarantee that only one instance of a class exists. As a global, a singleton injects a dependency, which ignores the interface of a function. This is due to the fact that singletons as static variables are typically invoked directly: `Singleton::getInstance()` as shown in the two lines of the main function. The direct invocation of the singleton has a few serious consequences. You cannot *unit test* a function having a singleton because there is no unit. Additionally, you cannot fake your singleton and replace it during run time because the singleton is not part of the function interface. To make it short: Singletons break the testability of your code.

Implementing a singleton seems like a piece of cake but is not. You are faced with a few challenges:

- Who is responsible for destroying the singleton?
- Should it be possible to derive from the singleton?
- How can you initialize a singleton in a thread-safe way?
- In which sequence are singletons initialized when they depend on each other and are in different translation units? This is to scare you. This challenge is called the *static initialization order problem*.

The bad reputation of the singleton is, in particular, due to an additional fact. Singletons were heavily overused. I see programs that consist entirely of singletons. There are no objects because the developer wants to prove that they apply design patterns.

Dependency injection as a cure

When an object uses a singleton, it injects a hidden dependency into the object. Thanks to dependency injection, this dependency is part of the interface, and the service is injected from the outside. Consequently, there is no dependency between the client and the injected service. Typical ways to inject dependencies are constructors, setter members, or template parameters.

The following program shows how you can replace a logger using dependency injection.

```cpp
// dependencyInjection.cpp

#include <chrono>
#include <iostream>
#include <memory>

class Logger {
public:
    virtual void write(const std::string&) = 0;
    virtual ~Logger() = default;
};

class SimpleLogger: public Logger {
    void write(const std::string& mess) override {
        std::cout << mess << std::endl;
    }
};

class TimeLogger: public Logger {
    using MySecondTick = std::chrono::duration<long double>;
    long double timeSinceEpoch() {
        auto timeNow = std::chrono::system_clock::now();
        auto duration = timeNow.time_since_epoch();
        MySecondTick sec(duration);
        return sec.count();
    }
    void write(const std::string& mess) override {
        std::cout << std::fixed;
        std::cout << "Time since epoch: " << timeSinceEpoch()
    }

};

class Client {
public:
    Client(std::shared_ptr<Logger> log): logger(log) {}
    void doSomething() {
        logger->write("Message");
    }
    void setLogger(std::shared_ptr<Logger> log) {
        logger = log;
    }
```

```
private:
    std::shared_ptr<Logger> logger;
};


int main() {

    std::cout << '\n';

    Client cl(std::make_shared<SimpleLogger>());       // (1)
    cl.doSomething();
    cl.setLogger(std::make_shared<TimeLogger>());     // (2)
    cl.doSomething();
    cl.doSomething();

    std::cout << '\n';

}
```

The client `cl` supports the constructor (1) and the member function `setLogger` (2) to inject the logger service. In contrast to the `SimpleLogger`, the `TimeLogger` includes the time since epoch in its message (see Figure 3.1).

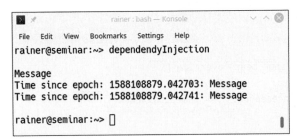

Figure 3.1 *Dependency injection*

Making good interfaces

Functions should not communicate via global variables but through interfaces. Now we are in the core of this chapter. According to the C++ Core Guidelines, here are the recommendations for interfaces. Interfaces should follow these rules:

- Make interfaces explicit (I.1).
- Make interfaces precise and strongly typed (I.4).

- Keep the number of function arguments low (I.23).

- Avoid adjacent unrelated parameters of the same type (I.24).

The first function `showRectangle` breaks all mentioned rules for interfaces:

```
void showRectangle(double a, double b, double c, double d) {
    a = floor(a);
    b = ceil(b);


    ...

}
```

```
void showRectangle(Point top_left, Point bottom_right);
```

Although the first function `showRectangle` should show only a rectangle, it modifies its arguments. Essentially, it has two purposes and has, as a consequence, a misleading name (I.1). Additionally, the function signature does not provide any information about what the arguments should be, nor in which sequence the arguments must be given (I.23 and I.24). Furthermore, the arguments are doubles without a constraint value range. This constraint must, therefore, be established in the function body (I.4). In contrast, the second function `showRectangle` takes two concrete points. Checking to see if a `Point` has valid value is the job of the constructor of `Point`. This responsibility should not be the job of the function.

I want to elaborate more on the rules *I.23* and *I.24* and the function *std::transform_reduce* from the Standard Template Library (STL). First, I need to define the term callable. A callable is something that behaves like a function. This can be a function but also a function object, or a lambda expression. If a callable accepts one argument, it is called a unary callable; if it takes two arguments, it is called a binary callable.

`std::transform_reduce` first applies a unary callable to one range or a binary callable to two ranges and then a binary callable to the resulting range. When you use `std::transform_reduce` with a unary lambda expression, the call is easy to use correctly:

```
std::vector<std::string> strVec{"Only", "for", "testing", "purpose"};

std::size_t res = std::transform_reduce(
        std::execution::par,
        strVec.begin(), strVec.end(),
        0,
        [](std::size_t a, std::size_t b) { return a + b; },
```

```
    [](std::string s) { return s.size(); }
);
```

The function `std::transform_reduce` transforms each string onto its length (`[]
(const std::string s) { return s.size(); }`) and applies the binary callable (`[]
(std::size_t a, std::size_t b) { return a + b; }`) to the resulting range. The
initial value for the summation is 0. The whole calculation is performed in parallel:
`std::execution::par`.

When you use the overload, which accepts two binary callables, the declaration of
the function becomes quite complicated and error prone. Consequently, it breaks the
rules *I.23* and *I.24*.

```
template<class ExecutionPolicy,
         class ForwardIt1, class ForwardIt2, class T,
         class BinaryOp1, class BinaryOp2>
T transform_reduce(ExecutionPolicy&& policy,
                   ForwardIt1 first1, ForwardIt1 last1,
                   ForwardIt2 first2,
                   T init, BinaryOp1 binary_op1, BinaryOp2 binary_op2);
```

Calling this overload would require six template arguments and seven function arguments. Using the binary callables in the correct sequence may also be a challenge.

```
transform | reduce
```

The main reason for the complicated function `std::transform_reduce` is that two
functions are combined into one. Defining two separate functions `transform` and
`reduce` and supporting function composition via the pipe operator would be a better
choice: `transform | reduce`.

I.13   Do not pass an array as a single pointer

The guideline that you should not pass an array as a single pointer is special. I can
tell you from experience that this rule is a common cause of undefined behavior. For
instance, the function copy_n is quite error prone.

```
template <typename T>
void copy_n(const T* p, T* q, int n); // copy from [p:p+n) to [q:q+n)

...
```

```
int a[100] = {0, };
int b[100] = {0, };

copy_n(a, b, 101);
```

Maybe you had an exhausting day and you miscounted by one. The result is an off-by-one error and, therefore, undefined behavior. The cure is simple. Use a container from the STL such as std::vector and check the size of the container in the function body. C++20 offers std::span, which solves this issue more elegantly. A std::span is an object that can refer to a contiguous sequence of objects. A std::span is never an owner. This contiguous memory can be an array, a pointer with a size, or a std::vector.

```
template <typename T>
void copy(std::span<const T> src, std::span<T> des);

int arr1[] = {1, 2, 3};
int arr2[] = {3, 4, 5};


...


copy(arr1, arr2);
```

copy doesn't need the number of elements. Hence, a common cause of errors is eliminated with std::span<T>.

I.27   For stable library ABI, consider the Pimpl idiom

An application binary interface (ABI) is the interface between two binary programs.

Thanks to the PImpl idiom, you can isolate the users of a class from its implementation and, therefore, avoid recompilation. PImpl stands for pointer to implementation and is a programming technique in C++ that removes implementation details from a class by placing them in a separate class. This separate class is accessed by a pointer. This is done because private data members participate in class layout and private member functions participate in overload resolution. These dependencies mean that changes to those implementation details require recompilation of all users of a class. A class holding a pointer to implementation (PImpl) can isolate the users of a class from changes in its implementation at the cost of an indirection.

The C++ Core Guidelines show a typical implementation.

- **Interface:** `Widget.h`

```cpp
class Widget {
    class impl;
    std::unique_ptr<impl> pimpl;
 public:
    void draw(); // public API that will be forwarded
                 // to the implementation
    Widget(int); // defined in the implementation file
    ~Widget();   // defined in the implementation file,
                 // where impl is a complete type
    Widget(Widget&&) = default;
    Widget(const Widget&) = delete;
    Widget& operator = (Widget&&); // defined in the
                                   // implementation file
    Widget& operator = (const Widget&) = delete;
};
```

- **Implementation:** `Widget.cpp`

```cpp
class Widget::impl {
    int n; // private data
 public:
    void draw(const Widget& w) { /* ... */ }
    impl(int n) : n(n) {}
};
void Widget::draw() { pimpl->draw(*this); }
Widget::Widget(int n) : pimpl{std::make_unique<impl>(n)} {}
Widget::~Widget() = default;
Widget& Widget::operator = (Widget&&) = default;
```

cppreference.com provides more information about the PImpl idiom. Additionally, the rule "C.129: When designing a class hierarchy, distinguish between implementation inheritance and interface inheritance" shows how to apply the PImpl idiom to dual inheritance.

Related rules

I present the rule "I.10: Use exceptions to signal a failure to perform a required task" in Chapter 11, Error Handling, the rule "I.11: Never transfer ownership by a raw pointer (T*) or reference (T&)" in Chapter 4, Functions, the rule "I.22: Avoid complex initialization of global objects" in Chapter 8, Expressions and Statements, and the rule "I.25: Prefer abstract classes as interfaces to class hierarchies" in Chapter 5, Classes and Class Hierarchies.

Distilled

Important

- Don't use global variables. They introduce hidden dependencies.
- Singletons are global variables in disguise.
- Interfaces and in particular functions should express their intent.
- Interfaces should be strongly typed and have few arguments that cannot be easily confused.
- Don't take a C-array by pointer but use a `std::span`.
- If you want to separate the users of a class from its implementation, use the PImpl idiom.

Chapter 4

Functions

Cippi uses functions to solve the challenge.

Software developers master complexity by dividing complex tasks into smaller units. After the small units are addressed, they put the smaller units together to master the complex task. A function is a typical unit and, therefore, the basic building block for a program. Functions are "the most critical part in most interfaces . . ." (C++ Core Guidelines about functions).

The C++ Core Guidelines have about forty rules for functions. They provide valuable information on the definition of functions, how you should pass the arguments (e.g., by copy or by reference), and what that means for the ownership semantics. They also state rules about the semantics of the return value and other functions such as lambdas. Let's dive into them.

Function definitions

Presumably, the most important principle for good software is good names. This principle is often ignored and holds true in particular for functions.

Good names

The C++ Core Guidelines dedicate the first three rules to good names: "F.1: 'Package' meaningful operations as carefully named functions," "F.2: A function should perform a single logical operation," and "F.3: Keep functions short and simple."

Let me start with a short anecdote. A few years ago, a software developer asked me, "How should I call my function?" I told him to give the function a name such as verbObject. In case of a member function, a verb may be fine because the function already operates on an object. The verb stands for the operation that is performed on the object. The software developer replied that this is not possible; the function must be called getTimeAndAddToPhonebook or just processData because the functions perform more than one job (single-responsibility principle). When you don't find a meaningful name for your function (F.1), that's a strong indication that your function does more than one logical operation (F.2) and that your function isn't short and simple (F.3). A function is too long if it does not fit on a screen. A screen means roughly 60 lines by 140 characters, but your measure may differ. Now you should identify the operations of the function and package these operations into carefully named functions.

The guidelines present an example of a bad function:

```
void read_and_print() {    // bad
    int x;
    std::cin >> x;
    // check for errors
    std::cout << x << '\n';
}
```

The function `read_and_print` is bad for many reasons. The function is tied to a specific input and output and cannot be used in a different context. Refactoring the function into two functions solves these issues and makes it easier to test and to maintain:

```
int read(std::istream& is) {  // better
    int x;
    is >> x;
    // check for errors
    return x;
}

void print(std::ostream& os, int x) {
    os << x << '\n';
}
```

F.4   **If a function may have to be evaluated at compile-time, declare it `constexpr`**

A `constexpr` function is a function that has the potential to run at compile time. When you invoke a `constexpr` function within a constant expression, or you take the result of a `constexpr` with a `constexpr` variable, it runs at compile time. You can invoke a `constexpr` function with arguments that can be evaluated only at run time, too. `constexpr` functions are implicit `inline`.

The result of `constexpr` evaluated at compile time is stored in the ROM (read-only memory). Performance is, therefore, the first big benefit of a `constexpr` function. The second is that `constexpr` functions evaluated at compile time are const and, therefore, thread safe.

Finally, a result of the calculation is made available at run time as a constant in ROM.

```
// constexpr.cpp

constexpr auto gcd(int a, int b) {
    while (b != 0) {
        auto t = b;
        b = a % b;
        a = t;
    }
    return a;
```

```
}

int main() {

    constexpr int i = gcd(11, 121);    // (1)

    int a = 11;
    int b = 121;
    int j = gcd(a, b);                 // (2)

}
```

Figure 4.1 shows the output of Compiler Explorer and depicts the assembly code generated by the compiler for this function. I used the Microsoft Visual Studio Compiler 19.22 without optimization.

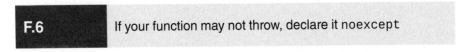

```
32   main    PROC
33   $LN3:
34           sub     rsp, 56                      ; 00000038H
35           mov     DWORD PTR i$[rsp], 11
36           mov     DWORD PTR a$[rsp], 11
37           mov     DWORD PTR b$[rsp], 121       ; 00000079H
38           mov     edx, DWORD PTR b$[rsp]
39           mov     ecx, DWORD PTR a$[rsp]
40           call    int gcd(int,int)             ; gcd
41           mov     DWORD PTR j$[rsp], eax
42           xor     eax, eax
43           add     rsp, 56                      ; 00000038H
44           ret     0
45   main    ENDP
```

Figure 4.1 *Assembler instructions to the program* constexpr.cpp

Based on the colors, you can see that (1) in the source code corresponds to line 35 in the assembler instructions and (2) in the source code corresponds to lines 38–41 in the assembler instructions. The call constexpr int i = gcd(11, 121); boils down to the value 11, but the call int j = gcd(a, b); results in a function call.

F.6 If your function may not throw, declare it noexcept

By declaring a function as noexcept, you reduce the number of alternative control paths; therefore, noexcept is a valuable hint to the optimizer. Even if your function can throw, noexcept often makes much sense. noexcept means in this case: I don't care. The reason may be that you have no way to react to an exception. Therefore, the only way to deal with exceptions is to invoke std::terminate(). This noexcept declaration is also a piece of valuable information for the reader of your code.

The next function just crashes if it runs out of memory.

```
std::vector<std::string> collect(std::istream& is) noexcept {
    std::vector<std::string> res;
    for (std::string s; is >> s;) {
        res.push_back(s);
    }
    return res;
}
```

The following types of functions should never throw: destructors (see the section Failing Destructor in Chapter 5), swap functions, move operations, and default constructors.

F.8   Prefer pure functions

Pure functions are functions that always return the same result when given the same arguments. This property is also called referential transparency. Pure functions behave like infinite big lookup tables.

The function template square is a pure function:

```
template<class T>
auto square(T t) {
    return t * t;
}
```

Conversely, impure functions are functions such as random() or time(), which can return a different result from call to call. To put it another way, functions that interact with state outside the function body are impure.

Pure functions have a few very interesting properties. You should, therefore, prefer pure functions, if possible.

Pure functions can

- Be tested in isolation
- Be verified or refactorized in isolation

- Cache their result
- Automatically be reordered or be executed on other threads

Pure functions are also often called mathematical functions. Functions in C++ are by default not pure such as in the pure functional programming language Haskell. Using pure functions is based on the discipline of the programmer. constexpr functions are pure when evaluated at compile time. Template metaprogramming is a pure functional language embedded in the imperative language C++.

Chapter 13, Templates and Generic Programming, gives a concise introduction to programming at compile time, including template metaprogramming.

Parameter passing: in and out

The C++ Core Guidelines have a few rules to express various ways to pass parameters in and out of functions.

| F.15 | Prefer simple and conventional ways of passing information |

The first rule presents the big picture. First, it provides an overview of the various ways to pass information in and out of a function (see Table 4.1).

Table 4.1 *Normal parameter passing*

	Cheap to copy or impossible to copy	Cheap to move or moderate cost to move or don't know	Expensive to move
In	func(X)	func(const X&)	
In & retain "copy"			
In/Out	func(X&)		
Out	X func()		func(X&)

The table is very concise: The headings describe the characteristics of the data regarding the cost of copying and moving. The rows indicate the direction of parameter passing.

- Kind of data

  - **Cheap to copy or impossible to copy:** int or std::unique_ptr

- **Cheap to move:** `std::vector<T>` or `std::string`

- **Moderate cost to move:** `std::array<std::vector>` or `BigPOD` (POD stands for Plain Old Data—that is, a class without constructors, destructors, and virtual member functions.)

- **Don't know:** template

- **Expensive to move:** `BigPOD[]` or `std::array<BigPOD>`

- Direction of parameter passing

  - **In:** input parameter

  - **In & retain "copy":** caller retains its copy

  - **In/Out:** parameter that is modified

  - **Out:** output parameter

A cheap operation is an operation with a few `ints`; moderate cost is about one thousand bytes without memory allocation.

These normal parameter passing rules should be your first choice. However, there are also advanced parameter passing rules (see Table 4.2). Essentially, the case with the "in & move from" semantics was added.

Table 4.2 *Advanced parameter passing*

	Cheap to copy or impossible to copy	Cheap to move or moderate cost to move or don't know	Expensive to move
In	`func(X)`	`func(constX&)`	
In & retain "copy"			
In & move from	`func(X&&)`		
In/Out	`func(X&)`		
Out	`X func()`		`func(X&)`

After the "in & move from" call, the argument is in the so-called moved-from state. Moved-from means that it is in a valid but not nearer specified state. Essentially, you have to initialize the moved-from object before using it again.

The remaining rules to parameter passing provide the necessary background information for these tables.

F.16	For "in" parameters, pass cheaply-copied types by value and others by reference to `const`

The rule is straightforward to follow. Input values should be copied by default if possible. When they cannot be cheaply copied, take them by const reference. The C++ Core Guidelines give a rule of thumb to the question, Which objects are cheap to copy or expensive to copy?

- You should pass a parameter par by value if `sizeof(par) < 3 * sizeof(void*)`.
- You should pass a parameter par by const reference if `sizeof(par) > 3 * sizeof(void*)`.

```cpp
void f1(const std::string& s);   // OK: pass by reference to const;
                                 // always cheap

void f2(std::string s);          // bad: potentially expensive

void f3(int x);                  // OK: unbeatable

void f4(const int& x);           // bad: overhead on access in f4()
```

F.19	For "forward" parameters, pass by TP&& and only `std::forward` the parameter

This rule stands for a special input value. Sometimes you want to forward the parameter par. This means an lvalue is copied and an rvalue is moved. Therefore, the constness of an lvalue is ignored and the rvalueness of an rvalue is preserved.

The typical use case for forwarding parameters is a factory function that creates an arbitrary object by invoking its constructor. You do not know if the arguments are rvalues nor do you know how many arguments the constructor needs.

```cpp
// forwarding.cpp

#include <string>
```

```
#include <utility>

template <typename T, typename ... T1>   // (1)
T create(T1&& ... t1) {
    return T(std::forward<T1>(t1)...);
}

struct MyType {
    MyType(int, double, bool) {}
};

int main() {

    // lvalue
    int five=5;
    int myFive= create<int>(five);

    // rvalues
    int myFive2= create<int>(5);

    // no arguments
    int myZero= create<int>();

    // three arguments; (lvalue, rvalue, rvalue)
    MyType myType = create<MyType>(myZero, 5.5, true);

}
```

The three dots (ellipsis) in the function create (1) denote a parameter pack. We call a template using a parameter pack a variadic template.

Packing and unpacking of the parameter pack

When the ellipsis is on the left of the type parameter T1, the parameter pack is packed; when on the right, it is unpacked. This unpacking in the return statement T(std::forward<T1>(t1)...) essentially means that the expression std::forward<T1>(t1) is repeated until all arguments of the parameter pack are consumed and a comma is put between each subexpression. For the curious, C++ Insights shows this unpacking process.

The combination of forwarding together with variadic templates is the typical creation pattern in C++. Here is a possible implementation of `std::make_unique<T>`.

```
template<typename T, typename... Args>
std::unique_ptr<T> make_unique(Args&&... args) {
    return std::unique_ptr<T>(new T(std::forward<Args>(args)...));
}
std::make_unique<T> creates a std::unique_ptr for T
```

F.17   For "in-out" parameters, pass by reference to non-`const`

The rule communicates its intention to the caller: This function modifies its argument.

```
std::vector<int> myVec{1, 2, 3, 4, 5};

void modifyVector(std::vector<int>& vec) {
    vec.push_back(6);
    vec.insert(vec.end(), {7, 8, 9, 10});
}
```

F.20   For "out" output values, prefer return values to output parameters

The rule is straightforward. Just return the value, but don't use a `const` value because it has no added value and interferes with move semantics. Maybe you think that copying a value is an expensive operation. Yes and no. Yes, you are right, but no, the compiler applies RVO (Return Value Optimization) or NRVO (Named Return Value Optimization). RVO means that the compiler is allowed to remove unnecessary copy operations. What was a possible optimization step becomes in C++17 a guarantee.

```
MyType func() {
    return MyType{};        // no copy with C++17
}
MyType myType = func();     // no copy with C++17
```

Two unnecessary copy operations can happen in these few lines, the first in the return call and the second in the function call. With C++17, no copy operation takes place. If the return value has a name, we call it NRVO. Maybe you guessed that.

```cpp
MyType func() {
    MyType myValue;
    return myValue;             // one copy allowed
}
MyType myType = func();         // no copy with C++17
```

The subtle difference is that the compiler can still copy the value `myValue` in the return statement according to C++17. But no copy will take place in the function call.

Often, a function has to return more than one value. Here, the rule F.21 kicks in.

F.21	To return multiple "out" values, prefer returning a struct or tuple

When you insert a value into a `std::set`, overloads of the member function `insert` return a `std::pair` of an iterator to the inserted element and a `bool` set to `true` if the insertion was successful. std::tie with C++11 or structured binding with C++17 are two elegant ways to bind both values to a variable.

```cpp
// returnPair.cpp; C++17

#include <iostream>
#include <set>
#include <tuple>

int main() {

    std::cout << '\n';

    std::set<int> mySet;

    std::set<int>::iterator iter;
    bool inserted = false;
    std::tie(iter, inserted) = mySet.insert(2011); // (1)
    if (inserted) std::cout << "2011 was inserted successfully\n";

    auto [iter2, inserted2] = mySet.insert(2017);  // (2)
```

```
    if (inserted2) std::cout << "2017 was inserted successfully\n";

    std::cout << '\n';

}
```

Line (1) uses `std::tie` to unpack the return value of insert into `iter` and `inserted`. Line (2) uses structured binding to unpack the return value of insert into `iter2` and `inserted2`. `std::tie` needs, in contrast to structured binding, a predeclared variable. See Figure 4.2.

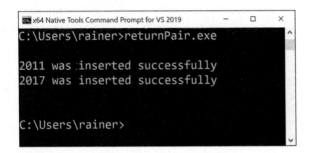

Figure 4.2 *Returning a std::pair*

Parameter passing: ownership semantics

The last section was about the flow of parameters: which parameters are input, input/output, or output values. But there is more to arguments than the direction of the flow. Passing parameters is about ownership semantics. This section presents five typical ways to pass parameters: by copy, by pointer, by reference, by `std::unique_ptr`, or by `std::shared_ptr`. Only the rules to smart pointers are inside this section. The rule to pass by copy is part of the previous section Parameter Passing: In and Out, and the rules to pointers and references are part of Chapter 3, Interfaces.

Table 4.3 provides the first overview.

Table 4.3 *Ownership semantics of parameter passing*

Example	Ownership	Rule
`func(value)`	func is a single owner of the resource.	F.16
`func(pointer*)`	func has borrowed the resource.	I.11 and F.7
`func(reference&)`	func has borrowed the resource.	I.11 and F.7
`func(std::unique_ptr)`	func is a single owner of the resource.	F.26
`func(std::shared_ptr)`	func is a shared owner of the resource.	F.27

Here are more details:

- **func(value):** The function func has its own copy of the value and is its owner. func automatically releases the resource.

- **func(pointer*):** func has borrowed the resource and is, therefore, not authorized to delete the resource. func has to check before each usage that the pointer is not a null pointer.

- **func(reference&):** func has borrowed the resource. In contrast to the pointer, the reference always has a valid value.

- **func(std::unique_ptr):** func is the new owner of the resource. The caller of the func has explicitly transferred the ownership of the resource to the callee. func automatically releases the resource.

- **func(std::shared_ptr):** func is an additional owner of the resource. func extends the lifetime of the resource. At the end of func, func ends its ownership of the resource. This end causes the release of the resource if func was the last owner.

Who is the owner?

It's very important to indicate ownership clearly. Just imagine that your program is written in legacy C++, and you have only a raw pointer at your disposal to express the four kinds of ownership by pointer, by reference, by std::unique_ptr, or by std::shared_ptr. The key question in legacy C++ is, Who is the owner?

The following code snippet makes my point:

```
void func(double* ptr) {
   ...
}


double* ptr = new double[];
func(ptr);
```

The critical question is, Who is the owner of the resource? The callee of func that uses the array, or the caller of the func that created the array? If func is the owner, it has to release the resource. If not, func is not allowed to release the resource. This condition is not satisfactory. If func does not release the resource, a memory leak may happen. If func does release the resource, undefined behavior may be the result.

In consequence, ownership needs to be documented. Defining the contract using the type system in modern C++ is a big step in the right direction to eliminate this ambiguity in documentation.

Using std::move on application level is not about moving. Using std::move on application level is about the transfer of ownership—for example, applying std::move to a std::unique_ptr transfers the ownership of the memory to another std::unique_ptr. The smart pointer uniquePtr1 is the original owner, but uniquePtr2 becomes the new owner.

```
auto uniquePtr1 = std::make_unique<int>(2011);
std::unique_ptr<int> uniquePtr2{ std::move(uniquePtr1) };
```

Here are five variants of ownership semantics in practice.

```
1  // ownershipSemantic.cpp
2
3  #include <iostream>
4  #include <memory>
5  #include <utility>
6
7  class MyInt {
8  public:
9      explicit MyInt(int val): myInt(val) {}
10     ~MyInt() noexcept {
11         std::cout << myInt << '\n';
12     }
13 private:
14     int myInt;
15 };
16
17 void funcCopy(MyInt myInt) {}
18 void funcPtr(MyInt* myInt) {}
19 void funcRef(MyInt& myInt) {}
20 void funcUniqPtr(std::unique_ptr<MyInt> myInt) {}
21 void funcSharedPtr(std::shared_ptr<MyInt> myInt) {}
22
23 int main() {
24
25     std::cout << '\n';
26
27     std::cout <<  "=== Begin" << '\n';
28
29     MyInt myInt{1998};
```

```
30      MyInt* myIntPtr = &myInt;
31      MyInt& myIntRef = myInt;
32      auto uniqPtr = std::make_unique<MyInt>(2011);
33      auto sharedPtr = std::make_shared<MyInt>(2014);
34
35      funcCopy(myInt);
36      funcPtr(myIntPtr);
37      funcRef(myIntRef);
38      funcUniqPtr(std::move(uniqPtr));
39      funcSharedPtr(sharedPtr);
40
41      std::cout << "==== End" << '\n';
42
43      std::cout << '\n';
44
45 }
```

The type `MyInt` displays in its destructor (lines 10–12) the value of `myInt` (line 14). The five functions in the lines 17–21 implement each of the ownership semantics. The lines 29–33 have the corresponding values. See Figure 4.3.

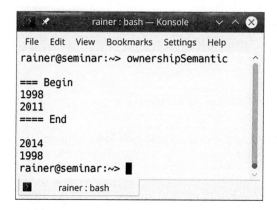

Figure 4.3 *The five ownership semantics*

The screenshot shows that two destructors are called before and two destructors are called at the end of the `main` function. The destructors of the copied `myInt` (line 35) and the moved `uniquePtr` (line 38) are called before the end of `main`. In both cases, `funcCopy` or `funcUniqPtr` becomes the owner of the resource. The lifetime of the functions ends before the lifetime of `main`. This end of the lifetime does not hold for the original `myInt` (line 29) and the `sharedPtr` (line 33). Their lifetime ends with `main`, and therefore, the destructor is called at the end of the `main` function.

Value return semantics

The seven rules in this section are in accordance with the previously mentioned rule "F.20: For 'out' output values, prefer return values to output parameters." The rules of this section are, in particular, about special use cases and don'ts.

When to return a pointer (T*) or an lvalue reference (T&)

As we know from the last section (Parameter Passing: Ownership Semantics), a pointer or a reference should never transfer ownership.

F.42	Return a T* to indicate a position (only)

A pointer should indicate only a position. This is exactly what the function `find` does.

```
Node* find(Node* t, const string& s) {
    if (!t || t->name == s) return t;
    if ((auto p = find(t->left, s))) return p;
    if ((auto p = find(t->right, s))) return p;
    return nullptr;
}
```

The pointer indicates that the `Node` is holding the position of `s`.

F.44	Return a T& when copy is undesirable and "returning no object" isn't needed

When return no object is not an option, using a reference instead of a pointer comes into play.

Sometimes you want to chain operations without unnecessary copying and destruction of temporaries. Typical use cases are input and output streams or assignment operators ("F.47: Return T& from assignment operators"). What is the subtle difference between returning by T& or returning by T in the following code snippet?

```
A& operator = (const A& rhs) { ... };
A operator = (const A& rhs) { ... };
```

```
A = a1, a2, a3;
a1 = a2 = a3;
```

The copy assignment operator returning a copy (A) triggers the creation of two additional temporary objects of type A.

A reference to a local

Returning a reference (pointer) to a local is undefined behavior.

Undefined behavior essentially means this: Don't make any assumptions about your program. Fix undefined behavior. The program lambdaFunctionCapture.cpp returns a reference to a local.

```
// lambdaFunctionCapture.cpp

#include <functional>
#include <iostream>
#include <string>

auto makeLambda() {
  const std::string val = "on stack created";
  return [&val]{return val;};              // (2)
}

int main() {

  auto bad = makeLambda();                 // (1)
  std::cout << bad();                       // (3)

}
```

The main function calls the function makeLambda() (1). The function returns a lambda expression, which has a reference to the local variable val (2).

The call bad() (3) causes the undefined behavior because the lambda expression uses a reference to the local val. As local, its lifetime ends with the scope of makeLambda().

Executing the program gives unpredictable results. Sometimes I get the entire string, sometimes a part of the string, or sometimes just the value 0. As an example, here are two runs of the program.

In the first run, arbitrary characters are displayed until the string terminating symbol (\0) ends it (see Figure 4.4).

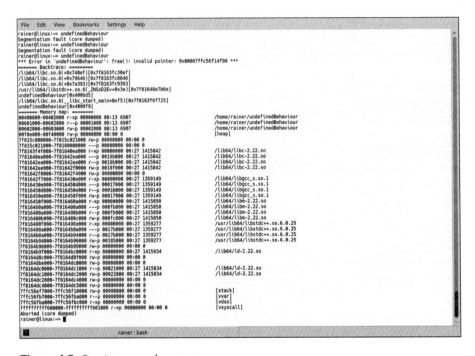

Figure 4.4 *Displaying arbitrary characters*

In the second run, the program causes a core dump (see Figure 4.5).

Figure 4.5 *Causing a core dump*

F.45	Don't return a T&&

and

F.48	Don't return std::move(local)

Both rules are very rigorous.

T&&

You should not use a T&& as a return type. Here is a small example to demonstrate the issue.

```
// returnRvalueReference.cpp

int&& returnRvalueReference() {
    return int{};
}


int main() {

    auto myInt = returnRvalueReference();

}
```

When compiled, the GCCcompiler complains immediately about a reference to a temporary (see Figure 4.6). To be precise, the lifetime of the temporary ends with the end of the full expression auto myInt = returnRvalueReference();.

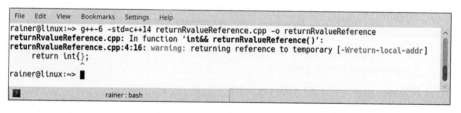

Figure 4.6 *Returning a reference to a temporary*

std::move(local)

Thanks to copy elision with RVO and NRVO, using return std::move(local) is not an optimization but a pessimization. Pessimization means that your program may become slower.

F.46	int is the return type for main()

According to the C++ standard, there are two variations of the main function:

```
int main() { ... }
int main(int argc, char** argv) { ... }
```

The second version is equivalent to `int main(int argc, char* argv[]) { ... }`.

The `main` function does not need a return statement. If control reaches the end of the `main` function without encountering a return statement, the effect is that of executing `return 0;`. `return 0` stands for the successful execution of the program.

Other functions

The rules in this section advise on when to use lambdas and compare `va_arg` with fold expressions.

Lambdas

F.50	Use a lambda when a function won't do (to capture local variables, or to write a local function)

This rule states the use case for lambdas. This immediately raises the question, When do you have to use a lambda or a function? Here are two obvious reasons.

1. If your callable has to capture local variables or is declared in a local scope, you have to use a lambda function.

2. If your callable should support overloading, use a function.

Now I want to present my crucial arguments for lambdas that are often ignored.

Expressiveness

"Explicit is better than implicit." This meta-rule from Python (PEP 20—The Zen of Python) also applies to C++. It means that your code should explicitly express its intent (see rule "P.1: Express ideas directly in code"). Of course, this holds true in particular for lambdas.

```
std::vector<std::string> myStrVec = {"523345", "4336893456", "7234",
                    "564", "199", "433", "2435345"};

std::sort(myStrVec.begin(), myStrVec.end(),
        [](const std::string& f, const std::string& s) {
            return f.size() < s.size();
        }
);
```

Compare this lambda with the function `lessLength`, which is subsequently used.

```
std::vector<std::string> myStrVec = {"523345", "4336893456", "7234",
                                     "564", "199", "433", "2435345"};
```

```
bool lessLength(const std::string& f, const std::string& s) {
    return f.size() < s.size();
}
```

```
std::sort(myStrVec.begin(), myStrVec.end(), lessLength);
```

Both the lambda and the function provide the same order predicate for the sort algorithm. Imagine that your coworker named the function `foo`. This means you have no idea what the function is supposed to do. As a consequence, you have to document the function.

```
// sorts the vector ascending, based on the length of its strings
std::sort(myStrVec.begin(), myStrVec.end(), foo);
```

Further, you have to hope that your coworker did it right. If you don't trust them, you have to analyze the implementation. Maybe that's not possible because you have the declaration of the function. With a lambda, your coworker cannot fool you. The code is the truth. Let me put it more provocatively: *Your code should be so expressive that it does not require documentation.*

Expressiveness versus don't repeat yourself (DRY)

The design rule to write expressive code with lambdas often contradicts another important design rule: Don't repeat yourself (DRY). DRY means that you should not write the same code more than once. Making a reusable unit such as a function and giving it a self-explanatory name is the appropriate cure for DRY. In the end, you have to decide in the concrete case if you rate expressiveness higher than DRY.

F.52   Prefer capturing by reference in lambdas that will be used locally, including passed to algorithms

and

F.53	Avoid capturing by reference in lambdas that will be used nonlocally, including returned, stored on the heap, or passed to another thread

Both rules are strongly related, and they boil down to the following observation: A lambda should operate only on valid data. When the lambda captures the data by copy, the data is by definition valid. When the lambda captures data by reference, the lifetime of the data must outlive the lifetime of the lambda. The previous example with a reference to a local showed different results of a lambda referring to invalid data.

Sometimes the issue is not so easy to catch.

```cpp
int main() {

    std::string str{"C++11"};

    std::thread thr([&str]{ std::cout << str << '\n'; });
    thr.detach();

}
```

Okay, I hear you say, "That is easy." The lambda expression used in the created thread `thr` captures the variable `str` by reference. Afterward, `thr` is detached from the lifetime of its creator, which is the main thread. Therefore, there is no guarantee that the created thread `thr` uses a valid string `str` because the lifetime of `str` is bound to the lifetime of the main thread. Here is a straightforward way to fix the issue. Capture `str` by copy:

```cpp
int main() {

    std::string str{"C++11"};

    std::thread thr([str]{ std::cout << str << '\n'; });
    thr.detach();

}
```

Problem solved? No! The crucial question is, Who is the owner of `std::cout`? `std::cout`'s lifetime is bound to the lifetime of the process. This means that the thread thr may be gone before `std::cout` prints C++11 onscreen. The way to fix this problem is to join the thread `thr`. In this case, the creator waits until the created is done, and therefore, capturing by reference is also fine.

```
int main() {

    std::string str{"C++11"};

    std::thread thr([&str]{ std::cout << str << '\n'; });
    thr.join();

}
```

F.51	Where there is a choice, prefer default arguments over overloading

If you need to invoke a function with a different number of arguments, prefer default arguments over overloading if possible. Therefore, you follow the DRY principle (don't repeat yourself).

```
void print(const string& s, format f = {});
```

The equivalent functionality with overloading requires two functions:

```
void print(const string& s);  // use default format
void print(const string& s, format f);
```

F.55	Don't use va_arg arguments

The title of this rule is too short. Use variadic templates instead of `va_arg` arguments when your function should accept an arbitrary number of arguments.

Variadic functions are functions such as `std::printf` that can take an arbitrary number of arguments. The issue is that you have to assume that the correct types were passed. Of course, this assumption is very error prone and relies on the discipline of the programmer.

To understand the implicit danger of variadic functions, here is a small example.

```cpp
// vararg.cpp

#include <iostream>
#include <cstdarg>

int sum(int num, ... ) {

  int sum = 0;

  va_list argPointer;
  va_start(argPointer, num );
  for( int i = 0; i < num; i++ )
    sum += va_arg(argPointer, int );
  va_end(argPointer);

  return sum;
}

int main() {

  std::cout << "sum(1, 5): " << sum(1, 5) << '\n';
  std::cout << "sum(3, 1, 2, 3): " << sum(3, 1, 2, 3) << '\n';
  std::cout << "sum(3, 1, 2, 3, 4): "
            << sum(3, 1, 2, 3, 4)  << '\n';  // (1)
  std::cout << "sum(3, 1, 2, 3.5): "
            << sum(3, 1, 2, 3.5) << '\n';    // (2)

}
```

sum is a variadic function. Its first argument is the number of arguments that should be summed up. The following background information about va_arg macros helps with understanding the code.

- **va_list:** holds the necessary information for the following macros
- **va_start:** enables access to the variadic function arguments
- **va_arg:** accesses the next variadic function argument
- **va_end:** ends the access of the variadic function arguments

For more information, read cppreference.com about variadic functions.

In (1) and (2), I had a bad day. First, the number of the arguments num is wrong; second, I provided a double instead of an int. The output shows both issues. The last element in (1) is missing, and the double is interpreted as int (2). See Figure 4.7.

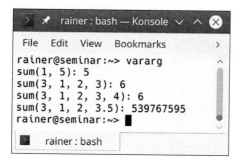

Figure 4.7 *Summation with* va_arg

These issues can be easily overcome with fold expressions in C++17. In contrast to va_args, fold expressions automatically deduce the number and the type of their arguments.

```
// foldExpressions.cpp

#include <iostream>

template<class ... Args>
auto sum(Args ... args) {
    return (... + args);
}

int main() {

    std::cout << "sum(5): " << sum(5) << '\n';
    std::cout << "sum(1, 2, 3): " << sum(1, 2, 3) << '\n';
    std::cout << "sum(1, 2, 3, 4): " << sum(1, 2, 3, 4)  << '\n';
    std::cout << "sum(1, 2, 3.5): " << sum(1, 2, 3.5) << '\n';

}
```

The function sum may look scary to you. It requires at least one argument and uses C++11 variadic templates. These are templates that can accept an arbitrary number of arguments. The arbitrary number is held by a so-called parameter pack denoted by an ellipsis (. . .). Additionally, with C++17, you can directly reduce a parameter pack with a binary operator. This addition, based on variadic templates, is called fold expressions. In the case of the sum function, the binary + operator (...+ args) is applied. If you want to know more about fold expressions in C++17, details are at https://www.modernescpp.com/index.php/fold-expressions.

The output of the program is as expected (see Figure 4.8).

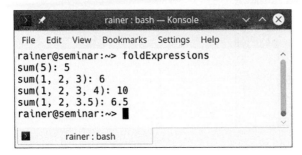

Figure 4.8 *Summation with fold expressions*

Related rules

An additional rule to lambdas is in Chapter 8, Expressions and Statements: "ES.28: Use lambdas for complex initialization, especially of `const` variables."

I skipped the C++20 feature `std::span` in this chapter and provided basic information on `std::span` in Chapter 7, Resource Management.

Distilled

Important

- A function should perform one operation, be short and simple, and have a carefully chosen name.

- Make functions that could run at compile-time `constexpr`.

- Make your functions pure if possible.

- Distinguish between the in, in/out, and out parameters of a function. Use passing by value or by `const` reference for in, use passing by reference for in/out, and use passing by value for the out parameter.

- Passing parameters to functions is a question of ownership semantics. Passing by value makes the function an independent owner of the resource. Passing by pointer or reference means the function only borrows the resource. A `std::unique_ptr` transfers the ownership to the function. `std::shared_ptr` makes the function a shared owner.

- Use variadic templates instead of `va_arg` arguments when your function should accept an arbitrary number of arguments.

Chapter 5

Classes and Class Hierarchies

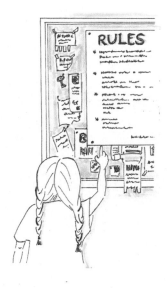

Cippi reasons about the rule of zero, five, or six.

A class is a user-defined type for which the programmer can specify the representation, the operations, and the interface. Class hierarchies are used to organize related structures.

The C++ Core Guidelines have about a hundred rules for user-defined types.

The guidelines start with summary rules before they dive into the special rules for

- Concrete types
- Constructors, assignments, and destructors
- Class hierarchies
- Overloading and overloaded operators
- Unions

The eight summary rules provide the background for the special rules.

Summary rules

The summary rules are quite short and don't go into much detail. They provide broad but valuable insight into classes.

Syntactic differences between `class` and `struct`

This section often refers to the semantic differences between classes and structs. First of all: What are the syntactic differences? The differences are minimal but important: In a `struct`, all members are `public` by default; in a `class`, all members are `private` by default. The same holds for inheritance. The base classes of a `struct` are `public` by default; the base classes of a `class` are `private` by default.

C.1	Organize related data into structures (`structs` or `classes`)

How can draw's interface be improved?

```
void draw(int fromX, fromY, int toX, int toY);
```

It is not obvious what the `ints` stand for. Consequently, you may invoke the function with a wrong sequence of arguments. Compare the previous function `draw` with the new one:

```
void draw(Point from, Point to);
```

By putting related elements together into a structure, the function signature becomes self-documenting and is, therefore, less error prone than the previous one.

C.2	Use `class` if the class has an invariant; use `struct` if the data members can vary independently

A class invariant is an invariant used for constraining instances of a class. Member functions have to preserve this invariant. The invariant constrains the possible values for the instances of a class.

This is a common question in C++: When do I have to use a `class` or a `struct`? The C++ Core Guidelines give the following recommendation. Use a `class` if the class has an invariant. A class invariant can be that (y, m, d) together represent a valid calendar date.

```
struct Pair {  // the members can vary independently
    string name;
    int volume;
};

class Date {
 public:
    // validate that {yy, mm, dd} is a valid date and initialize
    Date(int yy, Month mm, char dd);
    // ...
 private:
    int y;
    Month m;
    char d;    // day
};
```

The class invariant is initialized and checked in the constructor. The data type `Pair` has no invariant because all values for `name` and `volume` are valid. `Pair` is a simple data holder and needs no explicitly provided constructor.

C.3   Represent the distinction between an interface and an implementation using a class

The public member functions of a class are the interface of a class, and the private part is the implementation.

```
class Date {
 public:
    Date();
    // validate that {yy, mm, dd} is a valid date and initialize
    Date(int yy, Month mm, char dd);

    int day() const;
    Month month() const;
    // ...
 private:
    // ... some representation
};
```

From a maintainability perspective, the implementation of the class Date can be changed without affecting the user of the class.

C.4   Make a function a member only if it needs direct access to the representation of a class

If a function needs no access to the internals of the class, it should not be a member. Hence, you get loose coupling, and a change of the internals of the class will not affect the helper functions.

```
class Date {
    // ... relatively small interface ...
};

// helper functions:
Date next_weekday(Date);
bool operator == (Date, Date);
```

The operators =, ( ), [ ], and -> have to be members.

C.5	Place helper functions in the same namespace as the class they support

A helper function should be in the namespace of the class because it is part of the interface to the class. In contrast to a member function, a helper function does not need direct access to the representation of the class.

```
namespace Chrono { // here we keep time-related services

    class Date { /* ... */ };

    // helper functions:
    bool operator == (Date, Date);
    Date next_weekday(Date);
    // ...
}
...
if (date1 == date2) {  ...            // (1)
```

Thanks to argument-dependent lookup (ADL), the comparison date1 == date2 will additionally look for the equality operator in the Chrono namespace. ADL is, in particular, important for overloaded operators such as the output operator: << .

C.7	Don't define a class or enum and declare a variable of its type in the same statement

Defining a class and declaring a variable of its type in the same statement confuses and should, therefore, be avoided.

```
// bad
struct Data { /*...*/ } data { /*...*/ };

// good
struct Data { /*...*/ };
Data data{ /*...*/ };
```

C.8	Use `class` rather than `struct` if any member is non-public

When your user-defined type has nonpublic members, you probably want to protect their invariants from the outside. It is the job of the constructor to establish the invariants. Accordingly, you should use a `class` instead of a `struct`.

C.9	Minimize exposure of members

Data hiding and encapsulation is one of the cornerstones of object-oriented class design. You encapsulate the members in the class and allow access only via public member functions. You should think about two interfaces to your class: a `public` interface for the outside in general and a `protected` interface for derived classes. The remaining members should be `private`.

Concrete types

This section has only two rules but introduces the terms concrete and regular type.

A concrete type is "the simplest kind of a class" according to the C++ Core Guidelines. It is often called a value type and is not part of a type hierarchy.

A regular type is a type that "behaves like an int" and has, therefore, to support copy and assignment, equality, and order. To be more formal, a regular type X behaves like an int and supports the following operations:

- **Default constructor:** `X()`
- **Copy constructor:** `X(const X&)`
- **Copy assignment:** `operator = (const X&)`
- **Move constructor:** `X(X&&)`
- **Move assignment:** `operator = (X&&)`
- **Destructor:** `~(X)`
- **Swap operator:** `swap(X&, X&)`
- **Equality operator:** `operator == (const X&, const X&)`

C.10	Prefer concrete types over class hierarchies

If you do not have a use case for a class hierarchy, use a concrete type. A concrete type is way easier to implement, smaller, and faster. You do not have to worry about inheritance, virtuality, references, or pointers including memory allocation and deallocation. There is no virtual dispatch and, therefore, no run-time overhead.

To make a long story short: Apply the KISS principle (keep it simple, stupid). Your type behaves like a value.

C.11	Make concrete types regular

Regular types (`ints`) are easier to understand. They are per se intuitive. This means that if you have a concrete type, think about upgrading it to a regular type.

The built-in types such as `int` or `double` are regular but so are the user-defined types such as `std::string` or containers such as `std::vector` or `std::unordered_map`.

C++20 supports the concept of `regular`.

Constructors, assignments, and destructors

This section about constructors, assignments, and destructors has by far the most rules to classes and class hierarchies. They control the life cycle of objects: creation, copy, move, and destruction. In short, we call them the big six. Here are the six special member functions:

- **Default constructor:** `X()`
- **Copy constructor:** `X(const X&)`
- **Copy assignment:** `operator = (const X&)`
- **Move constructor:** `X(X&&)`
- **Move assignment:** `operator = (X&&)`
- **Destructor:** `~(X)`

The compiler can generate default implementations for the big six. The section starts with rules regarding default operations; continues with rules about constructors, copy and move operations, and destructors; and ends with rules for the other default operations that do not fall into the previous four categories.

Based on the declaration of the default constructor, you may have the impression that the default constructor takes no arguments. This is wrong. A default constructor can be invoked without argument, but it may have default arguments for each parameter.

Default operations

By default, the compiler can generate the big six if needed. You can define the six special member functions but can also explicitly ask the compiler to provide them with = default or delete them with = delete.

C.20	If you can avoid defining any default operations, do

This rule is also known as "the rule of zero." That means that you can avoid writing any custom constructors, copy/move constructors, assignment operators, or destructors by using types that support the appropriate copy/move semantics. This applies to the regular types such as the built-in types bool or double but also the containers of the Standard Template Library (STL) such as std::vector or std::string.

```
class Named_map {
public:
    // ... no default operations declared ...
private:
    std::string name;
    std::map<int, int> rep;
};
```

```
Named_map nm;        // default construct
Named_map nm2 {nm};  // copy construct
```

The default construction and the copy construction work because they are already defined for std::string and std::map. When the compiler auto-generates the copy constructor for a class, it invokes the copy constructor for all members and all bases of the class.

| C.21 | If you define or =delete any default operation, define or =delete them all |

The big six are closely related. Due to this relationship, you have to define or =delete all six. Consequently, this rule is called "the rule of six." Sometimes you hear "the rule of five" because the default constructor is special and, therefore, sometimes excluded.

Dependencies between the special member functions

Howard Hinnant developed in his talk at the ACCU 2014 conference an overview of the automatically generated special member functions (see Figure 5.1). Howard's table demands a deep explanation.

		compiler implicitly declares				
		default constructor	destructor	copy constructor	copy assignment	move constructor	move assignment
user declares	Nothing	defaulted	defaulted	defaulted	defaulted	defaulted	defaulted
	Any constructor	not declared	defaulted	defaulted	defaulted	defaulted	defaulted
	default constructor	user declared	defaulted	defaulted	defaulted	defaulted	defaulted
	destructor	defaulted	user declared	defaulted	defaulted	not declared	not declared
	copy constructor	not declared	defaulted	user declared	defaulted	not declared	not declared
	copy assignment	defaulted	defaulted	defaulted	user declared	not declared	not declared
	move constructor	not declared	defaulted	deleted	deleted	user declared	not declared
	move assignment	defaulted	defaulted	deleted	deleted	not declared	user declared

Figure 5.1 *Automatically generated special member functions*

First of all, user declared means for one of these six special member functions that you define it explicitly or auto request it from the compiler with =default. Deletion of the special member function with =delete is also regarded as defined. Essentially, when you just use the name, such as the name of the default constructor, it counts as user declared.

When you define any constructor, you get no default constructor. A default constructor is a constructor that can be invoked without an argument.

When you define or delete a default constructor with =default or =delete, none of the other six special member functions is affected.

When you define or delete a destructor, a copy constructor, or a copy-assignment operator with =default or =delete, you get no compiler-generated move-constructor and move-assignment constructor. This means move operations such as move construction or move assignment fall back to copy operations such as copy construction or copy assignment. This fallback automatism is marked in red in the table.

When you define or delete with =default or =delete a move constructor or a move-assignment operator, you get only the defined =default or =delete move constructor or move-assignment operator. Consequently, the copy constructor and the copy-assignment operator are set to =delete. Invoking a copy operation such as copy construction or copy assignment causes, therefore, a compilation error.

When you don't follow this rule, you get very unintuitive objects. Here is an unintuitive example from the guidelines.

```cpp
// doubleFree.cpp

#include <cstddef>

class BigArray {

public:
    BigArray(std::size_t len): len_(len), data_(new int[len]) {}

    ~BigArray(){
        delete[] data_;
    }

private:
    size_t len_;
    int* data_;
};

int main(){
```

```
BigArray bigArray1(1000);

BigArray bigArray2(1000);

bigArray2 = bigArray1;     // (1)

}                          // (2)
```

Why does this program have undefined behavior? The default copy-assignment operation bigArray2 = bigArray1 (1) of the example copies all members of bigArray2. Copying means, in particular, that pointer data is copied but not the data. Hence, the destructor for bigArray1 and bigArray2 is called (2), and we get undefined behavior because of double free.

The unintuitive behavior of the example is that the compiler-generated copy-assignment operator of BigArray makes a shallow copy of BigArray, but the explicit implemented destructor of BigArray assumes ownership of data.

AddressSanitizer makes the undefined behavior visible (see Figure 5.2).

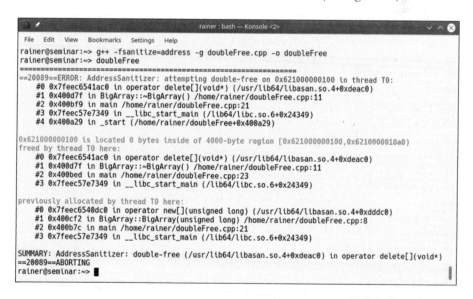

Figure 5.2 *Double free detected with AddressSanitizer*

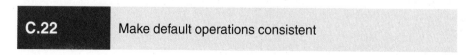
C.22   Make default operations consistent

This rule is related to the previous rule. If you implement the default operations with different semantics, the users of the class may become very confused. This strange behavior may also appear if you partially implement the member functions and partially request them via =default. You cannot assume that the compiler-generated special member functions have the same semantics as yours.

As an example of the odd behavior, here is the class Strange. Strange includes a pointer to int.

```
1 // strange.cpp
2
3 #include <iostream>
4
5 struct Strange {
6
7   Strange(): p(new int(2011)) {}
8
9   // deep copy
10   Strange(const Strange& a) : p(new int(*a.p)) {}
11
12   // shallow copy
13   // equivalent to Strange& operator = (const Strange&) = default;
14   Strange& operator = (const Strange& a) {
15     p = a.p;
16     return *this;
17   }
18
19   int* p;
20
21 };
22
23 int main() {
24
25   std::cout << '\n';
26
27   std::cout << "Deep copy" << '\n';
28
29   Strange s1;
30   Strange s2(s1);
31
32   std::cout << "s1.p: " << s1.p << "; *s1.p: " << *s1.p << '\n';
33   std::cout << "s2.p: " << s2.p << "; *s2.p: " << *s2.p << '\n';
34
35   std::cout <<  "*s2.p = 2017" << '\n';
36   *s2.p = 2017;
37
```

```
38   std::cout << "s1.p: " << s1.p << "; *s1.p: " << *s1.p << '\n';
39   std::cout << "s2.p: " << s2.p << "; *s2.p: " << *s2.p << '\n';
40
41   std::cout << '\n';
42
43   std::cout << "Shallow copy" << '\n';
44
45   Strange s3;
46   s3 = s1;
47
48   std::cout << "s1.p: " << s1.p << "; *s1.p: " << *s1.p << '\n';
49   std::cout << "s3.p: " << s3.p << "; *s3.p: " << *s3.p << '\n';
50
51
52   std::cout <<  "*s3.p = 2017" << '\n';
53   *s3.p = 2017;
54
55   std::cout << "s1.p: " << s1.p << "; *s1.p: " << *s1.p << '\n';
56   std::cout << "s3.p: " << s3.p << "; *s3.p: " << *s3.p << '\n';
57
58   std::cout << '\n';
59
60   std::cout << "delete s1.p" << '\n';
61   delete s1.p;
62
63   std::cout << "s2.p: " << s2.p << "; *s2.p: " << *s2.p << '\n';
64   std::cout << "s3.p: " << s3.p << "; *s3.p: " << *s3.p << '\n';
65
66   std::cout << '\n';
67
68 }
```

The class `Strange` has a copy constructor (line 10) and a copy-assignment operator
(line 14). The copy constructor applies deep copy, and the assignment operator
applies shallow copy. By the way, the compiler-generated copy constructor or copy-
assignment operator also applies shallow copy. Most of the time, you want deep
copy semantics (value semantics) for your types, but you probably never want to have
different semantics for these two related operations. The difference is that deep copy
semantics creates two new separate storage `p(new int(*a.p))` while shallow copy
semantics just copies the pointer `p = a.p`. Let's play with the `Strange` types. Figure
5.3 shows the output of the program.

```
rainer : bash — Konsole
File  Edit  View  Bookmarks  Settings  Help
rainer@seminar:~> strange

Deep copy
s1.p: 0x22ea280; *s1.p: 2011
s2.p: 0x22ea2a0; *s2.p: 2011
*s2.p = 2017
s1.p: 0x22ea280; *s1.p: 2011
s2.p: 0x22ea2a0; *s2.p: 2017

Shallow copy
s1.p: 0x22ea280; *s1.p: 2011
s3.p: 0x22ea280; *s3.p: 2011
*s3.p = 2017
s1.p: 0x22ea280; *s1.p: 2017
s3.p: 0x22ea280; *s3.p: 2017

delete s1.p
s2.p: 0x22ea2a0; *s2.p: 2017
s3.p: 0x22ea280; *s3.p: 0

rainer@seminar:~> █
```

Figure 5.3 *Output of* `strange.cpp`

Line 30 uses the copy constructor to create s2. Displaying the addresses of the pointer and changing the value of the pointer s2.p (line 36) shows that s1 and s2 are two distinct objects. This is not the case for s1 and s3. The copy-assignment operation in line 46 performs a shallow copy. The result is that changing the pointer s3.p (line 53) also affects the pointer s1.p because both pointers refer to the same value.

The fun starts if I delete the pointer s1.p (line 61). Thanks to the deep copy, nothing bad happens to s2.p, but the value of s3.p becomes an invalid pointer. To be more precise: Dereferencing an invalid pointer such as in *s3.p (line 63) is undefined behavior.

Constructor

Thirteen rules deal with the construction of objects. Roughly speaking, they fall into five categories:

- Constructors in general
- Default constructor
- Constructor with a single argument
- Initialization of the members
- Special constructors such as an inheriting or a delegating constructor

In the end, I have a warning. Don't call a virtual function from a constructor. I refer to this warning in a broader context, including destructors, in the section Other Default Operations later in this chapter.

Constructors in general

I skipped the rule "C.40: Define a constructor if a class has an invariant" because I already wrote about it in the rule "C.2: Use `class` if the class has an invariant; use `struct` if the data members can vary independently." Therefore, two closely related guidelines are left: "C.41: A constructor should create a fully initialized object" and "C.42: If a constructor cannot construct a valid object, throw an exception."

 C.41   A constructor should create a fully initialized object

It is the job of the constructor to create a fully initialized object. A class having an `init` member function is asking for trouble.

```
class DiskFile { // BAD: default constructor not sufficient
    FILE* f;     // call init() before any other function
    // ...
public:
    DiskFile() = default;
    void init();   // initialize f
    void read();   // read from f
    // ...
};


int main() {
    DiskFile file;
    file.read();   // crash or bad read!
    // ...
    file.init();   // too late
    // ...
}
```

The user might mistakenly invoke `read` before `init` or might just forget to invoke `init`. Making the member function `init` private and calling it from all constructors is better but not optimal. When you have common actions for all constructors of a class, use a delegating constructor.

C.42	If a constructor cannot construct a valid object, throw an exception

According to the previous rule, throw an exception if you cannot construct a valid object. There is not much to add. If you work with an invalid object, you always have to check the state of the object before its usage. This is extremely tedious, inefficient, and in particular, error prone. Here is an example from the guidelines, violating this rule:

```cpp
class DiskFile { // BAD: constructor leaves a nonvalid object behind
    FILE* f;
    bool valid;
    // ...
public:
    explicit DiskFile(const string& name)
        :f{fopen(name.c_str(), "r")}, valid{false} {
        if (f) valid = true;
        // ...
    }

    bool is_valid() const { return valid; }
    void read();   // read from f
    // ...
};

int main() {
    DiskFile file {"Heraclides"};
    file.read();   // crash or bad read!
    // ...
    if (file.is_valid()) {
        file.read();
        // ...
    }
    else {
        // ... handle error ...
    }
    // ...
}
```

Default constructor

The next two rules answer the question: When does and when doesn't a class need a default constructor?

C.43	Ensure that a copyable (value type) class has a default constructor

Informally said, a class needs no default constructor when instances of the class have no meaningful default. For example, a human being has no meaningful default, but a type such as a bank account has one. The initial value of a bank account may be zero. Having a default constructor makes it easier to use your type. Many constructors of the STL containers rely on the fact that your type has a default constructor—for example, for the value of an ordered associative container such as `std::map`. If all the members of the class have a default constructor, the compiler generates one for your class if possible (read the previous section in this chapter Dependencies between the Special Member Functions for more details).

Now to the case where a default constructor should not be provided.

C.45	Don't define a default constructor that only initializes data members; use member initializers instead

Often, code says more than a thousand words.

```cpp
1  // classMemberInitializerWidget.cpp
2
3  #include <iostream>
4
5  class Widget {
6  public:
7    Widget(): width(640), height(480),
8             frame(false), visible(true) {}
9    explicit Widget(int w): width(w), height(getHeight(w)),
10                          frame(false), visible(true) {}
11   Widget(int w, int h): width(w), height(h),
12                          frame(false), visible(true) {}
13
14   void show() const {
15       std::cout << std::boolalpha << width << "x" << height
16          << ", frame: " << frame
17          << ", visible: " << visible << '\n';
18   }
19  private:
20    int getHeight(int w) { return w*3/4; }
21    int width;
```

```
22    int height;
23    bool frame;
24    bool visible;
25 };
26
27 class WidgetImpro {
28  public:
29    WidgetImpro() = default;
30    explicit WidgetImpro(int w): width(w), height(getHeight(w)) {}
31    WidgetImpro(int w, int h): width(w), height(h) {}
32
33    void show() const {
34        std::cout << std::boolalpha << width << "x" << height
35            << ", frame: " << frame
36            << ", visible: " << visible << '\n';
37    }
38
39  private:
40    int getHeight(int w) { return w * 3 / 4; }
41    int width{640};
42    int height{480};
43    bool frame{false};
44    bool visible{true};
45 };
46
47
48  int main() {
49
50  std::cout << '\n';
51
52    Widget wVGA;
53    Widget wSVGA(800);
54    Widget wHD(1280, 720);
55
56    wVGA.show();
57    wSVGA.show();
58    wHD.show();
59
60    std::cout << '\n';
61
62    WidgetImpro wImproVGA;
63    WidgetImpro wImproSVGA(800);
64    WidgetImpro wImproHD(1280, 720);
```

```
65
66    wImproVGA.show();
67    wImproSVGA.show();
68    wImproHD.show();
69
70    std::cout << '\n';
71
72 }
```

The class `Widget` uses its three constructors (lines 7–12) exclusively to initialize its members. The refactored class `WidgetImpro` initializes its members directly in the class body (lines 41–44). See Figure 5.4. By moving the initialization from the constructor to the class body, the three constructors (lines 29–31) become easier to comprehend and the class easier to maintain. For example, when you add a new member to the class, you have only to add the initialization in the class body, not to all constructors. Additionally, there is no need to think about and take care of putting initializers in constructors in correct order. Consequently, you cannot have a partially initialized object when you create a new object.

Of course, both objects behave identically.

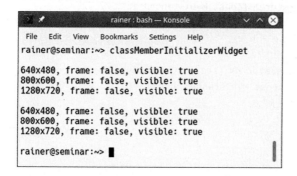

Figure 5.4 *Directly initializing in the class*

Here is the approach that I follow when I design a new class: *Define the default behavior in the class body. Use explicitly defined constructors only to vary the default behavior.*

Did you notice the keyword `explicit` in the previous constructor taking one argument?

C.46   By default, declare single-argument constructors `explicit`

To say it more explicitly: A single-argument constructor without `explicit` is a converting constructor. A converting constructor takes an argument and makes an object of the class out of it. This behavior is often the cause of big surprises.

The program `convertingConstructor.cpp` uses user-defined literals.

```cpp
// convertingConstructor.cpp

#include <iomanip>
#include <iostream>
#include <ostream>

namespace Distance {
    class MyDistance {
    public:
        MyDistance(double d):m(d) {}                         // (5)

        friend MyDistance operator + (const MyDistance& a,   // (2)
                                      const MyDistance& b) {
            return MyDistance(a.m + b.m);
        }
        friend std::ostream& operator << (std::ostream &out, // (3)
                                const MyDistance& myDist) {
            out << myDist.m << " m";
            return out;
        }
    private:
        double m;

    };

    namespace Unit{
        MyDistance operator "" _km(long double d) {          // (1)
            return MyDistance(1000*d);
        }
        MyDistance operator "" _m(long double m) {
            return MyDistance(m);
        }
        MyDistance operator "" _dm(long double d) {
```

```
            return MyDistance(d/10);
        }
        MyDistance operator "" _cm(long double c) {
            return MyDistance(c/100);
        }
    }
}

using namespace Distance::Unit;

int main() {

    std:: cout << std::setprecision(7) << '\n';

    std::cout << "1.0_km + 2.0_dm + 3.0_cm: "
              << 1.0_km + 2.0_dm + 3.0_cm << '\n';
    std::cout << "4.2_km + 5.5_dm + 10.0_m + 0.3_cm: "
              << 4.2_km + 5.5 + 10.0_m + 0.3_cm << '\n';      // (4)

    std::cout << '\n';

}
```

A call such as 1.0_km goes to the literal operator "" _km(long double d) (1), which creates a MyDistance(1000.0) object that stands for 1000.0 meters. Additionally, MyDistance overloads the + operator (2) and the output operator (3). The main reason for user-defined literals is to define a type-safe arithmetic. Each number has its units attached. See Figure 5.5.

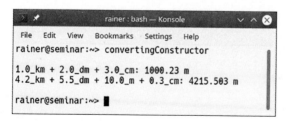

Figure 5.5 *Converting constructor*

Fine? No! I made an error and wrote 5.5 (4) instead of 5.5_dm. The converting constructor made a MyDistance object out of it. What should be a decimeter ended up being a meter. This implicit conversion from double would not have happened if the constructor (5) had been defined as explicit: explicit MyDistance(double d);.

Initialization of the members

Three rules deal with the initialization of members. The first rule has the potential for a big surprise.

 Define and initialize member variables in the order of member declaration

The class members are initialized in the order of their declaration. If you initialize them in the member initialization list in a different order, you may get a surprise.

```cpp
// memberDeclarationOrder.cpp

#include <iostream>

class Foo {
    int m1;
    int m2;
public:
    Foo(int x) :m2{x}, m1{++x} { // BAD: misleading initializer order
        std::cout << "m1: " << m1 << '\n';
        std::cout << "m2: " << m2 <<
    }
};

int main() {

    std::cout << '\n';
    Foo foo(1);
    std::cout<< '\n';

}
```

Many people assume that first m2 is initialized and then m1. As a consequence, m2 would have the value 1 and m1 the value 2.

The class members are destructed exactly in the reverse order of their initialization (see Figure 5.6).

Figure 5.6 *Wrong initialization order of member variables*

C.48 Prefer in-class initializers to member initializers in constructors for constant initializers

This rule is kind of similar to the previous rule "C.45: Don't define a default constructor that only initializes data members; use member initializers instead." In-class initializers make it a lot easier to define the constructors. Additionally, you cannot forget to initialize a member.

```
class X {   // BAD
    int i;
    string s;
    int j;
public:
    X() :i{666}, s{"qqq"} {}      // j is uninitialized
    explicit X(int ii) :i{ii} {}  // s is "" and j is uninitialized
    // ...
};

class X2 {
    int i{0};
    std::string s{"qqq"};
    int j{0}
public:
    X2() = default; // all members are initialized to their defaults
    explicit X2(int ii) :i{ii} {}     // s and j initialized
                                      // to their defaults
    // ...
};
```

While the in-class initialization establishes the default behavior of an object, the constructor allows the variation of the default behavior.

C.49   Prefer initialization to assignment in constructors

The most obvious pros of initialization to the assignment are twofold: First, you cannot forget to assign a value and use it uninitialized; second, initialization may be faster but never slower than an assignment. The following code snippet from the guidelines shows why.

```
class Bad {
    std::string s1;
public:
    Bad(const std::string& s2) { s1 = s2; } // BAD: default
    // constructor followed by assignment
    // ...
};
```

First, the default constructor of `std::string` is called, and second, the assignment takes place in the constructor.

To the contrary, the constructor in the class `Good` initializes the `std::string`.

```
class Good {
    std::string s1;
public:
    Good(const std::string& s2): s1{s2} {} // Good: initialization

    // ...
};
```

Special constructors

Since C++11, a constructor can delegate its work to another constructor of the same class and constructors can be inherited from the parent class. Both techniques allow the programmer to write more concise and more expressive code.

C.51   Use delegating constructors to represent common actions for all constructors of a class

A constructor can delegate its work to another constructor of the same class. Delegating is the modern way in C++ to put common actions for all constructors into one constructor. Before C++11, a special initialization function, which was typically called `init`, had to be used.

```cpp
class Degree {
public:
    explicit Degree(int deg) {              // (1)
        degree = deg % 360;
        if (degree < 0) degree += 360;
    }

    Degree(): Degree(0) {}                  // (2)

    explicit Degree(double deg):            // (3)
        Degree(static_cast<int>(std::ceil(deg))) {}

private:
    int degree;
};
```

The constructors (2) and (3) of the class `Degree` delegate its initialization work to the constructor (1), which verifies its arguments. Invoking constructors recursively is undefined behavior.

A simplified implementation initializes `Degree` in the class and skips the default constructor.

```cpp
class Degree {
public:
    explicit Degree(int deg) {              // (1)
        degree= deg % 360;
        if (degree < 0) degree += 360;
    }

    explicit Degree(double deg):            // (3)
        Degree(static_cast<int>(std::ceil(deg))) {}

private:
    int degree = 0;
};
```

C.52   Use inheriting constructors to import constructors into a derived class that does not need further explicit initialization

Reuse the constructors of the base class in the derived class if you can. This idea of reuse applies when your derived class has no members. If you don't reuse constructors when you could, you violate the DRY (don't repeat yourself) principle. The inherited constructors keep all characteristics from their definition in the base class, such as access specifiers or attributes `explicit` or `constexpr`.

```cpp
class Rec {
    // ... data and lots of nice constructors ...
};

class Oper : public Rec {
    using Rec::Rec;
    // ... no data members ...
    // ... lots of nice utility functions ...
};

struct Rec2 : public Rec {
    int x;
    using Rec::Rec;
};

Rec2 r {"foo", 7};
int val = r.x;              // uninitialized
```

There is a danger of using inherited constructors. If your derived class, such as `Rec2`, has its own members, such as `int x`, they are not initialized unless they have in-class initializers (see "C.48: Prefer in-class initializers to member initializers in constructors for constant initializers").

Copy and move

Although the C++ Core Guidelines have eight rules regarding copy and move, they boil down to three classes of rules: copy- and move-assignment operations, the semantics of copy and move, and the infamous slicing.

Assignment

Syntax

The two rules "C.60: Make copy assignment non-virtual, take the parameter by const&, and return by non-const&" and "C.63: Make move assignment non-virtual, take the parameter by &&, and return by non-const&" state explicitly the syntax of the copy- and move-assignment operator. `std::vector` follows the proposed syntax. Here is a simplified version:

```cpp
// copy assignment
vector& operator = (const vector& other);
```

```
// move assignment
vector& operator = (vector&& other);              // until C++17
vector& operator = (vector&& other) noexcept ;    // since C++17
```

The small code snippet shows that the move-assignment operator is noexcept. With C++17, the rule is quite obvious: "C.66: Make move operations noexcept." Move operations include the move constructor and the move-assignment operator. A noexcept declared function is an optimization opportunity for the compiler. The following code snippet shows the declaration of the move operations for std::vector.

```
vector(vector&& other) noexcept ;                 // since C++17
vector& operator = (vector&& other) noexcept ;    // since C++17
```

Self-assignment

Both rules address self-assignment: "C.62: Make copy assignment safe for self-assignment" and "C.65: Make move assignment safe for self-assignment." Safe for self-assignment means that the operation x = x should not change the value of x.

Copy/move assignment of the containers of the STL, std::string, and built-in types such as int are safe for self-assignment. The automatic generated copy/move assignment operator is safe for self-assignment. The same holds for an automatically generated copy/move assignment operator that uses types that are safe for self-assignment.

The following class Foo does the right job. No self-assignment could happen.

```
class Foo {
    std::string s;
    int i;
public:
    Foo& Foo::operator = (const Foo& a) {
        s = a.s;
        i = a.i;
        return *this;
    }
    Foo& Foo::operator = (Foo&& a) noexcept {
        s = std::move(a.s);
        i = a.i;
        return *this;
    }
    // ....
};
```

Any redundant and expensive check for self-assignment is a pessimization in this case.

```cpp
class Foo {
  std::string s;
  int i;
public:
  Foo& Foo::operator = (const Foo& a) {
    if (this == &a) return *this;    // redundant self-assignment check
    s = a.s;
    i = a.i;
    return *this;
  }
  Foo& Foo::operator = (Foo&& a) noexcept {
    if (this == &a) return *this;    // redundant self-assignment check
    s = std::move(a.s);
    i = a.i;
    return *this;
  }
  // ....
};
```

Semantics

The two guidelines for this section sound obvious: "C.61: A copy operation should copy" and "C.64: A move operation should move and leave its source in a valid state." What does that mean?

- Copy operation

  - After copying (a = b), a and b must be the same: (a == b).

  - Copying can be deep or shallow. Deep copying means that both objects a and b are afterward independent of each other (value semantics). Shallow copying means that both objects a and b share an object afterward (reference semantics).

- Move operation

  - The C++ standard requires that the moved-from object must be afterward in an unspecified but valid state. Often, this moved-from state is in the default state of the source of the move operation.

C.67   A polymorphic class should suppress copying

This rule sounds innocuous but is often the reason for undefined behavior. First of all: What is a polymorphic class?

A polymorphic class is a class that defines or inherits at least one virtual function.

Copying a polymorphic class may end in slicing. Slicing is one of the darkest parts of C++.

Slicing

Slicing means you want to copy an object during assignment or initialization and you get only a part of the object. Let me give you a simple example:

```cpp
// slice.cpp

struct Base {
  int base{1998};
};

struct Derived : Base {
  int derived{2011};
};

void needB(Base b) {
    // ...
};

int main() {

  Derived d;
  Base b = d;       // (1)
  Base b2(d);       // (2)
  needB(d);         // (3)

}
```

The expressions (1), (2), and (3) have all the same effect: The Derived part of d is removed. I assume that was not your intention.

Now, it becomes really dangerous. Slicing kicks in when you copy a polymorphic class.

```cpp
1 // sliceVirtuality.cpp
2
3 #include <iostream>
4 #include <string>
5
6 struct Base {
7    virtual std::string getName() const {
8        return "Base";
9    }
10 };
11
12 struct Derived : Base {
13    std::string getName() const override {
14        return "Derived";
15    }
16 };
17
18 int main() {
19
20    std::cout << '\n';
21
22    Base b;
23    std::cout << "b.getName(): " << b.getName() << '\n';
24
25    Derived d;
26    std::cout << "d.getName(): " << d.getName() << '\n';
27
28    Base b1 = d;  // slicing
29    std::cout << "b1.getName():  " << b1.getName() << '\n';
30
31    Base& b2 = d;
32    std::cout << "b2.getName():  " << b2.getName() << '\n';
33
34    Base* b3 = new Derived;
35    std::cout << "b3->getName(): " << b3->getName() << '\n';
36
37    std::cout << '\n';
38
39 }
```

The program has a small hierarchy consisting of the `Base` and the `Derived` classes. Each object of this class hierarchy returns its name. The member function `getName` is virtual (line 7) and class `Derived` overrides it in line 13. Class `Base` is a polymorphic class. This means that I can use a derived object via a reference (line 31) or a pointer to a base object (line 34) to get polymorphic behavior. Under the hood, the object is of type `Derived`.

This behavior does not hold if I copy `Derived d` to `Base b1` (line 28). In this case, slicing kicks in, and I have a `Base` object under the hood. See Figure 5.7. In the case of copying, the declared or static type is used. If you use an indirection such as a reference or a pointer, the current or dynamic type is used.

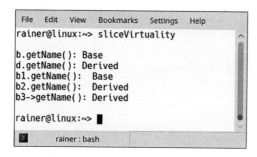

Figure 5.7 *Slicing*

If you want to make a deep copy, prefer a virtual `clone` function. Read the details about this technique in the rule "C.130: For making deep copies of polymorphic classes prefer a virtual `clone` function instead of copy construction/assignment."

Destructors

Does my class need a destructor? I often hear this question. Most of the time, the answer is no, and you are fine with the rule of zero. Sometimes the answer is yes, and we are back to the rule of five/six. To be more precise, the C++ Core Guidelines provide seven rules for destructors. They fall into four categories: when destructors are needed, how destructors should handle pointers and references, how base class destructors should be defined, and why destructors should not fail.

Need for destructors

The destructor of an object is automatically invoked at the end of its lifetime. To be more precise, the destructor of the object is invoked when the object goes out of scope.

C.30 Define a destructor if a class needs an explicit action at object destruction

The question is if the compiler-generated destructor is sufficient in your case. If you must execute extra code at the end of the lifetime of your user-defined type, you have to write a destructor. For example, your user-defined type wants to deregister itself from a registration. If you define the destructor, the rule of five/six kicks in.

To put it the other way around, if no member of your class needs additional cleanup, there is no need to define a destructor such as in the following code snippet from the guidelines:

```cpp
class Foo {   // bad; use the default destructor
public:
    // ...
    ~Foo() { s = ""; i = 0; vi.clear(); }  // clean up
private:
    std::string s;
    int i;
    std::vector<int> vi;
};
```

C.31 All resources acquired by a class must be released by the class's destructor

This rule sounds quite obvious and helps you to prevent resource leaks. Right? But you have to consider which of your class members have a full set of default operations. Now we are once more back to the rule of zero or the rule of five/six.

In the following example, while the `std::ifstream` class has a destructor, the class `File` might not have one, and therefore, we get a memory leak if instances of `MyClass` go out of scope.

```cpp
class MyClass {
    std::ifstream fstream;    // may own a file
    File* file_;              // may own a file
    ...
};
```

Pointers and references
If your class has raw pointers or references, you have to answer the crucial question: Who is the owner?

C.32	If a class has a raw pointer (T*) or reference (T&), consider whether it might be owning

If a class has a raw pointer or a reference, you have to be specific about ownership. This means in the case of the pointer. If the ownership is obscure, you may delete a pointer to an object that you do not own or may not delete a pointer that you own. In the first case, you end up with undefined behavior because of double delete; in the second case, you end up with a memory leak. The corresponding reasoning holds about references.

The topic of this paragraph is already thoroughly answered in the chapter on the ownership semantics of function parameters. Read the details in the section Parameter Passing: Ownership Semantics in Chapter 4.

C.33	If a class has an owning pointer member, define a destructor

The reason for this rule is straightforward: If a class owns an object, it is responsible for its destruction. The destruction is the job of the destructor.

Admittedly, there is more to write about a class owning a pointer member. You should first answer the following question: Is the class the exclusive owner of the pointer? The answer can be yes or no. Make the class the exclusive owner by putting the pointer into a std::unique_ptr. Otherwise, make the class the shared owner by putting the pointer into a std::shared_ptr. Raising the abstraction level from a pointer to a smart pointer makes ownership semantics transparent and way less error prone.

What are the advantages of smart pointers over pointers? First and foremost, the lifetime of the smart pointer is automatically managed by the C++ run time. Second, a std::shared_ptr supports the big six. This means using a std::shared_ptr in a class does not impose any restriction on the class. To the contrary, a std::unique_ptr used in the class definition disables the copy semantics.

```
// classWithUniquePtr.cpp

#include <memory>

struct MyClass {
    std::unique_ptr<int> uniPtr = std::make_unique<int>(2011);
};
```

```
int main() {

    MyClass myClass;
    MyClass myClass2(myClass);
    MyClass myClass3;
    myClass3 = myClass;

}
```

Due to the `std::unique_ptr`, objects of type `MyClass` cannot be copied. Neither calling the copy constructor (`MyClass myClass2(myClass)`) nor calling the copy-assignment operator (`myClass3 = myClass`) is valid. See Figure 5.8.

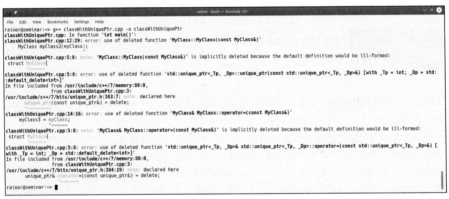

Figure 5.8 *A class with a* `std::unique_ptr`

C.35   A base class destructor should be either public and virtual, or protected and non-virtual

---

This rule is very interesting from the perspective of virtual functions. Let's divide it into two parts.

- **Public and virtual destructor**

    If the base class has a public and virtual destructor, you can destroy instances of a derived class through a base class pointer. The same holds for references.

    ```
    struct Base {  // no virtual destructor
        virtual void f() {};
    };
    ```

```
struct Derived : Base {
    std::string s {"a resource needing cleanup"};
    ~Derived() { /* ... do some cleanup ... */ }
};

    ...

Base* b = new Derived();
delete b;
```

The compiler generates for `Base` a nonvirtual destructor, but deleting an instance of `Derived` through a `Base` pointer is undefined behavior if the destructor of `Base` is nonvirtual.

- **Protected and nonvirtual destructor**

  This is quite easy to get. If the destructor of the base class is protected, you cannot destroy derived objects using a base class pointer or reference; therefore, the destructor need not be virtual.

Here are a few concluding remarks about the access specifiers for destructors of a `Base` class.

- If the destructor of a class `Base` is private, you cannot derive from it.

- If the destructor of a class `Base` is protected, you can derive only `Derived` from `Base` and use `Derived`.

```
struct Base {
    protected:
    ~Base() = default;
};

struct Derived: Base {};

int main() {
    Base b;   // Error: Base::~Base is protected within this context
    Derived d;
}
```

The declaration `Base  b;` causes an error because the destructor of `Base` is inaccessible.

Failing destructor

Two rules address the issue of failing destructors: "C.36: A destructor may not fail" and "C.37: Make destructors noexcept."

Clarification on C.37: Make destructors noexcept

The wording of the rule is misleading. A user-defined or implicitly generated destructor of a type MyType is noexcept by default. If one of the members or bases of MyType has a destructor without a noexcept guarantee, the destructor of MyType has no noexcept guarantee, too. *Consequently, there is no need to specify the destructor as noexcept.*

I think I should add a few words about noexcept.

noexcept

If you declare a function func such as a destructor as noexcept, an exception thrown in func calls std::terminate. std::terminate calls the currently installed std::terminate_handler, which is by default std::abort, and your program aborts. By declaring a function void func() noexcept; as noexcept, you state

- My function does not throw any exception.

- If my function throws an exception, it is fine to let the program abort.

The reason that you should explicitly declare your destructor as noexcept is obvious. There is no general way to write error-free code if the destructor could fail. If all of the members of a class have a noexcept destructor, the user-defined or compiler-generated destructor is implicitly noexcept.

Other default operations

The remaining rules related to constructors, assignments, and destructors have a broad focus. They cover when you should use =default and =delete explicitly and why you should not call virtual functions from constructors and destructors. The remaining rules make the story of regular types complete. The `swap` function (`swap(X&, X&)`) is the first rule, followed by the equality operator (`operator == (const X&)`).

Explicit use of `=default` and `=delete`

This section provides guidance about when to use `=default` and `=delete` explicitly.

C.80	**Use `=default` if you have to be explicit about using the default semantics**

Do you remember the rule of five? It means that if you define one of the five special member functions, you have to define them all. The five special member functions are all the special member functions excluding the default constructor.

When I define the destructor such as in the following example, I have to define the copy and move constructor and the copy- and move-assignment operators. Requesting the remaining four by `=default` is the easiest way.

```cpp
class Tracer {
    std::string message;
public:
    explicit Tracer(const std::string& m) : message{m} {
        std::cerr << "entering " << message << '\n';
    }
    ~Tracer() { std::cerr << "exiting " << message << '\n'; }

    Tracer(const Tracer&) = default;
    Tracer& operator = (const Tracer&) = default;
    Tracer(Tracer&&) = default;
    Tracer& operator = (Tracer&&) = default;
};
```

This was easy! Right? Providing your own implementation is boring and also very prone to mistakes. For example, the user-defined move constructor and move-assignment operator in the following example are not declared noexcept.

```cpp
class Tracer {
    std::string message;
public:
    explicit Tracer(const std::string& m) : message{m} {
        std::cerr << "entering " << message << '\n';
    }
    ~Tracer() { std::cerr << "exiting " << message << '\n'; }
```

```
    Tracer(const Tracer& a) : message{a.message} {}
    Tracer& operator = (const Tracer& a) {
        message = a.message; return *this;
    }
    Tracer(Tracer&& a) :message{a.message} {}
    Tracer& operator = (Tracer&& a) {
        message = a.message; return *this;
    }
};
```

C.81	Use =delete when you want to disable default behavior (without wanting an alternative)

Sometimes, you want to disable the default operations. Here comes =delete into play. C++ eats its own dog food. The copy constructor of almost all types from the threading API is set to delete. This holds true for data types such as mutexes, locks, or futures.

You can use delete to create strange types. Instances of Immortal cannot be destructed.

```
// immortal.cpp

class Immortal {
public:
    ~Immortal() = delete;    // do not allow destruction
};

int main() {
    Immortal im;           // (1)
    Immortal* pIm = new Immortal;

    delete pIm;            // (2)
}
```

An implicit call of the destructor (1) or an explicit call of the destructor (2) causes a compile-time error. See Figure 5.9.

Figure 5.9 *delete the destructor*

C.82	Don't call virtual functions in constructors and destructors

Calling a pure virtual function from a constructor or a destructor is undefined behavior. Calling a virtual function from a constructor or a destructor does not work the way you may expect. For protection reasons, the virtual call mechanism is disabled in the constructor or destructor, and you get a nonvirtual call.

Hence, the `Base` version of the virtual function `f` will be called in the following example.

```cpp
// virtualCall.cpp

#include <iostream>

struct Base {
    Base() {
        f();
    }
    virtual void f() {
        std::cout << "Base called" << '\n';
    }
};
```

```
struct Derived: Base {
    void f() override {
        std::cout << "Derived called" << '\n';
    }
};

int main() {

    std::cout << '\n';

    Derived d;

    std::cout << '\n';

};
```

Figure 5.10 shows the surprising behavior.

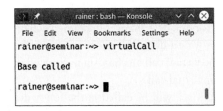

Figure 5.10 *Calling a virtual function in the constructor*

swap *function*

For a type to be a regular type, it has to support a swap function. A more informal term for a regular type is a value-like type, and this is the wording the first rule uses: "C.83: For value-like types, consider providing a noexcept swap function." According, to the first rule, a swap should not fail ("C.84: A swap may not fail") and should, therefore, be declared as noexcept: "C.85: Make swap noexcept."

The data type Foo from the C++ Core Guidelines has a swap function.

```
class Foo {
public:
    void swap(Foo& rhs) noexcept {
        m1.swap(rhs.m1);
        std::swap(m2, rhs.m2);
    }
```

```
private:
    Bar m1;
    int m2;
};
```

For convenience reasons, you should consider supporting a nonmember `swap` function based on the already implemented swap member function.

```
void swap(Foo& a, Foo& b) noexcept {
    a.swap(b);
}
```

If you do not provide a nonmember `swap` function, then the standard library algorithms that require swapping (such as `std::sort` and `std::rotate`) will fall back to the `std::swap` template, which is defined in terms of move construction and move assignment.

```
template<typename T>
void std::swap(T& a, T& b) noexcept {
    T tmp(std::move(a));
    a = std::move(b);
    b = std::move(tmp);
}
```

The C++ standard offers more than 40 overloads of `std::swap`. You can use the `swap` function as a building block for many idioms such as copy construction or move assignment. A `swap` function should not fail; therefore, you should declare it as `noexcept`.

The copy-and-swap idiom

If you use the copy-and-swap idiom to implement the copy-assignment and move-assignment operator, you must define your own swap — either as a member function or as a friend. I added a `swap` function to the class `Cont` and use it in the copy-assignment and move-assignment operator.

```
class Cont {
public:
    // ...
    Cont& operator = (const Cont& rhs);
    Cont& operator = (Cont&& rhs) noexcept;
```

```
            friend void swap(Cont& lhs, Cont& rhs) noexcept {
                swap(lhs.size, rhs.size);
                swap(lhs.pdata, rhs.pdata);
            }
    private:
        int* pData;
        std::size_t size;
    };

    Cont& Cont::operator = (const Cont& rhs) {
        Cont tmp(rhs);
        swap(*this, tmp);
        return *this;
    }

    Cont& Cont::operator = (Cont&& rhs) {
        Cont tmp(std::move(rhs));
        swap(*this, tmp);
        return *this;
    }
```

Both assignment operators make a temporary copy tmp of the source object and then apply the swap function to it.

When a swap function is based on copy semantics instead of move semantics, a swap function may fail because of memory exhaustion. The following implementation contradicts the already mentioned rule "C.84: A swap must not fail." This is the C++98 implementation of std::swap.

```
template<typename T>
void std::swap(T& a, T& b) {
    T tmp = a;
    a = b;
    b = tmp;
}
```

In this case, memory exhaustion causes a std::bad_alloc exception.

Equality operator
To be regular, a data type also has to support the equality operator.

C.86 Make == symmetric with respect to operand types and noexcept

If you don't want to surprise your user, you should make the equality operator symmetric.

The following code snippet shows an unintuitive equality operator that is defined inside the class.

```cpp
class MyInt {       // BAD: unsymmetric ==
    int num;
public:
    MyInt(int n): num(n) {};
    bool operator == (const MyInt& rhs) const noexcept {
        return num == rhs.num;
    }
};


int main() {
  MyInt(5) == 5;      // OK
   5 == MyInt(5);      // ERROR
}
```

The call `MyInt(5) == 5` is valid because the constructor converts the `int` to an instance of `MyInt`. The last line (`5 == MyInt(5)`) gives an error. An object of type `int` cannot be compared with a `MyInt` object, and there is no conversion from `MyInt` to `int` possible.

The elegant way to solve this asymmetry is to declare a friend `operator ==` inside the class `MyInt`. Here is the improved version of `MyInt`.

```cpp
class MyInt {
  int num;
public:
  MyInt(int n): num(n) {};
  friend bool operator == (const MyInt& lhs, const MyInt& rhs) noexcept {
    return lhs.num == rhs.num;
  }
};


int main() {
  MyInt(5) == 5;   // OK
   5 == MyInt(5);   // OK
}
```

If you carefully read this book, you may recall that a constructor taking one argument should be explicit ("C.46: By default, declare single-argument constructors explicit"). Honestly, you are right.

```cpp
class MyInt {
  int num;
public:
  explicit MyInt(int n): num(n) {};
  friend bool operator == (const MyInt& lhs, const MyInt& rhs) noexcept {
    return lhs.num == rhs.num;
  }
};


int main() {
  MyInt(5) == 5;  // ERROR
  5 == MyInt(5);  // ERROR
}
```

Making the constructor `explicit` breaks the implicit conversion from `int` to `MyInt`. Providing two additional overloads solves the issue. One overload takes an `int` as the left and the other an `int` as the right argument.

```cpp
// equalityOperator.cpp

class MyInt {
  int num;
public:
  explicit MyInt(int n): num(n) {};
  friend bool operator == (const MyInt& lhs, const MyInt& rhs) noexcept {
    return lhs.num == rhs.num;
  }
  friend bool operator == (int lhs, const MyInt& rhs) noexcept {
    return lhs == rhs.num;
  }
  friend bool operator == (const MyInt& lhs, int rhs) noexcept {
    return lhs.num == rhs;
  }
};


int main() {
  MyInt(5) == 5;   // OK
  5 == MyInt(5);   // OK
}
```

The surprises continue with the equality operator.

C.87   Beware of == on base classes

Writing a foolproof equality operator for a hierarchy is hard. The guidelines give a nice example of the complications involved. Here is the hierarchy.

```cpp
// equalityOperatorHierarchy.cpp

#include <string>

struct Base {
    std::string name;
    int number;
    virtual bool operator == (const Base& a) const {
        return name == a.name && number == a.number;
    }
};

struct Derived: Base {
    char character;
    virtual bool operator == (const Derived& a) const {
        return name == a.name &&
               number == a.number &&
               character == a.character;
    }
};

int main() {

    Base b;
    Base& base = b;
    Derived d;
    Derived& derived = d;

    base == derived;  // compares name and number, but        (1)
                      // ignores derived's character
    derived == base;  // error: no == defined                 (2)
    Derived derived2;
    derived == derived2; // compares name, number, and character
    Base& base2 = derived2;
    base2 == derived; // compares name and number, but         (3)
```

```
                        // ignores derived2's and derived's character

}                       // ignores derived2's and derived's character
```

Comparing instances of `Base` or instances of `Derived` works. But mixing instances of `Base` and `Derived` does not work as expected. Using `Base`'s `==` operator ignores `Derived`'s character (3). Using `Derived`'s operator does not work for instances of `Base` (4). The line causes a compilation error. The last line (3) is quite tricky. The equality operator of `Base` is used. Why? The `==` operator of `Derived` overwrote the `==` operator of `Base`. No! Both operators have different signatures. One operator takes an instance of `Base`; the other operator takes an instance of `Derived`. `Derived`'s version does not overwrite `Base`'s version.

These observations also hold for the other five comparison operators: `!=`, `<`, `<=`, `>`, and `>=`. This misbehaving is another facet of the slicing issue: "C.67: A polymorphic class should suppress copying."

Class hierarchies

The C++ Core Guidelines have about thirty rules in total addressing class hierarchies.

But first, what is a class hierarchy? The C++ Core Guidelines give a clear answer. Let me rephrase it. A class hierarchy represents a set of hierarchically organized concepts. Base classes typically act as interfaces. There are two uses for interfaces. One is often named interface inheritance and the other implementation inheritance.

Interface inheritance uses public inheritance. It separates users from implementations to allow derived classes to add or change functionality of the base class without affecting the users of base classes.

For example, if you derive `public` a class `Handball` from a `Ball`, you can use `Handball` instead of a `Ball`. A `Handball` is also a `Ball`. This principle is called the Liskov substitution principle.

Implementation inheritance often uses private inheritance. Typically, the derived class provides its functionality by adapting functionality from base classes.

A prominent example of implementation inheritance is the adapter pattern if you implement it with multiple inheritance. The idea of the adapter pattern is to adapt an existing interface to a new one. The adapter uses `private` inheritance from the implementation and `public` inheritance from the new interface. The new interface uses the existing implementation to provide its services to the user.

The first three rules for class hierarchies have a general focus. They provide a kind of summary for the more detailed rules for the designing of classes and the accessing of objects in class hierarchies.

General rules

The first rules describe when to use class hierarchies and introduce the idea of abstract classes.

C.120	Use class hierarchies to represent concepts with inherent hierarchical structure (only)

This rule makes a software system intuitive and easy to comprehend. If you model something in the code that has an inherently hierarchical structure, you should use a hierarchy. Often, the easiest way to reason about code is if you have a natural match between the code and the world.

For example, your job as a software architect is to model a complex system such as a defibrillator. This system consists of many subsystems. For example, a subsystem is the user interfaces. The requirement for the defibrillator is that different input devices such as a keyboard, a touch screen, or a few buttons could be used as a user interface. This system consisting of various subsystems such as a user interface is inherently hierarchical and should, therefore, be modeled hierarchically. The great benefit is that the complex system is now easy to explain in a top-down fashion because there is a natural match between the real hardware and the software.

Of course, the classic example of using a hierarchy is in the design of a graphical user interface (GUI). This is the example the C++ Core Guidelines use.

```cpp
class DrawableUIElement {
public:
    virtual void render() const = 0;
// ...
};


class AbstractButton : public DrawableUIElement {
public:
    virtual void onClick() = 0;
// ...
};


class PushButton : public AbstractButton {
    void render() const override;
    void onClick() override;
// ...
};
```

```
class Checkbox : public AbstractButton {
// ...
};
```

If something is not inherently hierarchical, you should not model it in a hierarchical way. Have a look here.

```
template<typename T>
class Container {
public:
    // list operations:
    virtual T& get() = 0;
    virtual void put(T&) = 0;
    virtual void insert(Position) = 0;
    // ...
    // vector operations:
    virtual T& operator [] (int) = 0;
    virtual void sort() = 0;
    // ...
    // tree operations:
    virtual void balance() = 0;
    // ...
};
```

Why is the example terrible? Read the comments! The class template `Container` consists of pure virtual functions for modeling a list, a vector, and a tree. That means if you use `Container` as an interface, you have to implement three disjunctive concepts.

Interface segregation principle

The class template `Container` breaks the interface segregation principle (ISP), coined by the software engineer and instructor Robert C. Martin, popularly known as "Uncle Bob." The interface-segregation principle states that no client such as a derived class should be forced to depend on member functions it does not use. In the concrete case of the class template `Container`, each class implementing the interface has to implement all abstract methods.

The ISP splits interfaces that are too large and consist of too many member functions into smaller and more specific ones.

C.121	If a base class is used as an interface, make it an abstract class

An abstract class is a class that has at least one pure virtual function. A pure virtual function (`virtual void function() = 0`) is a function that must be implemented by a derived class if that class should not be abstract. An abstract class cannot be instantiated.

I want to add for completeness: An abstract class can provide an implementation for a pure virtual function. A derived class can, therefore, use this implementation.

Interfaces should usually consist of `public` pure virtual functions, don't have data members, and have a default/empty virtual destructor (`virtual ~My_interface() = default`).

C.122	Use abstract classes as interfaces when complete separation of interface and implementation is needed

Abstract classes are about the separation of interface and implementation. If the client, such as in this case an application, depends only on the interface `Device`, it can use different implementations during run time. Additionally, a modification in the implementation does not necessarily affect the interface and, therefore, the application.

```
struct Device {
    virtual void write(std::span<const char> outbuf) = 0;
    virtual void read(std::span<char> inbuf) = 0;
};

class Mouse : public Device {
// ... data ...
    void write(std::span<const char> outbuf) override;
    void read(std::span<char> inbuf) override;
};

class TouchScreen : public Device {
// ... different data ...
    void write(std::span<const char> outbuf) override;
    void read(std::span<char> inbuf) override;
};
```

Designing classes

The 12 rules for designing classes target the following topics: constructors for abstract classes, virtuality, access specifiers for data members, multiple inheritance, and typical traps.

C.126	An abstract class typically doesn't need a constructor

Let me combine the already presented rules "C.2: Use `class` if the class has an invariant; use `struct` if the data members can vary independently" and "C.41: A constructor should create a fully initialized object" to get the actual rule. An invariant is a condition on a class data member that has to be established by the constructor. Conversely, an abstract base class does not have any data and needs, therefore, no declared constructor.

Virtuality

There a few rules to virtual functions you should keep in mind when designing class hierarchies.

C.128	Virtual functions should specify exactly one of `virtual`, `override`, or `final`

Since C++11, we have had three keywords to control overriding.

- **`virtual`:** declares a virtual function that can be overridden in derived classes
- **`override`:** verifies that the function is virtual and overrides a virtual function of a base class
- **`final`:** verifies that the function is virtual and cannot be overridden by a member function of a derived class

According to the guidelines, the rules for the usage of the three keywords are straightforward: "Use `virtual` only when declaring a new virtual function. Use `override` only when declaring an overrider. Use `final` only when declaring a final overrider."

```
struct Base{
    virtual void testGood() {}
    virtual void testBad() {}
};
```

```
struct Derived: Base{
    void testGood() final {}
    virtual void testBad() final override {}
};

int main() {
    Derived d;
}
```

The member function testBad() in the class Derived provides much redundant information.

- You should use final or override only if the function is virtual. Skip virtual: void testBad() final override {}.

- Using the keyword final without the virtual keyword is valid only if the function is already virtual; therefore, the function must override a virtual function of a base class. Skip override: void testBad() final {}.

C.130	For making deep copies of polymorphic classes prefer a virtual clone function instead of copy construction/ assignment

This rule is a continuation of rule "C.67: A polymorphic class should suppress copying." Rule C.67 explicitly shows that copying a polymorphic class may lead to the slicing problem. To overcome this issue, override a virtual clone function that copies the actual type and returns an owning pointer (std::unique_ptr) to the new object. In the derived class, return the derived type by using the so-called covariant return type.

Covariant return type: allows for an overriding member function to return a derived type of the return type of the overridden member function.

Let me illustrate this recommendation with an example.

```
// cloneFunction.cpp

#include <iostream>
#include <memory>
#include <string>

struct Base { // GOOD: base class suppresses copying
```

```
  Base() = default;
  virtual ~Base() = default;
  Base(const Base&) = delete;
  Base& operator = (const Base&) = delete;
  virtual std::unique_ptr<Base> clone() {
    return std::make_unique<Base>();
    }
  virtual std::string getName() const { return "Base"; }
};

struct Derived : public Base {
  Derived() = default;
  std::unique_ptr<Base> clone() override {
    return std::make_unique<Derived>();
    }
    std::string getName() const override { return "Derived"; }
};

int main() {

  std::cout << '\n';

  auto base1 = std::make_unique<Base>();
  auto base2 = base1->clone();
  std::cout << "base1->getName(): " << base1->getName() << '\n';
  std::cout << "base2->getName(): " << base2->getName() << '\n';

  auto derived1 = std::make_unique<Derived>();
  auto derived2 = derived1->clone();
  std::cout << "derived1->getName(): " << derived1->getName() << '\n';
  std::cout << "derived2->getName(): " << derived2->getName() << '\n';

  std::cout << '\n';


}
```

The clone member function returns the newly created object in a std::unique_ptr. The ownership of the newly created objects goes, therefore, to the caller. Now the virtual dispatch happens as expected. See Figure 5.11.

It's obligatory for the covariant return type that the Derived::clone member function's return type is std::unique_ptr<Base> and not std::unique_ptr<Derived>. When I change the return type of Derived::clone to std::unique_ptr<Derived>, the compilation fails (see Figure 5.12).

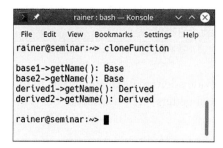

Figure 5.11 *A virtual* `clone` *member function*

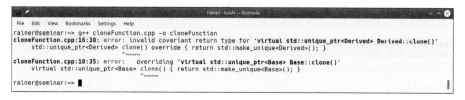

Figure 5.12 *A virtual* `clone` *member function without covariant return type*

C.132	Don't make a function `virtual` without reason

A virtual function is a feature that does not come for free.
A virtual function

- Increases the run time and the object code size
- Is open for errors because it can be overridden in derived classes

Access specifiers for data members

Typically, the access specifier for all data members of a class is the same: All data members are either `public` or `private`.

- `public` if there is no invariant on the data members. Use a `struct`.
- `private` if there is an invariant on the data members. Use a `class`.

C.131   Avoid trivial getters and setters

Getters or setters are trivial if they do not provide additional semantic value to the data members. Here are two examples of trivial getters and setters from the C++ Core Guidelines:

```
class Point {   // Bad: verbose
public:
    Point(int xx, int yy) : x{xx}, y{yy} { }
    int get_x() const { return x; }
    void set_x(int xx) { x = xx; }
    int get_y() const { return y; }
    void set_y(int yy) { y = yy; }
    // no behavioral member functions
private:
    int x;
    int y;
};
```

x and y can have arbitrary values. This means an instance of `Point` maintains no invariant on x and y. x and y are just values. Using a `struct` as a collection of values is more appropriate, and x and y should, consequently, become `public`.

```
struct Point {
    int x{0};
    int y{0};
};
```

C.133   Avoid `protected` data

`protected` data make your program complex and error prone. If you put `protected` data into a base class, you cannot reason about derived classes in isolation and, therefore, you break encapsulation. You always have to reason about the entire class hierarchy.

This means you have to answer at least these three questions.

1. Do I have to implement a constructor to initialize the `protected` data?

2. What is the actual value of the `protected` data if I use them?

3. Who is affected if I modify the `protected` data?

Answering these questions becomes more and more difficult as your class hierarchy becomes more and more complex.

To put it the other way, `protected` data is a kind of global data in the scope of the class hierarchy. And you know non-const global data is bad.

C.134	Ensure all non-`const` data members have the same access level

The previous rule, C.133, stated that you should avoid protected data. Consequently, all of your non-const data members should be either `public` or `private`. An object can have data members that do not represent the invariants of the object. Non-const data members that do not represent the invariants of an object should be `public`. In contrast, non-const `private` data members are used for the object invariants. As a reminder: A data member having an invariant cannot have all the values of the underlying type.

Based on this observation and the additional observation that you should not mix data members representing/not representing invariants in one class, all your non-const data members should be either `public` or `private`. Imagine if you have a class with `public` and `private` data members that are non-const. Now your data type is confusing. Does your data type maintain an invariant, or is it merely a collection of unrelated values?

Multiple inheritance

There are two typical use cases for multiple inheritance: separating interface inheritance from implementation inheritance and implementing multiple distinct interfaces.

C.129	When designing a class hierarchy, distinguish between implementation inheritance and interface inheritance

Interface inheritance is about the separation of interface and implementation, so that a derived class can be changed without affecting the user of the base class; implementation inheritance is the use of inheritance to support new functionality by extending existing functionality.

Pure interface inheritance is if your base class has only pure virtual functions. In contrast, if your base class has data members or implemented functions, this is implementation inheritance. Consequently, you break the previous rule "C.121: If a base class is used as an interface, make it an abstract class." The C++ Core Guidelines give an example of mixing both concepts.

```cpp
class Shape {   // BAD, mixed interface and implementation
public:
    Shape(Point ce = {0, 0}, Color co = none):
        cent{ce}, col {co} {
        /* ... */
    }

    Point center() const { return cent; }
    Color color() const { return col; }

    virtual void rotate(int) = 0;
    virtual void move(Point p) { cent = p; redraw(); }

    virtual void redraw() const;

    // ...
public:
    Point cent;
    Color col;
};

class Circle : public Shape {
public:
    Circle(Point c, int r) :Shape{c}, rad{r} { /* ... */ }

    // ...
private:
    int rad;
};

class Triangle : public Shape {
public:
    Triangle(Point p1, Point p2, Point p3); // calculate center
    // ...
};
```

Mixing the concepts of interface inheritance and implementation inheritance is bad. Why?

- As the Shape class evolves, it may become more and more difficult and error prone to maintain the various constructors.
- The member functions of the Shape class may never be used.
- If you add data to the Shape class, a recompilation becomes probable.

How can we get the best of those two worlds: stable interfaces with interface hierarchies and code reuse with implementation inheritance? One possible answer, which I implement in this chapter, is dual inheritance. Another answer is the PImpl idiom. PImpl stands for **p**ointer to **impl**ementation. It moves implementation details in a separate class that can be accessed through a pointer.

Let's continue with dual inheritance. Dual inheritance implements a quite sophisticated recipe.

1. **Define the base Shape of the class hierarchy as pure interface.**

```
class Shape {
public:
    virtual Point center() const = 0;
    virtual Color color() const = 0;

    virtual void rotate(int) = 0;
    virtual void move(Point p) = 0;

    virtual void redraw() const = 0;

    // ...
};
```

2. **Derive a pure interface Circle from the Shape.**

```
class Circle : public virtual Shape {
public:
    virtual int radius() = 0;
    // ...
};
```

3. Provide the implementation class `Impl::Shape`.

```cpp
class Impl::Shape : public virtual Shape {
public:
    // constructors, destructor
    // ...
    Point center() const override { /* ... */ }
    Color color() const override { /* ... */ }

    void rotate(int) override { /* ... */ }
    void move(Point p) override { /* ... */ }

    void redraw() const override { /* ... */ }

    // ...
};
```

4. Implement the class `Impl::Circle` by inheriting from the interface and the implementation.

```cpp
class Impl::Circle : public Circle, public Impl::Shape {
public:
    // constructors, destructor

    int radius() override { /* ... */ }
    // ...
};
```

5. If you want to extend the class hierarchy, you have to derive from the interface and from the implementation.

```cpp
class Smiley : public Circle {
public:
    // ...
};
```

```cpp
                    // implementation
class Impl::Smiley : public virtual Smiley, public Impl::Circle {
public:
    // constructors, destructor
    // ...
}
```

This is the big picture of the two hierarchies.

- **Interface:** `Smiley -> Circle -> Shape`
- **Implementation:** `Impl::Smiley -> Impl::Circle -> Impl::Shape`

By reading the last lines, maybe you had déjà vu. You are right. This technique of multiple inheritance is similar to the adapter pattern, implemented with multiple inheritance. The adapter pattern is from the well-known Gang of Four (GoF) design pattern book, *Design Patterns: Elements of Reusable Object-Oriented Software*, authored by Erich Gamma, Richard Helm, Ralph Johnson, and John Vlissides.

C.135	Use multiple inheritance to represent multiple distinct interfaces

It is a good idea that your interfaces support only one aspect of your design. What does that mean? If you provide a pure interface consisting only of pure virtual functions, a concrete class has to implement all functions. If the interface is too broad, the class has to implement functions it doesn't need or that make no sense.

An example of two distinct interfaces is `istream` and `ostream` from C++'s input and output streams library.

```
class iostream : public istream, public ostream { // very simplified
    // ...
};
```

Typical traps

There are two typical traps when it comes to the design of a class hierarchy.

C.138	Create an overload set for a derived class and its bases with `using`

This rule holds for virtual and nonvirtual functions. If you don't use the `using` declaration, member functions in the derived class hide the entire overload set. This process is also often called shadowing (see Figure 5.13). Shadowing is a behavior that contradicts the intuition of many C++ developers because an overload may be chosen that doesn't seem like the best match.

```cpp
// overloadSet.cpp

#include <iostream>

class Base {
public:
    void func(int i) { std::cout << "Base::func(int) \n"; }
    void func(double d) { std::cout << "Base::func(double) \n"; }
};

class Derived: public Base {  // Bad: shadowing func of Base
public:
    void func(int i) { std::cout << "Derived::func(int) \n"; }
};

int main() {

    std::cout << '\n';

    Derived der;
    der.func(2011);
    der.func(2020.5);

    std::cout << '\n';

}
```

The line der.func(2020.5) with a double argument is called, but the int overload of class Derived is used. Consequently, a narrowing conversion from double to int happens. That is most of the time not the behavior that you want.

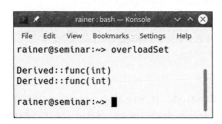

Figure 5.13 *Shadowing of member functions*

To use the `double` overload of class `Base`, you have to introduce it in the scope of `Derived`.

```
class Derived: public Base {   // good: Base::func is introduced
public:
    void func(int i) { std::cout << "f(int) \n"; }
    using Base::func; // exposes func(double)
};
```

C.140	Do not provide different default arguments for a virtual function and an overrider

If you provide different default arguments for a virtual function and an overrider, your class may cause lots of confusion.

```
// overrider.cpp

#include <iostream>

class Base {
public:
    virtual int multiply(int value, int factor = 2) = 0;
};

class Derived : public Base {  // Bad: different defaults
                               // for virtual functions
public:
    int multiply(int value, int factor = 10) override {
        return factor * value;
    }
};

int main() {

    std::cout << '\n';

    Derived d;
    Base& b = d;

    std::cout << "b.multiply(10): " << b.multiply(10) << '\n';
    std::cout << "d.multiply(10): " << d.multiply(10) << '\n';
```

```
    std::cout << '\n';


}
```

Figure 5.14 shows the surprising output of the program.

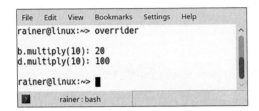

Figure 5.14 *Different default arguments for virtual functions*

What's happening? Both objects b and d call the same function. The function is virtual and, therefore, late binding happens. Late binding applies to member functions, but not to data members of a class including default arguments. They are statically bound, and early binding happens for that part.

Accessing objects

Although this section has nine rules, only about four of them are covered, for two reasons. First, the rule "C.145: Access polymorphic objects through pointers and references" adds nothing new to the rule "C.67: A polymorphic class should suppress copying." Second, the C++ Core Guidelines dedicate an entire section to smart pointers. The section about resource management provides complete details.

The remaining rules are about the dynamic_cast and the erroneous assignment of a pointer to an array of derived class objects.

dynamic_cast

Before I write about the dynamic_cast, let me emphasize that casts, including dynamic_cast, are used way too often. The job description of the dynamic_cast, according to cppreference.com, is "Safely converts pointers and references to classes up, down, and sideways along the inheritance hierarchy."

Let's first start with the use case of a dynamic_cast.

C.146	Use dynamic_cast where class hierarchy navigation is unavoidable

It's the job of a dynamic_cast to navigate in a class hierarchy.

```
struct Base {   // an interface
    virtual void f();
    virtual void g();
};

struct Derived : Base {   // a wider interface
    void f() override;
    virtual void h();
};

void user(Base* pb) {
    if (Derived* pd = dynamic_cast<Derived*>(pb)) {
        // ... use Derived's interface ...
    }
    else {
        // ... make do with Base's interface ...
    }
}
```

To detect the right type for pb during run time, a dynamic_cast is necessary: dynamic_cast<Derived*>(pb). If the cast fails, you get a null pointer.

A downcast can also be performed with static_cast, which avoids the cost of the run-time check. static_cast is only safe if the object is definitely Derived.

The following rules are two options you have for dynamic_cast.

C.147	Use dynamic_cast to a reference type when failure to find the required class is considered an error

and

C.148	Use dynamic_cast to a pointer type when failure to find the required class is considered a valid alternative

To make it short: You can apply a dynamic_cast to a pointer or to a reference. If the dynamic_cast fails, you get back a null pointer in the case of a pointer and a std::bad_cast exception in the case of a reference. Consequently, use a dynamic_cast to a pointer if a failure is a valid option; if a failure is not a valid option, use a reference.

The program badCast.cpp shows both cases.

```
// badCast.cpp

struct Base {
    virtual void f() {}
};
struct Derived : Base {};

int main() {

    Base a;

    Derived* b1 = dynamic_cast<Derived*>(&a);  // nullptr
    Derived& b2 = dynamic_cast<Derived&>(a);   // std::bad_cast


}
```

The g++ compiler complains about both dynamic_casts at compile time. At run time, the program throws the expected exception std::bad_cast for the reference (see Figure 5.15).

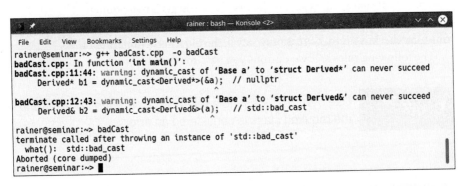

Figure 5.15 *dynamic_cast causes a* std::bad_cast *exception*

C.152	Never assign a pointer to an array of derived class objects to a pointer to its base

This may not happen very often, but when it happens, the consequences are terribly bad. The result may be an invalid object access or memory corruption. The code snippet shows the invalid object access.

```
struct Base { int x; };
struct Derived : Base { int y; };

Derived a[] = {{1, 2}, {3, 4}, {5, 6}};
Base* p = a; // Bad: a decays to &a[0] which is converted to a Base*
p[1].x = 7;  // overwrite Derived[0].y
```

The last assignment should update the Base member x of the second array element, but due to pointer arithmetic, it points to the second int after p[0].x. This happens to be memory of a[0].y! The reason is that Base* was assigned a pointer to an array of derived objects Derived. During this assignment (Base* p = a;), the array a decays to &a[0], which is converted to a Base*.

Decay is the name of an implicit conversion that applies lvalue-to-rvalue, array-to-pointer, and function-to-pointer conversions, removing const and volatile qualifiers. This means that you can call a function accepting Derived* with an array of Deriveds. Necessary information such as the length of the array of Deriveds is lost.

In the following code snippet, the function func takes its array as a pointer to the first element.

```
void func(Derived* d);
Derived d[] = {{1, 2}, {3, 4}, {5, 6}};
```

```
func(d);
```

The array-to-pointer decay is perfectly fine in this func case but causes problems in the previous p[1].x case.

Overloading and overloaded operators

You can overload functions, member functions, template functions, and operators. You cannot overload function objects, and therefore, you cannot overload lambdas.

The seven rules to overloading and overloaded operators follow one key idea: Build intuitive software systems for your users. Let me rephrase this key idea with a well-known golden rule in software development: Follow the principle of least astonishment (also known as the principle of least surprise). The principle of least astonishment essentially means that the components of a system should behave in a way that most users will expect them to behave. This principle is very important for overloading and overloaded operators because with great power comes great responsibility.

Although the seven rules address the intuitive behavior of overloading and overloaded operators, they take different perspectives. They address their conventional usage, the implicit conversion of operators, the equivalence of overloaded operations, and the idea that you should overload operators in the namespace of their operands.

Conventional usage

Conventional usage means that the user should not be surprised by unexpected behavior or mysterious side effects of the operators.

C.167	Use an operator for an operation with its conventional meaning

Conventional meaning includes that you use the appropriate operator. For example, here are a few operators that we are used to:

- **==, !=, <, <=, >, and >=:** comparison operations
- **+, -, *, /, and %:** arithmetic operations
- **->, unary *, and []:** access of objects
- **=:** assignment of objects
- **<<, >>:** input and output operations

C.161	Use nonmember functions for symmetric operators

Conventional meaning includes that your data type should behave like a number if it models a number. This rule is a kind of a generalization of the rule "C.86: Make == symmetric with respect to operand types and noexcept."

In general, the implementation of a symmetric operator such as + inside the class is not possible.

Assume that you want to implement a type `MyInt`. `MyInt` should support the addition of `MyInt`s and built-in `int`s. Let's give it a try.

```cpp
// MyInt.cpp

struct MyInt {
    MyInt(int v):val(v) {};
    MyInt operator + (const MyInt& oth) const {
        return MyInt(val + oth.val);
    }
    int val;
};

int main() {

    MyInt myFive = MyInt(2) + MyInt(3);
    MyInt myFive2 = MyInt(3) + MyInt(2);

    MyInt myTen = myFive + 5;           // OK
    MyInt myTen2 = 5 + myFive;          // ERROR

}
```

Due to the implicit conversion constructor (`MyInt(int v):val(v)`), the expression `myFive + 5` is valid. Constructors taking one argument are conversion constructors because they take in the concrete case an `int` and return a `MyInt`. In contrast, the last expression `5 + myFive` is not valid because the + operator for `int` and `MyInt` is not overloaded (see Figure 5.16).

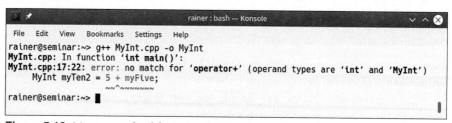

Figure 5.16 *Missing overload for* `int` *and* `MyInt`

The small program has many issues:

1. The + operator is not symmetric.

2. The val variable is public.

3. The conversion constructor is implicit.

It's quite easy to overcome the first two issues with a nonmember operator + that is in the class declared as a friend.

```cpp
// MyInt2.cpp

class MyInt2 {
public:
    MyInt2(int v):val(v) {};
    friend MyInt2 operator + (const MyInt2& fir, const MyInt2& sec) {
        return MyInt2(fir.val + sec.val);
    }
private:
    int val;
};


int main() {

    MyInt2 myFive = MyInt2(2) + MyInt2(3);
    MyInt2 myFive2 = MyInt2(3) + MyInt2(2);

    MyInt2 myTen = myFive + 5;    // OK
    MyInt2 myTen2 = 5 + myFive;   // OK

}
```

Now implicit conversion from int to MyInt2 kicks in, and the variable val is private. Thanks to the implicit conversion, the 5 in the last line becomes a MyInt2(5).

According to rule "C.46: By default, declare single-argument constructors explicit," you should not use an implicit conversion constructor.

MyInt3 has an explicit conversion constructor.

```cpp
// MyInt3.cpp

class MyInt3 {
public:
    explicit MyInt3(int v):val(v) {};
```

```
    friend MyInt3 operator + (const MyInt3& fir, const MyInt3& sec) {
        return MyInt3(fir.val + sec.val);
    }
private:
    int val;
};


int main() {

    MyInt3 myFive = MyInt3(2) + MyInt3(3);
    MyInt3 myFive2 = MyInt3(3) + MyInt3(2);

    MyInt3 myTen = myFive + 5;      // ERROR
    MyInt3 myTen2 = 5 + myFive;     // ERROR


}
```

Making the conversion constructor explicit breaks the compilation (see Figure 5.17).

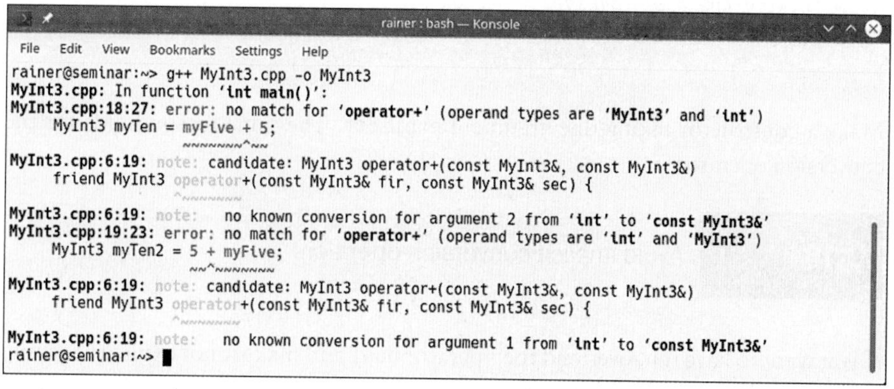

Figure 5.17 *Using an* explicit *constructor*

The general way to solve the challenge is to implement two additional + operators for MyInt4. One takes an int as the left argument, and one takes an int as the right argument.

```
// MyInt4.cpp

class MyInt4 {
public:
```

```
    explicit MyInt4(int v):val(v) {};
    friend MyInt4 operator + (const MyInt4& fir, const MyInt4& sec) {
        return MyInt4(fir.val + sec.val);
    }
    friend MyInt4 operator + (const MyInt4& fir, int sec) {
        return MyInt4(fir.val + sec);
    }
     friend MyInt4 operator + (int fir, const MyInt4& sec) {
        return MyInt4(fir + sec.val);
    }
private:
    int val;
};

int main() {

    MyInt4 myFive = MyInt4(2) + MyInt4(3);
    MyInt4 myFive2 = MyInt4(3) + MyInt4(2);

    MyInt4 myTen = myFive + 5;     // OK
    MyInt4 myTen2 = 5 + myFive;    // OK

}
```

Make a constructor taking one argument explicit. The same reason holds for the conversion operator.

C.164   Avoid implicit conversion operators

If you want to have fun, overload the operator bool and make it not explicit. Making it not explicit means that integer promotion from bool to int can happen silently.

Let me design a data type MyHouse that can be bought. I implement the operator bool to easily check to see if a family has already bought the house.

```
1 // implicitConversion.cpp
2
3 #include <iostream>
4 #include <string>
5
```

```
 6 struct MyHouse {
 7    MyHouse() = default;
 8    explicit MyHouse(const std::string& fam): family(fam) {}
 9
10    operator bool(){ return not family.empty(); }
11    // explicit operator bool(){ return not family.empty(); }
12
13    std::string family = "";
14 };
15
16 int main() {
17
18    std::cout << std::boolalpha << '\n';
19
20    MyHouse firstHouse;
21    if (not firstHouse) {
22        std::cout << "firstHouse is not sold." << '\n';
23    }
24
25    MyHouse secondHouse("grimm");
26    if (secondHouse) {
27        std::cout << "Grimm bought secondHouse." << '\n';
28    }
29
30    std::cout << '\n';
31
32    int myNewHouse = firstHouse + secondHouse;
33    int myNewHouse2 = (20 * firstHouse - 10 * secondHouse)
34                          / secondHouse;
35
36    std::cout << "myNewHouse: " << myNewHouse << '\n';
37    std::cout << "myNewHouse2: " << myNewHouse2 << '\n';
38
39    std::cout << '\n';
40
41 }
```

Now I can easily check with the operator bool (line 10) to see if a family (line 21) or no family (line 26) lives in the house. Fine. Due to the implicit operator bool, I can use objects of MyHouse in arithmetic expressions (lines 32 and 33). Supporting arithmetic was not my intention. See Figure 5.18.

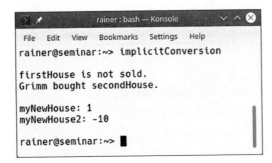

Figure 5.18 *Implicit operator bool*

This is weird!

Since C++11, you can make a conversion operator explicit; therefore, no implicit conversion to int kicks in. If I use the explicit operator bool (line 11), the arithmetic of houses is not possible anymore, but houses can be used in logical expressions. See Figure 5.19.

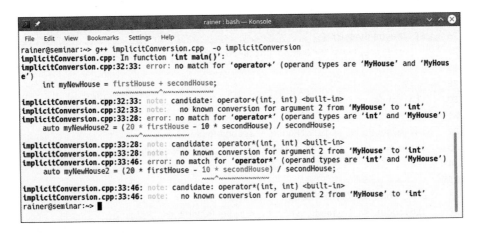

Figure 5.19 *Explicit operator bool*

C.162	Overload operations that are roughly equivalent

and

C.163	Overload only for operations that are roughly equivalent

Both rules are closely related. Equivalent operations should have the same name. Or the other way around: Nonequivalent operations should not have the same name.

Here is the example from the C++ Core Guidelines.

```
void print(int a);
void print(const string&);
...
print(5);
```

Invoking print(5) feels like generic programming. You don't have to care which version of print is used. This observation will not hold if the functions have different names.

```
void print_int(int a);
void print_string(const string&);
 ...
print_int(5)
```

If nonequivalent operations have the same name, the names are too general or just wrong. This is confusing and error prone.

```
std::string translate(const std::string& text); // translate into English
Code translate(const Code& code);                 // compile the code
```

C.168	Define overloaded operators in the namespace of their operands

Have you ever wondered why the following program works and displays Test?

```
#include <iostream>
int main() {
    std::cout << "Test\n";
}
```

First of all, when you execute the program, it essentially becomes the following program:

```
#include <iostream>
int main() {
    operator << (std::cout, "Test\n");
}
```

`std::cout << "Test\n"` boils down to `operator << (std::cout, "Test\n");`. There is no operator `<<` in the global namespace, but argument-dependent lookup (ADL) examines the `std` namespace. The `operator <<` finds `std::operator << (std::ostream&, const char*)` because `std::cout` is in the `std::` namespace.

Argument-dependent lookup (ADL, also called Koenig lookup) means that for unqualified function calls, the functions in the namespace of the function arguments are considered by the C++ compile time.

Let me rephrase the definition of ADL using operands and operators. The C++ run time also considers for operators the namespace of the operands. Consequently, you should define overloaded operators in the namespace of their operands.

Unions

A union is a special class type where all members start at the same address. A union can hold only one type at a time; therefore, you can save memory. A tagged union (aka discriminated union) is a union that keeps track of its types. `std::variant` is a tagged union.

The C++ Core Guidelines state that the job of unions is to save memory. You should not use naked unions but tagged unions such as `std::variant`.

C.180	Use unions to save memory

A union can hold only one type at one point in time, so you can save memory because the elements of a union share the same memory. The union will be as big as the biggest type.

```
union Value {
    int i;
    double d;
};
```

```
Value v = { 123 };          // initializes the first member with an int
std::cout << v.i << '\n';    // write 123
v.d = 987.654;              // now v holds a double
std::cout << v.d << '\n';    // write 987.654
```

`Value` is a "naked" union. You should not use it, according to the next rule.

C.181 Avoid "naked" unions

"Naked" unions are very error prone because you have to keep track of the underlying type.

```cpp
// nakedUnion.cpp

#include <iostream>

union Value {
    int i;
    double d;
};

int main() {

    std::cout << '\n';

    Value v;
    v.d = 987.654;
    std::cout << "v.d: " << v.d << '\n';
    std::cout << "v.i: " << v.i << '\n';    // (1)

    std::cout << '\n';

    v.i = 123;
    std::cout << "v.i: " << v.i << '\n';
    std::cout << "v.d: " << v.d << '\n';    // (2)

    std::cout << '\n';

}
```

The union holds a `double` in the first section and an `int` value in the second section. If you read a `double` as an `int` (1), or an `int` as a `double` (2), you get undefined behavior (see Figure 5.20).

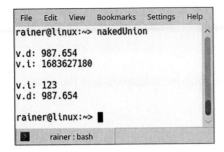

Figure 5.20 *Undefined behavior with a "naked" union*

To overcome this source of errors, you should use a tagged union.

C.182   Use anonymous unions to implement tagged unions

Implementing a tagged union is quite sophisticated. In case you are curious, have a look at the rule "C.182: Use anonymous unions to implement tagged unions."

To simplify the code sample below, I used the tagged union std::variant, which is part of C++17.

```
1 // variant.cpp; C++17
2
3 #include <variant>
4 #include <string>
5
6 int main() {
7
8    std::variant<int, float> v;
9    std::variant<int, float> w;
10
11   int i = std::get<int>(v);  // i is 0
12
13   v = 12;                    // v contains int
14   int j = std::get<int>(v);
15
16   w = std::get<int>(v);
17   w = std::get<0>(v);        // same effect as the previous line
18   w = v;                     // same effect as the previous line
19
20
```

```
21    //  std::get<double>(v);     // error: no double in [int, float]
22    //  std::get<3>(v);          // error: valid index values are 0 and 1
23
24    try{
25        std::get<float>(w);      // w contains int, not float: will throw
26    }
27    catch (std::bad_variant_access&) {}
28
29    v  = 5.5f;                   // switch to float
30    v = 5;                       // and back
31
32    std::variant<std::string> v2("abc"); // converting constructors ok
                                           // when unambiguous
33    v2 = "def";                  // converting assignment ok when unambiguous
34
35 }
```

Lines 8 and 9 define the two variants v and w. Both variants can have an int and a float value. Their initial value is 0 (line 11). The default value for the first underlying type int is 0. v gets in the line 13 the value 13. Thanks to std::get<int>(v), you can get the value for the underlying type. Line 16 and the following two lines show three possibilities to assign the variant v the variant w. You have to keep a few rules in mind. You can ask for the value of a variant by type or by index. The type must be unique, and the index valid (lines 21 and 22). If not, you get a std::bad_variant_ access exception. Lines 29 and 30 switch the variant v to float and back to int. If the constructor call or assignment call is unambiguous, a conversion takes place. This conversion is the reason you can construct a std::variant<std::string> with a C-string or assign a new C-string to the variant (lines 27 and 28).

Related rules

I have skipped two sections from the classes and class hierarchies part of the C++ Core Guidelines. The first one is the section on containers and other resource handles; the second one is the section related to function objects and lambdas.

I also skipped the six guidelines discussing containers and other resource handles because they lack content.

The four guidelines to function objects and lambdas are already part of Chapter 4, Functions, and Chapter 8, Expressions and Statements.

The rules related to smart pointers are presented in a bigger context in Chapter 7, Resource Management.

Distilled

Important

- Prefer concrete types over class hierarchies. Make your concrete type regular. Regular types support the big six (default constructor, destructor, copy and move constructor, copy- and move-assignment operator), the `swap` function, and the equality operator.

- If possible, let the compiler generate the big six. If not, request all the special member functions via `default`. If this is not possible, implement all of them explicitly and give them a consistent design. A copy constructor or copy-assignment operator should copy. A move constructor or move-assignment operator should move.

- A constructor should return a fully initialized object. Use the constructor to establish the invariant. Don't use a constructor to set the members to its defaults. Prefer in-class initialization to reduce repetition.

- Implement a destructor if you need cleanup action at object destruction. A base-class destructor should be `public` and `virtual` or `protected` and nonvirtual.

- Use class hierarchies to model only inherent hierarchical structures. Make the base class abstract if used as an interface to separate the interface from the implementation. An abstract class should have only a defaulted default constructor.

- Distinguish between interface inheritance and implementation inheritance. The objective of interface inheritance is to separate the user from the implementation; implementation inheritance is about reusing an existing implementation. Don't mix both concepts in a class.

- A class with virtual functions should have a `public` and `virtual` or `protected` destructor. Use exactly one of `virtual`, `override`, or `final` for a virtual function.

- Data members of a class should all be either `public` or `private`. Make them `private` and use a `class` if the class establishes an invariant. If not, make them `public` and use a `struct`.

- Make single-argument constructors and conversion operators `explicit`.

- Use unions to save memory, but don't use naked unions; prefer tagged unions such as `std::variant` from C++17.

Chapter 6

Enumerations

Cippi counts from one to five.

Enumerations are used to define sets of integer values and also a type for such sets of values. Although this section has eight rules about enums, there is a crucial rule. Prefer scoped enumerations to classic enumerations. Scoped enumerations are also called strongly typed enums or enum `classes`.

General Rules

Classical enumerations (before C++11) have many drawbacks. Let me explicitly compare plain (unscoped) enumerations and scoped enumerations because the difference is not explicitly mentioned in the C++ Core Guidelines.

Here is a classical enumeration:

```
enum Color {
    red,
    blue,
    green
};
```

What are the drawbacks of classical enumerations? The enumerators

- Have no scope.

- Implicitly convert `int`.

- Pollute the global namespace.

- Have an unknown type. The type has to be big enough to hold the enumerators.

By using the keyword `class` or `struct`, the enumeration becomes a scoped enumeration (class enum):

```
enum class ColorScoped {
    red,
    blue,
    green
};
```

Now you have to use the scope operator (`::`) to access the enumerators: `ColorScoped::red`. `ColorScoped::red` does not implicitly convert to `int` and, therefore, does not pollute the global namespace. This is the reason they are often called strongly typed.

Additionally, the underlying type is by default `int`, but you can choose a different integral type.

Now that the background information has been provided, let's dive directly into the most important rules.

Enum.1   Prefer enumerations over macros

Macros don't respect scope and have no type. This means you can override a previously set macro that specifies a color.

```
// webcolors.h
#define RED   0xFF0000
```

```
// productinfo.h
#define RED    0

int webcolor = RED;   // should be 0xFF0000
```

With `ColorScoped`, this would not have happened because you have to use the scope operator: `ColorScoped webcolor = ColorScoped::red;`.

Enum.2	Use enumerations to represent sets of related named constants

This rule is obvious because enumerators create a set of integers, which is a named type.

```
enum class Day {
    Mon,
    Tue,
    Wcd,
    Thu,
    Fri,
    Sat,
    Sun
};
```

Enum.3	Prefer enum classes over "plain" enums

The enumerators of a scoped enumerator (`enum class`) do not automatically convert to `int`. You have to access them with the scope operator.

```
// scopedEnum.cpp

#include <iostream>

enum class ColorScoped {
    red,
    blue,
    green
};
```

```
void useMe(ColorScoped color) {
    switch(color) {
    case ColorScoped::red:
        std::cout << "ColorScoped::red" << '\n';
        break;
    case ColorScoped::blue:
        std::cout << "ColorScoped::blue" << '\n';
        break;
    case ColorScoped::green:
        std::cout << "ColorScoped::green" << '\n';
        break;
    }
}


int main() {

    std::cout << static_cast<int>(ColorScoped::red) << '\n';   // 0
    std::cout << static_cast<int>(ColorScoped::green) << '\n'; // 2

    ColorScoped color{ColorScoped::red};
    useMe(color);                                  // ColorScoped::red

}
```

Enum.5   Don't use ALL_CAPS for enumerators

If you use ALL_CAPS for enumerators, you may get a conflict with macros because they are typically written in ALL_CAPS.

```
enum class ColorScoped{ RED };
```

```
#define RED 0xFF0000
```

Of course, this rule does not only apply to enumerators but to constants in general.

Enum.6   Avoid unnamed enumerations

Not every compile-time constant should be an enum. C++ also lets you define compile-time constants as constexpr variables. Use enums only for sets of *related* constants (Enum.2).

```
// bad
enum { red = 0xFF0000, scale = 4, is_signed = 1 };


// good
constexpr int red = 0xFF0000;
constexpr short scale = 4;
constexpr bool is_signed = true;
```

Enum.7	Specify the underlying type of an enumeration only when necessary

Since C++11, you can specify the underlying type of the enumeration and save memory. By default, the type of a scoped enum is int, and therefore, you can forward declare an enum.

```
// typeEnum.cpp

#include <iostream>

enum class Color1 {
    red,
    blue,
    green
};

enum struct Color2: char {
    red,
    blue,
    green
};

int main() {

    std::cout << sizeof(Color1) << '\n';  // 4
    std::cout << sizeof(Color2) << '\n';  // 1

}
```

Enum.8   Specify enumerator values only when necessary

By specifying the enumerator values, you may set a value twice. The following enumeration Col2 has this issue.

```
enum class Col1 { red, yellow, blue };
enum class Col2 { red = 1, yellow = 2, blue = 2 };    // typo
enum class Month { jan = 1, feb, mar,
                   apr, may, jun,
                   jul, aug, sep,
                   oct, nov, dec };                    // 1 is conventional
```

Sccoped enumerations check the value of their underlying enumerators at compile time.

```
// enumChecksRange.cpp

enum struct Color: char {
    red = 127,
    blue,
    green
};

int main() {

    Color color{Color::green};

}
```

The compilation of the program fails because the enumerators are too big to fit into the underlying type (see Figure 6.1).

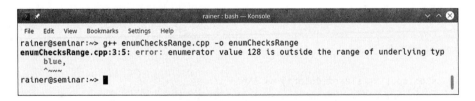

Figure 6.1 *The enumerators are too big for the underlying type*

With classical enumerators, the size of the underlying type would be just big enough.

Related rules

Chapter 8, Expressions and Statements, deepens the discussion to `constexpr` values.

Distilled

Important

- Use scoped enumerations instead of classical enumerations. As the name suggests, scoped enumerations have a scope, do not implicitly convert to `int`, do not pollute the global namespace, and have by default `int` as their underlying type.

- Specify the underlying type of the scoped enumerations and the values of the enumerators only when necessary.

Chapter 7

Resource Management

Cippi maintains the garden.

First, what is a resource? A resource is something that you have to manage. That means you have to acquire and release it because resources are limited, or you have to protect it. You can have only a limited amount of memory, sockets, processes, or threads; only one process can write a shared file or one thread can write a shared variable at one point in time. If you don't follow the protocol, many issues are possible.

If you think about resource management, it all boils down to one critical point: ownership. What I like in particular about modern C++ is that we can directly express our intention about ownership in code.

- **Local objects:** The C++ run time, as the owner, automatically manages the lifetime of these resources. The same holds for global objects or members of a class. The guidelines call them scoped objects.

- **References:** I'm not the owner. I only borrowed the resource that cannot be empty.

- **Raw pointers:** I'm not the owner. I only borrowed the resource that can be empty. I must not delete the resource.

- `std::unique_ptr`: I'm the exclusive owner of the resource. I may explicitly release the resource.

- `std::shared_ptr`: I share the resource with other `shared_ptrs` and release the resource if I'm the last owner. I may explicitly release my share of the ownership.

- `std::weak_ptr`: I'm not the owner of the resource, but I may temporarily become a shared owner of the resource by using the member function `std::weak_ptr.lock()`.

General rules

Although this section has six rules, only two of them, RAII and scoped objects, are original. Two of them are already part of other sections:

- R.2: In interfaces, use raw pointers to denote individual objects (only) (see I.13: Do not pass an array as a single pointer)

- R.6: Avoid non-const global variables (see I.2: Avoid non-const global variables)

The remaining four about the semantics of pointers and references extend existing rules.

The first general rule is idiomatic for C++: RAII. RAII stands for Resource Acquisition Is Initialization. The C++ standard library systematically relies on RAII.

R.1	Manage resources automatically using resource handles and RAII (Resource Acquisition Is Initialization)

The idea of RAII is simple. You create a kind of proxy object for your resource. The constructor of the proxy acquires the resource, and the destructor of the proxy releases the resource. The central idea of RAII is that the C++ run time is the owner of this proxy as a *local object* and, therefore, of the resource. When the proxy object as a local object goes out of the scope, the destructor of the proxy is automatically called. Consequently, we get deterministic destruction behavior in C++.

RAII is heavily used in the C++ ecosystem. Examples of RAII are the containers of the Standard Template Library (STL), smart pointers, and locks. Containers take care of their elements, smart pointers take care of their memory, and locks take care of their mutexes.

The following class `ResourceGuard` models RAII.

```cpp
1 // raii.cpp
2
3 #include <iostream>
4 #include <new>
5 #include <string>
6
7 class ResourceGuard {
8 public:
9     explicit ResourceGuard(const std::string& res):resource(res){
10        std::cout << "Acquire the " << resource << "." << '\n';
11    }
12    ~ResourceGuard(){
13        std::cout << "Release the "<< resource << "." << '\n';
14    }
15 private:
16    std::string resource;
17 };
18
19 int main() {
20
21    std::cout << '\n';
22
23    ResourceGuard resGuard1{"memoryBlock1"};
24
25    std::cout << "\nBefore local scope" << '\n';
26    {
27        ResourceGuard resGuard2{"memoryBlock2"};
28    }
29    std::cout << "After local scope" << '\n';
30
```

```
31      std::cout << '\n';
32
33
34      std::cout << "\nBefore try-catch block" << '\n';
35      try {
36          ResourceGuard resGuard3{"memoryBlock3"};
37          throw std::bad_alloc();
38      }
39      catch (const std::bad_alloc& e) {
40          std::cout << e.what();
41      }
42      std::cout << "\nAfter try-catch block" << '\n';
43
44      std::cout << '\n';
45
46 }
```

ResourceGuard is the guard that manages its resource. In this case, the resource is a simple string. ResourceGuard creates the resource in its constructor (lines 9–11) and releases the resource in its destructor (lines 12–14). It does its job very reliably. The creation and the releasing of the resource is only indicated in the constructor and in the destructor.

The C++ run time calls the destructor of resGuard1 (line 23) exactly at the end of the main function (line 46). The lifetime of resGuard2 (line 27) already ends in line 28. Therefore, the C++ run time calls the destructor once more. Even the throwing of the exception std::bad_alloc does not affect the reliability of resGuard3 (line 36). Its destructor is called at the end of the try block (lines 35–38).

Figure 7.1 displays the lifetime of the objects.

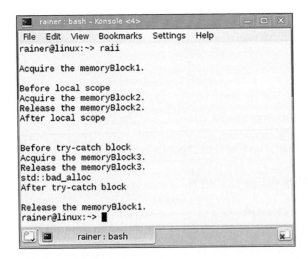

Figure 7.1 *Resource Acquisition Is Initialization*

R.3	A raw pointer (a T*) is non-owning

and

R.4	A raw reference (a T&) is non-owning

Both rules generalize the ownership aspect of the rule about passing pointers or references to functions and the rule about when to return a pointer (T*) or an lvalue reference (T&) from a function. The critical question for pointers and references is, Who is the owner of the resource? If you are not the owner but just borrowed it, you must not delete the resource.

R.5	Prefer scoped objects, don't heap-allocate unnecessarily

The rule about scoped objects is probably the most important rule for resource management in order to make it simple. If possible, use a scoped object.

A scoped object is an object with its scope. That may be a local object, a global object, or a member of a class. The C++ run time takes care of the scoped objects. There is no memory allocation and deallocation involved, and you cannot get a std::bad_alloc exception.

Why is the following example bad?

```cpp
void f(int n) {
    auto* p = new Gadget{n};
    // ...
    delete p;
}
```

There is no need to create Gadget on the heap. It costs time, and it is error prone. You may forget to deallocate the memory, or an exception may happen before the delete call. In the end, you have a memory leak. Just use a local object and you are safe by design.

```cpp
void f(int n) {
    Gadget g{n};
    // ...
}
```

The power of curly braces

It is handy to use extra curly braces to define an artificial scope. Thanks to the artificial scope, you can control the lifetime of a local object explicitly.

```cpp
int main() {

    {
        std::vector<int> myVec(SIZE);
        measurePerformance(myVec, "std::vector<int>(SIZE)");
    }


    {
        std::deque<int> myDec(SIZE);
        measurePerformance(myDec, "std::deque<int>(SIZE)");
    }

    {
        std::list<int> myList(SIZE);
        measurePerformance(myList, "std::list<int>(SIZE)");
    }

    {
        std::forward_list<int> myForwardList(SIZE);
        measurePerformance(myForwardList,
                          "std::forward_list<int>(SIZE)");
    }

    {
        std::string myString(SIZE,' ');
        measurePerformance(myString, "std::string(SIZE,' ')");
    }

}
```

The code snippet shows part of a performance test (measurePerformance) that includes substantial allocations. The temporarily created containers in each artificial scope are quite big. Without deleting them at the end of each artificial scope, your computer may run out of memory and you get a std::bad_alloc exception.

Allocation and deallocation

Maybe you are a little bit bewildered? The C++ Core Guidelines have only four rules for allocation and deallocation. Three of the four rules are about smart pointers. In the end, the essence of this section is that you should use smart pointers, which are the topic of the following section.

Before I dive into the four rules, let me give you a little background that is necessary for understanding the rules. Creating an object in C++ with new consists of two steps.

1. Allocate the memory for the object.

2. Construct the object into the allocated memory.

`operator new` or `operator new []` is the first step; the constructor is the second step.

The same strategy applies to the destruction but the other way around. First, the destructor (if any) is called, and then the memory is deallocated with `operator delete` or `operator delete []`.

R.10   Avoid `malloc()` and `free()`

What is the difference between `new` and `malloc`, or `delete` and `free`? The C functions `malloc` and `free` do only half of the job. `malloc` allocates the memory, and `free` deallocates the memory. Neither does `malloc` invoke the constructor nor does `free` invoke the destructor.

This means if you use an object that was just created via `malloc`, your program has undefined behavior.

```
// mallocVersusNew.cpp

#include <iostream>
#include <string>

struct Record {
    explicit Record(const std::string& na): name(na) {}
    std::string name;
};

int main() {
```

```
Record* p1 = static_cast<Record*>(malloc(sizeof(Record))); // (1)
std::cout << p1->name << '\n';

auto p2 = new Record("Record");                             // (2)
std::cout << p2->name << '\n';
```

}

I allocate memory only for the Record object (1). The result is that the output p1->name call in the following line is undefined behavior. Undefined behavior just means that you cannot make any assumption about the behavior of the program. On repeated runs, I got no output; the *expected* output, which is an empty string; and a core dump. See Figure 7.2.

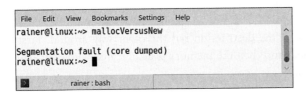

Figure 7.2 *Undefined behavior causes a core dump*

In contrast, the call (2) invokes the constructor.

R.11   Avoid calling new and delete explicitly

You should keep this rule in mind. The emphasis in this rule lies in the word *explicitly* because using smart pointers or containers of the STL gives you objects that *implicitly* use new and delete.

For example, here are a few variations to create std::unique_ptr and std::shared_ptr.

```
std::unique_ptr<int> uniq1(new int(2011));            // (1)
std::unique_ptr<int> uniq2 = std::make_unique<int>(2014);

std::shared_ptr<int> shar1(new int(2011));            // (1)
std::shared_ptr<int> share2 = std::make_shared<int>(2014);
```

If you don't know which version you should prefer, the rules "R.22: Use `make_shared()` to make `shared_ptrs`" and "R.23: Use `make_unique()` to make `unique_ptrs`" give you the definite answer.

You cannot entirely avoid the calls in (1). When you want to create a `std:::unique_ptr` or a `std::shared_ptr`, which shouldn't use the destructor of the underlying type, the following syntax is obligatory:

```
std::shared_ptr<int> shar1(new int(2011), MyIntDeleter());
```

R.12	Immediately give the result of an explicit resource allocation to a manager object

The C++ community loves acronyms. For memory allocation, there is a special name for this rule: NNN. NNN stands for No Naked New and means the result of a memory allocation should be given to a manager object. This manager object could be a `std::unique_ptr` or a `std::shared_ptr`. Of course, this rule has a broader context. For example, containers of the STL know how to take care of their elements, or locks know how to take care of their mutexes.

When you don't follow these rules, the danger of undefined behavior lurks.

```
// standaloneAllocation.cpp // Bad: because of double free

#include <iostream>
#include <memory>

struct MyInt{
  explicit MyInt(int myInt):i(myInt) {}
  ~MyInt() {
    std::cout << "Goodbye from " << i << '\n';
  }
  int i;
};

int main() {

    std::cout << '\n';

    MyInt* myInt = new MyInt(2011);

    std::unique_ptr<MyInt> uniq1 = std::unique_ptr<MyInt>(myInt);
```

```
    std::unique_ptr<MyInt> uniq2 = std::unique_ptr<MyInt>(myInt);

    std::cout << '\n';

}
```

The class `MyInt` displays in its destructor the value of the member attribute `i_`. The issue starts with the standalone allocation (`MyInt* myInt = new MyInt(2011)`). Either `uniq1` or `uniq2` is the owner of `myInt`, but not both. Due to the two owners, two deallocations of the memory happen, which is undefined behavior. See Figure 7.3.

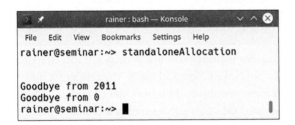

Figure 7.3 *Two owners with* `std::unique_ptr`

Two deallocations of `myInt` happen at the end of the `main` function. The first deallocation via the handle is fine, *but the second causes undefined behavior.* The value of the member attribute `i_` is 0 in the second case.

When using `std::make_unique`, you avoid the risk of double-free problems:

```
int main() {

    std::cout << '\n';

    std::unique_ptr<MyInt> uniq = std::make_unique<int>(2011);

    std::cout << '\n';

}
```

R.13	Perform at most one explicit resource allocation in a single expression statement

This rule is a little bit tricky.

```
void func(std::shared_ptr<Widget> sp1, std::shared_ptr<Widget> sp2) {
  ...
}

func(std::shared_ptr<Widget>(new Widget(1)),
     std::shared_ptr<Widget>(new Widget(2)));
```

This function call is not exception safe and may, therefore, result in a memory leak. Why? The reason is that four operations must be performed to initialize both shared pointers.

1. Allocate memory for `Widget(1)`.

2. Construct `Widget(1)`.

3. Allocate memory for `Widget(2)`.

4. Construct `Widget(2)`.

Up to C++14, the compiler is free to first allocate the memory for `Widget(1)` and `Widget(2)` and then construct both. From the optimization perspective, this makes much sense because one memory allocation of two `Widget`s is very likely faster than two allocations of one `Widget`. This means the following instructions could happen:

1. Allocate memory for `Widget(1)`.

2. Allocate memory for `Widget(2)`.

3. Construct `Widget(1)`.

4. Construct `Widget(2)`.

If one of the constructors throws an exception, the memory of the other object is not automatically freed and we get a memory leak.

It's easy to overcome this issue by using the factory function `std::make_shared` for creating a `std::shared_ptr`.

```
func(std::make_shared<Widget>(1), std::make_shared<Widget>(2));
```

`std::make_shared` guarantees that the function call has no effect if an exception is thrown. The analogous function `std::make_unique` for creating a `std::unique_ptr` gives the same guarantee.

Guaranteed evaluation order with C++17

Thanks to the guaranteed evaluation order in C++17, the already discussed code snippet in this rule cannot cause a memory leak.

```
void func(std::shared_ptr<Widget> sp1, std::shared_ptr<Widget> sp2) {
    ...
}

func(std::shared_ptr<Widget>(new Widget(1)),
     std::shared_ptr<Widget>(new Widget(2)));
```

The C++17 standard guarantees, in contrast to the C++14 standard, each subexpression in the function call `func` is evaluated before the other. In which sequence is still unspecified.

Smart pointers

From the library perspective, the smart pointers were the most important addition to the C++11 standard. The C++ Core Guidelines have more than ten rules related to `std::unique_ptr`, `std::shared_ptr`, and `std::weak_ptr`. The rules for smart pointers boil down to two categories: the basic usage of smart pointers as owners and smart pointers as function parameters.

Basic usage

I assume in this section a basic familiarity with smart pointers. If you want to know all the details, read the documentation for `std::unique_ptr`, `std::shared_ptr`, and `std::weak_ptr`.

R.20   Use `unique_ptr` or `shared_ptr` to represent ownership

For completeness, I also include `std::weak_ptr` in this rule. Modern C++ has three smart pointers for expressing three different kinds of ownership.

- **`std::unique_ptr`:** exclusive owner

- **std::shared_ptr:** shared owner

- **std::weak_ptr:** non-owning reference to an object that is managed by a std::shared_ptr

A std::unique_ptr is the exclusive owner of its resource. A std::unique_ptr cannot be copied, only moved.

```
auto uniquePtr1 = std::make_unique<int>(1998);
auto uniquePtr2(std::move(uniquePtr1));
```

In contrast, a std::shared_ptr shares ownership. If you copy or copy assign a shared pointer, the reference counter is increased; if you delete or reset a shared pointer, the reference counter is decreased. If the reference counter becomes zero, the underlying resource will be deleted.

```
auto sharedPtr1 = std::make_shared<int>(1998)    // reference count 1
auto sharedPtr2(sharedPtr1);                     // reference count 2
```

A std::weak_ptr is not a smart pointer. It has a reference to an object that is managed by a std::shared_ptr. Its interface is quite limited and doesn't allow the transparent access on the underlying resource. By using the member function lock on a std::weak_ptr, you can create a std::shared_ptr from a std::weak_ptr.

```
auto sharedPtr1 = std::make_shared<int>(1998) // reference count 1
std::weak_ptr<int> weakPtr1(sharedPtr1);      // reference count 1
auto sharedPtr2 = weakPtr1.lock();            // reference count 2
```

| **R.21** | Prefer unique_ptr over shared_ptr unless you need to share ownership |

The std::unique_ptr should always be your first choice if you need a smart pointer. A std::unique_ptr is per design as fast and as memory efficient as a raw pointer.

This observation does not hold for a std::shared_ptr. A std::shared_ptr needs to manage its reference counter and allocate extra memory for maintaining the control block. The control block is necessary to manage the lifetime of the controlled object. The std::shared_ptr shines when you need shared ownership. In this case, allocating the shared resource only once may spare memory and time.

Don't use a std::shared_ptr for convenience reasons because you want to copy it. A std::unique_ptr cannot be copied, but it can be moved.

```
 1 // moveUniquePtr.cpp
 2
 3 #include <algorithm>
 4 #include <iostream>
 5 #include <memory>
 6 #include <utility>
 7 #include <vector>
 8
 9 void takeUniquePtr(std::unique_ptr<int> uniqPtr) {
10     std::cout << "*uniqPtr: " << *uniqPtr << '\n';
11 }
12
13 int main() {
14
15     std::cout << '\n';
16
17     auto uniqPtr1 = std::make_unique<int>(2011);
18
19     takeUniquePtr(std::move(uniqPtr1));
20
21     auto uniqPtr2 = std::make_unique<int>(2014);
22     auto uniqPtr3 = std::make_unique<int>(2017);
23
24     std::vector<std::unique_ptr<int>> vecUniqPtr {};
25     vecUniqPtr.push_back(std::move(uniqPtr2));
26     vecUniqPtr.push_back(std::move(uniqPtr3));
27     vecUniqPtr.push_back(std::make_unique<int>(2020));
28
29     std::cout << '\n';
30
31     std::for_each(vecUniqPtr.begin(), vecUniqPtr.end(),
32                 [](std::unique_ptr<int>& uniqPtr) {
33                     std::cout << *uniqPtr << '\n';
34                 });
35
36     std::cout << '\n';
37
38 }
```

The function `takeUniquePtr` (line 9) takes a `std::unique_ptr` by value. The key observation is that you have to move the `std::unique_ptr` inside. The same argument holds for the `std::vector<std::unique_ptr<int>>` (line 24). `std::vector`, like all containers of the standard template, uses copy semantics. The container wants to own its elements but copying a `std::unique_ptr` is not possible. `std::move` solves this issue (lines 25 and 26). Directly constructing the `std::unique_ptr` is also possible (line 27). You can apply an algorithm such as `std::for_each` on the `std::vector<std::unique_ptr<int>>` (line 31) if no copy semantics is used internally.

Finally, Figure 7.4 shows the output of the program.

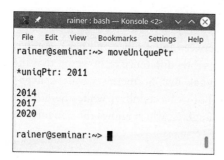

Figure 7.4 *Moving a* `std::unique_ptr`

R.22	Use make_shared() to make shared_ptrs

and

R.23	Use make_unique() to make unique_ptrs

There are two reasons to prefer `std::make_unique` to `std::unique_ptr` and to prefer `std::make_shared` to `std::shared_ptr`.

The first reason is exception safety. Read the details in the previous rule "R.13: Perform at most one explicit resource allocation in a single expression statement."

The second reason holds only for `std::shared_ptr`.

```
auto sharPtr1 = std::shared_ptr<int>(new int(1998));

auto sharPtr2 = std::make_shared<int>(1998);
```

When you call `std::shared_ptr<int>(new int(1998))`, two memory allocations are involved: one allocation for `new int(1998)` and the second for the control block of the `std::shared_ptr`. Memory allocation is expensive. Therefore, you should avoid it. `std::make_shared<int>(1998)` makes out of two memory allocations one and is, therefore, faster. Additionally, the allocated object (`new int(1998)`) and the control block are next to each other and can, therefore, be accessed faster.

R.24	Use std::weak_ptr to break cycles of shared_ptrs

You get cyclic references of std::shared_ptr if the std::shared_ptrs reference each other. For example, a doubly linked list creates cycles. If you implement the links with std::shared_ptr, your reference counter never becomes zero, and you end up with a memory leak. Here is a short example.

There are two cycles in Figure 7.5: first, between the mother and her daughter; second, between the mother and her son. The subtle difference is, however, that the mother references her daughter with a std::weak_ptr. So there's a std::shared_ptr cycle between mother and son keeping both objects alive, while there is no std::shared_ptr cycle between mother and daughter, which allows the daughter to be deleted.

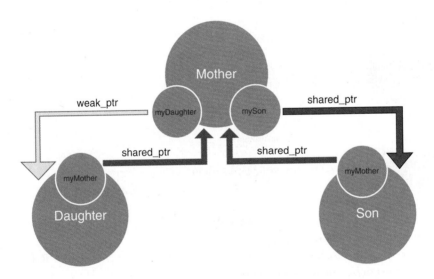

Figure 7.5 *Cycles of smart pointers*

If you don't like images, here is the corresponding source code.

```
1 // cycle.cpp
2
3 #include <iostream>
4 #include <memory>
5
```

```cpp
 6 struct Son;
 7 struct Daughter;
 8
 9 struct Mother {
10     ~Mother() {
11         std::cout << "Mother gone" << '\n';
12     }
13     void setSon(const std::shared_ptr<Son> s) {
14         mySon = s;
15     }
16     void setDaughter(const std::shared_ptr<Daughter> d) {
17         myDaughter = d;
18     }
19     std::shared_ptr<Son> mySon;
20     std::weak_ptr<Daughter> myDaughter;
21 };
22
23 struct Son {
24     explicit Son(std::shared_ptr<Mother> m): myMother(m) {}
25     ~Son() {
26         std::cout << "Son gone" << '\n';
27     }
28     std::shared_ptr<Mother> myMother;
29 };
30
31 struct Daughter {
32     explicit Daughter(std::shared_ptr<Mother> m): myMother(m) {}
33     ~Daughter() {
34         std::cout << "Daughter gone" << '\n';
35     }
36     std::shared_ptr<Mother> myMother;
37 };
38
39 int main() {
40
41     std::shared_ptr<Mother> m = std::make_shared<Mother>();
42     std::shared_ptr<Son> s = std::make_shared<Son>(m);
43     std::shared_ptr<Daughter> d = std::make_shared<Daughter>(m);
44     m->setSon(s);
45     m->setDaughter(d);
46
47 }
```

At the end of the main function, the lifetime of the mother, the son, and the daughter ends. Or to say it the other way around: mother, son, and daughter go out of scope, and therefore, the destructor of the class Mother (lines 10–12), Son (lines 25–27), and Daughter (lines 33–35) should automatically be invoked.

"Should" because only the destructor of the daughter is called. See Figure 7.6.

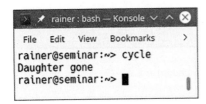

Figure 7.6 *Cycles of smart pointers*

Due to the cycle of std::shared_ptrs between the mother and the son, the reference counter is always greater than zero and the destructor is not automatically invoked. That observation is not true for the mother and the daughter. If the daughter goes out of scope, she is automatically deleted.

Function parameters

The remaining rules in this section answer the question, How should a function take smart pointers as parameters? Should the parameter be a std::unique_ptr or a std::shared_ptr? Should the argument be taken by const or by reference? You should perceive these rules for smart pointers as function parameters as a refinement of the more general previous rules for the parameter passing of function parameters: See Parameter Passing: In and Out and Parameter Passing: Ownership Semantics in Chapter 4.

Before I dive into the rules, Table 7.1 presents an overview first.

Table 7.1 *Smart pointers as function parameters*

Function signature	Semantics	Rule
func(std::unique_ptr<Widget>)	func takes ownership.	R.32
func(std::unique_ptr<Widget>&)	func meant to reseat Widget.	R.33
func(std::shared_ptr<Widget>)	func shares ownership.	R.34
func(std::shared_ptr<Widget>&)	func might reseat Widget.	R.35
func(const std::shared_ptr<Widget>&)	func might retain a reference count.	R.36

The table has five rules. Two rules for using smart pointers as parameters are still missing. First, we have to answer the question of when to use smart pointers as function parameters. Second, there are dangers involved if a function takes its parameters by reference.

Let's answer the first question: When should smart pointers be used as function parameters?

R.30	Take smart pointers as parameters only to explicitly express lifetime semantics

If you pass a smart pointer as a parameter to a function, and in this function, you use only the underlying resource of the smart pointer, you are doing something wrong. In this case, you should use a raw pointer or a reference as a function parameter because you don't need the lifetime semantics of a smart pointer.

Let me give you an example showing the quite sophisticated lifetime management of a smart pointer.

```
1 // lifetimeSemantic.cpp
2
3 #include <iostream>
4 #include <memory>
5
6 using std::cout;
7
8 void asSmartPointerGood(std::shared_ptr<int>& shr) {
9     cout << "asSmartPointerGood \n";
10    cout << " shr.use_count(): " << shr.use_count() << '\n';
11    shr.reset(new int(2011));
12    cout << " shr.use_count(): " << shr.use_count() << '\n';
13    cout << "asSmartPointerGood \n";
14 }
15
16 void asSmartPointerBad(std::shared_ptr<int>& shr) {
17    cout << "asSmartPointerBad(sharedPtr2) \n";
18    *shr += 19;
19 }
```

```
20
21 int main() {
22
23     cout << '\n';
24
25     auto sharedPtr1 = std::make_shared<int>(1998);
26     auto sharedPtr2 = sharedPtr1;
27     cout << "sharedPtr1.use_count(): " << sharedPtr1.use_count()
28         << '\n';
29     cout << '\n';
30
31     asSmartPointerGood(sharedPtr1);
32
33     cout << '\n';
34
35     cout << "*sharedPtr1: " << *sharedPtr1 << '\n';
36     cout << "sharedPtr1.use_count(): " << sharedPtr1.use_count()
37         << '\n';
38     cout << '\n';
39
40     cout << "*sharedPtr2: " << *sharedPtr2 << '\n';
41     cout << "sharedPtr2.use_count(): " << sharedPtr2.use_count()
42         << '\n';
43     cout << '\n';
44
45     asSmartPointerBad(sharedPtr2);
46     cout << "*sharedPtr2: " << *sharedPtr2 << '\n';
47
48     cout << '\n';
49
50 }
```

Let me start with the good case for a std::shared_ptr. The reference counter at line 27 is 2 because I used the shared pointer sharedPtr1 to initialize sharedPtr2. Let's have a closer look at the invocation of the function asSmartPointerGood (line 8). In line 10, the reference count of shr is 2, and then it becomes 1 in line 12. What happened in line 11? I reset shr to the new resource: new int(2011). Consequently, both the shared pointer sharedPtr1 and sharedPtr2 are immediately owners of different resources. You can observe the behavior in Figure 7.7.

Figure 7.7 *Lifetime semantics of smart pointers*

When you invoke `reset` on a shared pointer `sharedPtr`, a sophisticated workflow happens under the hood:

- If you invoke `reset` without an argument on `sharedPtr`, the reference counter is decreased by one. Afterward, `sharedPtr` is not an owner anymore.

- If you invoke `reset` with an argument and the reference counter is at least 2, you get two independent shared pointers owning different resources.

- If you invoke `reset` with or without an argument and the reference counter becomes 0, the resource is released.

The semantics of the argument of `asSmartPointerBad(std::shared_ptr<int>& shr)` suggests that you might reseat the smart pointer in the method, but the method does not have any intent to do so.

So the user of your method is pushed into the wrong direction.

This magic is overkill if you are only interested in the underlying resource of the shared pointer; therefore, a raw pointer or a reference is the right kind of parameter for the function `asSmartPointerBad` (line 16).

std::unique_ptr

There are two rules regarding std::unique_ptr parameters:

- R.32: Take a unique_ptr<widget> parameter to express that a function assumes ownership of a Widget
- R.33: Take a unique_ptr<widget>& parameter to express that a function reseats the Widget

Here are the two corresponding function signatures:

```
void sink(std::unique_ptr<Widget>)
void reseat(std::unique_ptr<Widget>&)
```

std::unique_ptr<Widget> When a function takes ownership of a Widget, you should take the std::unique_ptr<Widget> by value. The consequence is that the caller has to move the std::unique_ptr<Widget>.

```cpp
// uniqPtrMove.cpp

#include <memory>
#include <utility>

struct Widget {
    explicit Widget(int) {}
};

void sink(std::unique_ptr<Widget> uniqPtr) {
    // do something with uniqPtr, then dispose of it
}

int main() {

    auto uniqPtr = std::make_unique<Widget>(1998);

    sink(std::move(uniqPtr));     // OK
    sink(uniqPtr);                // ERROR

}
```

The call sink(std::move(uniqPtr)) is fine, but the call sink(uniqPtr) breaks because you cannot copy a std::unique_ptr. When your function only wants to use a Widget, it should take its parameter, according to the previous rule "R.30: Take smart pointers as parameters only to explicitly express lifetime semantics, by pointer or by reference."

std::unique_ptr<Widget>&   Sometimes a function wants to reseat a `Widget`. In this case, you should pass the `std::unique_ptr<Widget>` by a non-const reference.

```
// uniqPtrReference.cpp

#include <memory>
#include <utility>

struct Widget{
    Widget(int) {}
};

void reseat(std::unique_ptr<Widget>& uniqPtr) {
    uniqPtr.reset(new Widget(2003));
    // do something with uniqPtr
}

int main() {

    auto uniqPtr = std::make_unique<Widget>(1998);

    reseat(std::move(uniqPtr));      // ERROR
    reseat(uniqPtr);                 // OK

}
```

Now the call `reseat(std::move(uniqPtr))` fails because you cannot bind an rvalue to a non-const lvalue reference. This error does not hold for the call in the following line: `reseat(uniqPtr)`. An lvalue can be bound to an lvalue reference. By the way, the `uniqPtr.reset(new Widget(2003))` generates a new `Widget(2003)` and destructs the old `Widget(1998)`.

Two of the three rules for `std::shared_ptr` are repetitions; therefore, I will not bother you with details.

std::shared_ptr

There are three rules about parameters of type `std::shared_ptr`:

- R.34: Take a `shared_ptr<widget>` parameter to express that a function is part owner

- R.35: Take a `shared_ptr<widget>&` parameter to express that a function might reseat the shared pointer

- R.36: Take a const `shared_ptr<widget>&` parameter to express that it might retain a reference count to the object

Here are the relevant function signatures for `std::shared_ptr`:

```
void share(std::shared_ptr<Widget>);
void reseat(std::shared_ptr<Widget>&);
void mayShare(const std::shared_ptr<Widget>&);
```

Let's look at each function signature in isolation. What does this mean from the function perspective?

- **void share(std::shared_ptr<Widget>):** I'm a shared owner of the `Widget` during the lifetime of the function. At the beginning of the function, I increase the reference counter; at the end of the function, I decrease the reference counter; therefore, the `Widget` stays alive as long as I use it.

- **void reseat(std::shared_ptr<Widget>&):** I'm not a shared owner of the `Widget` because I do not change the reference counter. I have no guarantee that the `Widget` stays alive during the execution of the function, but I can reseat the resource.

- **void mayShare(const std::shared_ptr<Widget>&):** I only borrow the resource. I cannot extend the lifetime of the resource, nor can I reseat the resource. Honestly, it would be best if you used a pointer (`Widget*`) or a reference (`Widget&`) as a parameter instead because there is no added value in using a const `std::shared_ptr<Widget>&` as a parameter.

R.37	Do not pass a pointer or reference obtained from an aliased smart pointer

First of all, the title of this rule may be misleading. An aliased smart pointer (reference to a smart pointer) is a smart pointer, of which you are not the owner. Violating this rule often ends in a dangling pointer.

The code snippet exemplifies the problem.

```
void oldFunc(Widget* wid){
    // do something with wid
}
```

```
void shared(std::shared_ptr<Widget>& shaPtr){

    oldFunc(*shaPtr);
    // do something with shaPtr

}


auto globShared = std::make_shared<Widget>(2011);

...

shared(globShared);
```

globShared is a globally shared pointer. The function shared takes its argument by reference. Therefore, the reference counter of shaPtr as the aliased smart pointer is not increased and the function share does not extend the lifetime of Widget(2011). The issue begins with the call oldFunc(*shaPtr). oldFunc accepts a pointer to the Widget; therefore, oldFunc has no guarantee that the Widget stays alive during its execution. oldFunc only borrows the Widget.

The cure is simple. You have to ensure that the reference count of globShared is increased before the call to the function oldFunc.

- Pass the std::shared_ptr by value to the function shared:

  ```
  void shared(std::shared_ptr<Widget> shaPtr) {

      oldFunc(*shaPtr);

      // do something with shaPtr

  }
  ```

- Make a copy of the shaPtr in the function shared:

  ```
  void shared(std::shared_ptr<Widget>& shaPtr) {

      auto keepAlive = shaPtr;
      oldFunc(*shaPtr);

      // do something with keepAlive or shaPtr

  }
  ```

Let me formulate the cure as a straightforward rule: *You should access a shared resource only if you actually hold a share in its ownership.*

The same reasoning also applies to `std::unique_ptr`, but there is no simple cure because you cannot copy a `std::unique_ptr`.

Related rules

The general rules for resource management have a strong overlap with the existing rules regarding functions and interfaces (see Chapter 4, Functions).

The guidelines addressing smart pointers as function parameters are a refinement of the previous rules regarding the parameter passing of function parameters: See Parameter Passing: In and Out and Parameter Passing: Ownership Semantics in Chapter 4.

Distilled

Important

- Manage resources automatically. Create a kind of proxy object for your resource. The constructor of the proxy acquires the resource, and the destructor of the proxy releases the resource. The C++ run time takes care of the proxy.

- Use scoped objects, if possible. A scoped object is an object with its scope. That may be a local object, a global object, or a member of a class. The C++ run time takes care of the scoped objects.

- Don't use `malloc` and `free`, and avoid `new` and `delete`. Give the result of a resource allocation immediately to a resource manager such as `std::unique_ptr` or `std::shared_ptr`.

- Use the smart pointer `std::unique_ptr` to represent exclusive ownership and the smart pointer `std::shared_ptr` to represent shared ownership. Use `std::make_unique` to create a `std::unique_ptr` and `std::make_shared` to create a `std::shared_ptr`.

- Take smart pointers as function parameters if you want to express lifetime semantics. If not, use a plain pointer or a reference.

- Take smart pointers as function parameters by value to express ownership semantics; take smart pointers by reference to express that the function might reseat the smart pointer.

Chapter 8

Expressions and Statements

Cippi is back at school.

According to the C++ Core Guidelines, "expressions and statements are the lowest and most direct way of expressing actions and computation." This section has about sixty-five rules that list best practices for expressions and statements in general and declarations in arithmetic expressions in particular.

First of all, I want to give you an informal definition of what expressions and statements are:

- An **expression** evaluates to a value.

- A **statement** does something and is often composed of expressions or statements.

```
5 * 5;              // expression


std::cout <<  25;   // print statement
auto a = 10;        // assignment statement


auto b = 5 * 5;     // expression statement
```

Declarations in a block scope are statements. A block scope is something within curly braces.

General

The C++ Core Guidelines have two general rules with a particular focus on expressions and statements.

ES.1	Prefer the standard library to other libraries and to "handcrafted code"

There is no reason to write a raw loop to sum up a vector of doubles:

```
int max = v.size();
double sum = 0.0;
for (int i = 0; i < max; ++i) sum += v[i];
```

Instead, use the std::accumulate algorithm from the Standard Template Library (STL). This clearly communicates your intent and makes the code more readable.

```
auto sum = std::accumulate(std::begin(v), std::end(v), 0.0);
```

Maybe your next task is to build the product of the doubles. Just invoke std::accumulate with the suitable lambda.

```
auto pro = std::accumulate(std::begin(v), std::end(v), 1.0,
              [](double fir, double sec){ return fir * sec; });
```

The solution is good but not perfect. The C++ standard already defines many function objects such as multiplication.

```
auto pro = std::accumulate(std::begin(v), std::end(v), 1.0,
                          std::multiplies<>());
```

This rule reminds me of a quote from Sean Parent at the C++ Seasoning conference in 2013: "If you want to improve the code quality in your organization, replace all your coding guidelines with one goal: Prefer an algorithm to a raw loop." Or to say it more directly: *If you write a raw loop, you probably don't know the algorithms of the STL well enough.* The STL has more than 100 algorithms.

ES.2	Prefer suitable abstractions to direct use of language features

This is the next déjà vu. In one C++ seminar, I had a long discussion followed by an even more extended analysis of a few quite sophisticated and handmade functions for reading and writing `std::strstreams`. My students had to maintain a function, and after one week, they had no idea what was going on. The main reason why they got confused was that the functionality was not based on the right abstraction.

For example, consider this handmade function for reading a `std::istream`.

```
char** read1(istream& is, int maxelem, int maxstring, int* nread) {
    auto res = new char*[maxelem];
    int elemcount = 0;
    while (is && elemcount < maxelem) {
        auto s = new char[maxstring];
        is.read(s, maxstring);
        res[elemcount++] = s;
    }
    nread = &elemcount;
    return res;
}
```

In contrast, how easy is it to comprehend the following function?

```
std::vector<std::string> read2(std::istream& is) {
    std::vector<std::string> res;
    for (string s; is >> s;) res.push_back(s);
    return res;
}
```

The right abstraction often means that you don't have to think about ownership such as in the function read2. This concern does hold for the function read1. The caller of read1 is the owner of the result and has, therefore, to delete it.

Declarations

First of all, here is how a declaration is defined in the C++ Core Guidelines:

> A **declaration** is a statement. A declaration introduces a name into a scope and may cause the construction of a named object.

The rules for declarations are about names, the variables and their initialization, and macros.

Names

On the one hand, the following rules are obvious, and I describe them only briefly. On the other hand, I know many code bases that permanently break these rules. For example, I spoke with a former Fortran programmer who stated the following: Each name should have exactly three characters.

Let me first name the most important rule: *Good names are probably the most important rule for good software.*

ES.5	Keep scopes small

If a scope is small, you can put it on a screen and get an idea of what is going on. If a scope becomes too big, you should structure your code into functions or classes. Identify logical entities and use self-explanatory names in your refactoring process. Afterward, it becomes easier to think about your code.

ES.6	Declare names in for-statement initializers and conditions to limit scope

Since the first C++ standard, we can declare a variable in a for statement.

The Design and Evolution of C++ by Bjarne Stroustrup

Bjarne Stroustrup pointed out during the reviewing of this book that the definition of names in for statements was possible even before the first C++ standard. In case you are curious about the history of C++, I strongly suggest you read Bjarne's book *The Design and Evolution of C++*.

Since C++17, we can declare variables also in an `if` or a `switch` statement.

```
std::map<int,std::string> myMap;

if (auto result = myMap.insert(value); result.second) {
    useResult(*result.first);
    // ...
}
else {
    // ...
}   // result is automatically destroyed
```

The variable result is only valid inside the `if` and `else` branch of the `if` statement. result does not pollute the outer scope and is automatically destroyed. Before C++17, you had to declare result in the outer scope.

```
std::map<int,std::string> myMap;
auto result = myMap.insert(value)
if (result.second){
    useResult(*result.first);
    // ...
}
else {
    // ...
}
```

ES.7   Keep common and local names short, and keep uncommon and nonlocal names longer

This rule sounds strange, but we are already used to it. Giving a variable the name i or j or giving a variable the name T makes its intention immediately clear: i and j are indices, and T is a type for a template parameter.

```cpp
template<typename T>
void print(std::ostream& os, const std::vector<T>& v) {
    for (int i = 0; i < v.size(); ++i) os << v[i] << '\n';
}
```

i is an okay name for a loop control variable, a poor name for a function parameter, and a terrible name for a global variable.

There is a meta-rule underlying this rule. A name should be self-explanatory. In a brief context, you understand at a glance what the variable means. This will not automatically hold for longer contexts; therefore, use longer names.

ES.8   Avoid similar-looking names

Can you read this example without any hesitation?

```cpp
if (readable(i1 + l1 + ol + o1 + o0 + ol + o1 + I0 + l0)) surprise();
```

For example, I often have problems with the number 0 and the capital letter O. Depending on the font used, they look quite similar. A few years ago, it took me quite some time to log in to a server. My automatically generated password had a letter O.

ES.9   Avoid ALL_CAPS names

If you use ALL_CAPS, macro substitution may kick in because ALL_CAPS are commonly used for macros. The following code snippet may be a little surprising.

```cpp
// somewhere in some header:
#define NE !=

// somewhere else in some other header:
enum Coord { N, NE, NW, S, SE, SW, E, W };
```

```
// third, somewhere in some poor programmer's .cpp:
switch (direction) {
case N:
    // ...
case NE:
    // ...
// ...
}
```

ES.10   Declare one name (only) per declaration

Let me give you two examples. Do you spot two issues?

```
char* p, p2;
char a = 'a';
p = &a;
p2 = a;
```

```
int a = 7, b = 9, c, d = 10, e = 3;
```

p2 is just a char, and c is not initialized. With C++17, we acquired one exception to this rule: structured binding.

Now I can write the `if` statement with initializer in rule "ES.6: Declare names in for-statement initializers and conditions to limit scope" using a cleaner and more readable syntax.

```
std::map<int, std::string> myMap;

if (auto [iter, succeeded] = myMap.insert(value); succeeded) {
    useResult(iter);
    // ...
}
else {
    // ...
} // iter and succeeded are automatically destroyed
```

ES.11   Use auto to avoid redundant repetition of type names

If you use auto, changing your code may become a piece of cake.

The following code snippet only uses auto. You do not have to think about the types, and therefore, you cannot make an error. This means the type of res will be int at the end. Thanks to the typeid operator, you get a string representation of the type.

```
auto a = 5;
auto b = 10;
auto sum =  a * b * 3;
auto res = sum + 10;
std::cout << typeid(res).name() << '\n';      // i
```

If you decide to change the literal b from int to double (1), or use instead of the int literal 3 a float literal 3.1f (2), res always has the correct type. The compiler automatically deduces the correct type.

```
auto a = 5;
auto b = 10.5;                 // (1)
auto sum = a * b * 3;
auto res = sum * 10;
std::cout << typeid(res).name() << '\n';    // d
```

```
auto a = 5;
auto b = 10;
auto sum = a * b * 3.2f;       // (2)
auto res = sum * 10;
std::cout << typeid(res).name() << '\n';    // f
```

The GCC and the Clang compiler generated the type hints i, d, and f in the tree code snippets. The MSVC compiler would write more verbose type hints such as int, double, and float.

ES.12	Do not reuse names in nested scopes

For readability and maintenance reasons, you should not reuse names in nested scopes.

```
// shadow.cpp

#include <iostream>

int shadow(bool cond) {
```

```
    int d = 0;
    if (cond) {
        d = 1;
    }
    else {
        int d = 2;   // declare a local scoped d;
                     // hiding d of the parent scope
        d = 3;
    }                // the local scoped d is removed
    return d;
}

int main() {

    std::cout << '\n';

    std::cout << "shadow(true): " << shadow(true) << '\n';
    std::cout << "shadow(false): " << shadow(false) << '\n';

    std::cout << '\n';

}
```

What is the output of the program? Confused by the ds? Figure 8.1 shows the result.

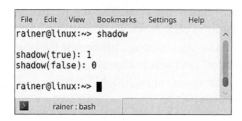

Figure 8.1 *Reusing names in nested scopes*

This was easy! Right? But the same behavior is quite surprising in a class hierarchy.

```
// shadowClass.cpp

#include <iostream>
#include <string>
```

```
struct Base {
    void shadow(std::string) {                    // (1)
        std::cout << "Base::shadow" << '\n';
    }
};

struct Derived: Base {
    void shadow(int) {                            // (2)
        std::cout << "Derived::shadow" << '\n';
    }
};

int main() {

    std::cout << '\n';

    Derived derived;

    derived.shadow(std::string{});                // (3)
    derived.shadow(int{});

    std::cout << '\n';

}
```

Both structs `Base` and `Derived` have a member function `shadow`. The one in the `Base` accepts a `std::string` (1) and the other one an `int` (2). When you invoke the object derived with a default-constructed `std::string` (3), you may assume that the base version is called. Wrong! The member function `shadow` is implemented in the class `Derived`. The member function of the base class is not considered during name resolution. Figure 8.2 shows the compilation error of GCC.

Figure 8.2 *Hiding member functions of a base*

Thanks to the using declaration, the base variant of shadow is visible in Derived.

```cpp
struct Derived: Base {
    using Base::shadow;
    void shadow(int) {
        std::cout << "Derived::shadow" << '\n';
    }
};
```

After adding the using Base::shadow into Derived, the program behaves as expected. The guideline "C.138: Create an overload set for a derived class and its bases with using" showed the issue of shadowing in a class hierarchy. See Figure 8.3.

Figure 8.3 *Change visibility with a using declaration*

Variables and their initialization

As in the previous section on names, the rules in this section regarding variables and their initialization are often quite obvious but sometimes provide precious insights. Consequently, I cover the intuitive rules quickly and write about the valuable insights in more depth.

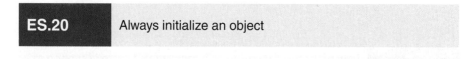

This is one of these elementary techniques that many professional C++ programmers get wrong. The simple question is: Which variable is initialized?

```cpp
struct T1 {};

class T2{
public:
    T2() {}
};
```

```
int n;                    // OK

int main() {
    int n2;               // BAD
    std::string s;        // OK
    T1 t1;                // OK
    T2 t2;                // OK
}
```

n has a global scope and has a fundamental type. Consequently, it is initialized to 0. The initialization does not happen for n2 because it has a local scope and is, therefore, not initialized. But if you use a user-defined type such as std::string, T1, or T2, it is initialized even in a local scope.

There is a simple fix to prevent this issue: Use auto. Now you cannot forget to initialize a variable.

```
struct T1 {};

class T2{
public:
    T2() {}
};

auto n = 0;

int main() {
  auto n2 = 0;
  auto s = ""s;
  auto t1 = T1();
  auto t2 = T2();
}
```

ES.21	Don't introduce a variable (or constant) before you need to use it

In the C standard C89, you must declare all of your variables at the beginning of a scope. We program in C++, not in C89.

ES.22	Don't declare a variable until you have a value to initialize it with

If you don't follow this rule, you may have a so-called use-before-set error. Have a look at the example from the guidelines.

```
int var;

if (cond) set(&var);        // some non-trivial condition
else if (cond2 || !cond3) {
    var = set2(3.14);
}


// use var
```

If cond3 holds but not cond, or cond2, then var is not initialized when it is used.

ES.23	Prefer the {}-initializer syntax

There are many reasons to use {}-initialization.
{}-initialization

- Is always applicable
- Overcomes the most vexing parse
- Prevents narrowing conversion

While the first two arguments make C++ more intuitive, the last argument often prevents undefined behavior.

Always applicable
{}-initialization is always applicable. Here are a few examples:

```
// uniformInitialization.cpp

#include <map>
#include <vector>
#include <string>

// Initialization of a C-array
class Array {
public:
    Array(): myData{1,2,3,4,5} {}
```

```cpp
private:
   const int myData[5];
};

class MyClass {
public:
   int x;
   double y;
};

class MyClass2 {
  public:
    MyClass2(int fir, double sec): x{fir}, y{sec} {};
  private:
    int x;
    double y;
};

int main() {

    // Direct initialization of standard containers
    int intArray[]= {1, 2, 3, 4, 5};
    std::vector<int> intArray1{1, 2, 3, 4, 5};
    std::map<std::string, int> myMap{ {"Scott", 1976},
                             {"Dijkstra", 1972} };

    Array arr;

    // Default initialization of arbitrary objects
    int i{};                 // i becomes 0
    std::string s{};         // s becomes ""
    std::vector<float> v{};  // v becomes an empty vector
    double d{};              // d becomes 0.0

    // Direct initialization of an object with public members
    MyClass myClass{2011, 3.14};
    MyClass myClass1 = {2011, 3.14};

    // Initialization of an object using the constructor
    MyClass2 myClass2{2011, 3.14};
    MyClass2 myClass3 = {2011, 3.14};

}
```

You should never say always. There is a weird behavior, which is fixed in C++17.

Type deduction with `auto`

Always applicable? Yes, but you have to keep a special rule in mind. If you use automatic type deduction with `auto` in combination with {}-initialization, you get a `std::initializer_list`.

```
auto initA{1};          // std::initializer_list<int>
auto initB = {2};       // std::initializer_list<int>
auto initC{1, 2};       // std::initializer_list<int>
auto initD = {1, 2};    // std::initializer_list<int>
```

This counterintuitive behavior changes with C++17.

```
auto initA{1};          // int
auto initB = {2};       // std::initializer_list<int>
auto initC{1, 2};       // error, no single element
auto initD = {1, 2};    // std::initializer_list<int>
```

Most vexing parse

The most vexing parse is well known, and almost any professional C++ developer has already fallen into this trap. The following short program demonstrates the trap.

```
// mostVexingParse.cpp

#include <iostream>

struct MyInt {
    MyInt(int arg = 0): i(arg) {}
    int i;
};


int main() {

    MyInt myInt(2011);
    MyInt myInt2();

    std::cout << myInt.i;
    std::cout << myInt2.i;

}
```

This simple-looking program does not compile! See Figure 8.4.

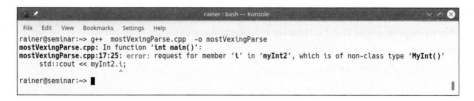

Figure 8.4 *The most vexing parse*

The error message is not very meaningful. The compiler can interpret the expression `MyInt myInt2()` as a call of a constructor or as a declaration of a function. When there is an ambiguity, it selects a function declaration. Consequently, the call `myInt2.i` is not valid.

Replacing round braces in the call `MyInt myInt2()` with curly braces, `MyInt myInt2{}`, solves the ambiguity.

```
// mostVexingParseSolved.cpp

#include <iostream>

struct MyInt {
    MyInt(int arg = 0): i(arg) {}
    int i;
};


int main() {

    MyInt myInt(2011);
    MyInt myInt2{};

    std::cout << myInt.i;
    std::cout << myInt2.i;

}
```

Narrowing conversion

Narrowing conversion is an implicit conversion of arithmetic values, including a loss of accuracy. That sounds extremely dangerous and is a common cause of undefined behavior.

The following code snippet exemplifies narrowing conversion for the two fundamental types `char` and `int`. It doesn't matter whether I use direct initialization or copy initialization.

```
// narrowingConversion.cpp

#include <iostream>

int main() {

    char c1(999);
    char c2 = 999;
    std::cout << "c1: " << c1 << '\n';
    std::cout << "c2: " << c2 << '\n';

    int i1(3.14);
    int i2 = 3.14;
    std::cout << "i1: " << i1 << '\n';
    std::cout << "i2: " << i2 << '\n';

}
```

The output of the program shows both issues. First, the `int` literal 999 doesn't fit into the type `char`; second, the `double` literal doesn't fit into the `int` type. See Figure 8.5.

Figure 8.5 *Narrowing conversion*

Narrowing conversion is not possible with {}-initialization.

```
// narrowingConversionSolved.cpp

#include <iostream>

int main() {
```

```
      char c1{999};
      char c2 = {999};
      std::cout << "c1: " << c1 << '\n';
      std::cout << "c2: " << c2 << '\n';

      int i1{3.14};
      int i2 = {3.14};
      std::cout << "i1: " << i1 << '\n';
      std::cout << "i2: " << i2 << '\n';

}
```

The program is ill formed because {}-initialization detects narrowing conversion. The compiler has at least to diagnose a warning. Most of the compilers treat narrowing conversion as an error. To be on the safe side, compile your program always with the narrowing flag set. Figure 8.6 shows the failing compilation with GCC.

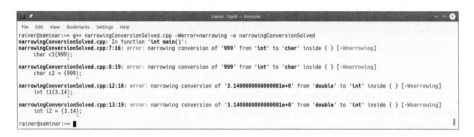

Figure 8.6 *Narrowing conversion detected*

ES.26   Don't use a variable for two unrelated purposes

Do you like the following code?

```
void use() {
    int i;
    for (i = 0; i < 20; ++i) { /* ... */ }
    for (i = 0; i < 200; ++i) { /* ... */ } // bad: i recycled
}
```

I hope not. Put the declaration of i into the for loop and you are fine. i is now bound to the lifetime of the for loop.

```
void use() {
    for (int i = 0; i < 20; ++i) { /* ... */ }
    for (int i = 0; i < 200; ++i) { /* ... */ }
}
```

With C++17, you can declare variables directly in an if statement or a switch statement.

ES.28	Use lambdas for complex initialization, especially of const variables

I often hear the question: Why should I invoke a lambda function in place? This rule answers this question. You can put complex initialization steps in a lambda. The in-place invocation of a lambda is, in particular, valuable if your variable should become const.

If you don't want to modify your variable after initialization, you should make it const. But sometimes, the initialization of the variable consists of more than one step. Consequently, you cannot make the variable const.

The widget x in the following example should be const after its initialization. It cannot be const because it is modified a few times during its initialization.

```
widget x;    // should be const, but:
for (auto i = 2; i <= N; ++i) {
    x += some_obj.do_something_with(i);
}

// from here, x should be const,
// but we can't say so in code in this style
```

Now a lambda expression comes to our rescue. Use a technique called Immediately Invoked Lambda Expression (IILE).

Put the initialization stuff into a lambda expression, capture the environment by reference, and initialize your const variable with the in-place invoked lambda function.

```
const widget x = [&]{
    widget val;
    for (auto i = 2; i <= N; ++i) {
```

```
        val += some_obj.do_something_with(i);
    }
    return val;
}();
```

Admittedly, it looks a little bit strange to invoke a lambda function just in place, but from the conceptional view, I like it. You put the whole initialization stuff just in the body of a lambda. The final pair of parentheses invokes the lambda.

Macros

If there is one unanimous consensus in the C++ standardization committee, then this is it: *Macros must go*. Macros are just text substitution without any C++ semantics. They transform the written code so that the compiler sees different code. This transformation is highly error prone and obscures the cause of the error.

But sometimes you have to deal with legacy code, which relies on macros. For completeness, the C++ Core Guidelines have four rules for macros.

- ES.30: Don't use macros for program text manipulation
- ES.31: Don't use macros for constants or "functions"
- ES.32: Use ALL_CAPS for all macro names
- ES.33: If you must use macros, give them unique names

Let me start with the don'ts. The following example shows the usage of the function-like macro max. I copied max from the param.h header file, which is part of the GNU C library.

```
// macro.cpp

#include <stdio.h>

#define max(a, b) ((a) > (b)) ? (a) : (b)

int main() {

    int a = 1, b = 2;
    printf("\nmax(a, b): %d\n", max(a, b));
    printf("a = %d, b = %d\n", a, b);

    printf("\nmax(++a, ++b): %d\n", max(++a, ++b));  // (1)
    printf("a = %d, b = %d\n\n", a, b);              // (2)

}
```

The output in (2) may surprise you. See Figure 8.7.

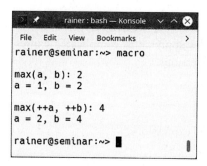

Figure 8.7 *Usage of the function-like macro* max

The variable b is two times evaluated and, therefore, incremented twice. Use instead of the function-like macro max a constexpr function or a max function template.

```
template<typename T>
T max (T i, T j) {
    return ((i > j) ? i : j);
}


constexpr int max (int i, int j){
    return ((i > j) ? i : j);
}
```

The same argumentation applies to macros as constants.

```
#define PI 3.14             // bad

constexpr double pi = 3.14  // good
```

If, for whatever reason, you have to use or to maintain macros, write them ALL_CAPS and give them unique names. The following code snippet breaks both rules. forever is written in lowercase letters and the macro CHAR may conflict with someone else using the name CHAR.

```
#define forever for (;;)

#define CHAR
```

Expressions

There are about twenty rules related to expressions. They are quite diverse and overlap with existing rules. Here I focus on the rules applying to complicated expressions, pointers, the order of evaluation, and conversions.

Complicated expressions

First and foremost, you should avoid complicated expressions.

ES.40	Avoid complicated expressions

What does complicated mean? Here is the example from the C++ Core Guidelines, including the explanation:

```cpp
// bad: assignment hidden in subexpression
while ((c = getc()) != -1)

// bad: two non-local variables assigned in a subexpression
while ((cin >> c1, cin >> c2), c1 == c2)

// better, but possibly still too complicated
for (char c1, c2; cin >> c1 >> c2 && c1 == c2;)

// OK: if i and j are not aliased (names for the same data)
int x = ++i + ++j;

// OK: if i != j and i != k
v[i] = v[j] + v[k];

// bad: multiple assignments "hidden" in subexpressions
x = a + (b = f()) + (c = g()) * 7;

// bad: relies on commonly misunderstood precedence rules
x = a & b + c * d && e ^ f == 7;

// bad: undefined behavior
x = x++ + x++ + ++x;
```

ES.41	If in doubt about operator precedence, parenthesize

On one hand, the guidelines say that if you are in doubt about operator precedence, use parentheses. On the other hand, they state that you should know enough not to need parentheses here. Finding the right balance is, therefore, the challenge and depends on the expertise of the users.

```
const unsigned int flag = 2;
unsigned int a = flag;

if (a & flag != 0)        // bad: means a&(flag != 0)

if (a < 0 || a <= max) { // good: quite obvious
    // ...
}
```

For an expert, the expression may be obvious, but for a beginner, it may be a challenge.

I have only two tips in mind:

1. If in doubt about precedence, use parentheses. The precedence table gives you all the details.

2. Program for the beginners! Keep the precedence table under your pillow.

ES.42	Keep use of pointers simple and straightforward

Let me quote the C++ Core Guidelines: "Complicated pointer manipulation is a major source of errors." Why should we care? Of course, our legacy code is full of pointer manipulations such as in the following code snippet.

```
void f(int* p, int count) {
    if (count < 2) return;

    int* q = p + 1;

    int n = *p++;
```

```
    if (count < 6) return;

    p[4] = 1;

    p[count - 1] = 2;

    use(&p[0], 3);
}

int myArray[100];

f(myArray, 100);
```

The main issue with these lines of code is that the caller must provide the correct length of the C-array. If not, undefined behavior kicks in.

Think about the last two lines of the code snippet for a few seconds. We start with a C-array and remove its type information by passing it to the function f. This process is called an array to pointer decay and is the reason for many errors. Maybe we counted the number of elements wrong or the size of the C-arrays changed. The result is the same in both cases: undefined behavior.

What should we do? We should use the appropriate data type. C++20 offers std:::span.

```
void f(std::span<int> a) {
    if (a.size() < 2) return;

    int n = a[0];      // OK

    std::span<int> q = a.subspan(1);

    if (a.size() < 6) return;

    a[4] = 1;

    a[count - 1] = 2;

    use(a.data(), a.size());
}
```

std::span knows its size. I hear your complaint. C++20 is not an option for you. To our rescue, C++ has templates; therefore, it's easy to overcome this restriction and write bounds-safe code.

```cpp
 1 // at.cpp
 2
 3 #include <algorithm>
 4 #include <array>
 5 #include <deque>
 6 #include <string>
 7 #include <vector>
 8
 9 template <typename T>
10 void use(T*, int) {}
11
12 template <typename T>
13 void f(T& a) {
14
15    if (a.size() < 2) return;
16
17    int n = a.at(0);
18
19    std::array<typename T::value_type , 99> q;
20    std::copy(a.begin() + 1, a.end(), q.begin());
21
22    if (a.size() < 6) return;
23
24    a.at(4) = 1;
25
26    a.at(a.size() - 1) = 2;
27
28    use(a.data(), a.size());
29 }
30
31 int main() {
32
33    std::array<int, 100> arr{};
34    f(arr);
35
36    std::array<double, 20> arr2{};
37    f(arr2);
38
39    std::vector<double> vec{1, 2, 3, 4, 5, 6, 7, 8, 9};
40    f(vec);
41
42    std::string myString= "123456789";
43    f(myString);
```

```
44
45    // std::deque<int> deq{1, 2, 3, 4, 5, 6, 7, 8, 9, 10};
46    // f(deq);
47
48 }
```

Now the function f works for std::arrays of different sizes and types (lines 34 and 37) but also for a std::vector (line 40) or a std::string (line 43). These containers have in common that their data is stored in a contiguous memory block. This is not the case for std::deque; therefore, the call a.data() in the comment (line 46) fails. The key observation in the example is that the at call on a container checks its boundaries and throws eventually a std::out_of_range exception.

The expression T::value_type helps to get the type of the elements of the container. T is a so-called dependent type because T is a type parameter of the function template f. This is the reason I have to give the compiler a hint that T::value_type is actually a type: typename T::value_type.

ES.45	Avoid "magic constants"; use symbolic constants

A symbolic constant is more explicit than a magic constant. The example in the C++ Core Guidelines starts with the magic constants 1 and 12 and ends with the symbolic constant first_month and last_month.

```
                    // don't: magic constants 1 and 12
for (int m = 1; m <= 12; ++m) std::cout << month[m] << '\n';
```

```
                    // months are indexed 1..12 (symbolic constant)
constexpr int first_month = 1;
constexpr int last_month = 12;
for (int m = first_month; m <= last_month; ++m) {
    std::cout << month[m] << '\n';
}
```

ES.55	Avoid the need for range checking

If you don't have to check the length of a range, you will not get an off-by-one error. Let's sum up the elements of a std::vector.

```cpp
// sumUp.cpp

#include <iostream>
#include <numeric>
#include <vector>

int main() {

    std::vector<int> vec{1, 2, 3, 4, 5, 6, 7, 8, 9, 10};

    // bad
    int sum1 = 0;
    auto sizeVec = vec.size();
    for (int i = 0; i < sizeVec; ++i) sum1 += vec[i];

    std::cout << sum1 << '\n';        // 55

    // better
    int sum2 = 0;
    for (auto v: vec) sum2 += v;
    std::cout << sum2 << '\n';        // 55

    // the best
    auto sum3 = std::accumulate(vec.begin(), vec.end(), 0);
    std::cout << sum3 << '\n';        // 55

}
```

Iterating explicitly through a container is very error prone. In contrast, iterating implicitly with a range-based for loop is safe. Additionally, the algorithm std::accumulate of the STL documents its intention.

Pointers

The rules for pointers start with null pointers and continue with the deletion and dereferencing of pointers.

ES.47   Use `nullptr` rather than `0` or `NULL`

Why should you not use 0 or NULL to denote a null pointer?

- **0**: The literal 0 can be the null pointer (void*)0 or the number 0. This is dependent on the context. Consequently, what started as null pointer could end up as number.

- **NULL**: NULL is a macro, and therefore, you don't know what's inside. A possible implementation according to cppreference.com could be the following:

```
#define NULL 0
//since C++11
#define NULL nullptr
```

Replace the null pointer 0 and NULL with the nullptr

I normally don't suggest refactoring existing code. Both null pointer 0 and NULL are an exception to this rule. Replace all occurrences of null pointer 0 and NULL with the null pointer nullptr.

```
int* a = 0;         // bad
int* b = NULL;      // bad

int* a = nullptr;   // good
int* b = nullptr;   // good
```

If your program compiles after the refactoring, fine. If you get a compiler error, you already know that you used a null pointer against its nature and you detected undefined behavior.

The null pointer nullptr avoids the ambiguity of the number 0 and the macro NULL. nullptr is and remains of type std::nullptr_t. You can assign a nullptr to an arbitrary pointer. The pointer becomes a null pointer and points, therefore, to no data. You cannot dereference a nullptr. The pointer of this type can on one hand be compared with all pointers and can on the other hand be converted to all pointers. You cannot compare and convert a nullptr to an integral type. There is one exception to this rule. nullptr can be explicitly or contextually converted to bool. Hence, you can use a nullptr in a logical expression.

Generic code

Using the three kinds of null pointers in generic code shows immediately the flaws of the number 0 and the macro NULL. Thanks to template argument deduction, the literals 0 and NULL deduce to integral types. The information that both literals should be null pointer constants is lost.

```cpp
// nullPointer.cpp

#include <cstddef>
#include <iostream>

template<class P >
void functionTemplate(P p) {
    int* a = p;
}

int main() {
    int* a = 0;
    int* b = NULL;
    int* c = nullptr;

    functionTemplate(0);       // (1)
    functionTemplate(NULL);    // (2)
    functionTemplate(nullptr);
}
```

You can use 0 and NULL to initialize the int pointer in (1) and (2). But if you use the values 0 and NULL as arguments to the function template, the compiler will loudly complain. See Figure 8.8.

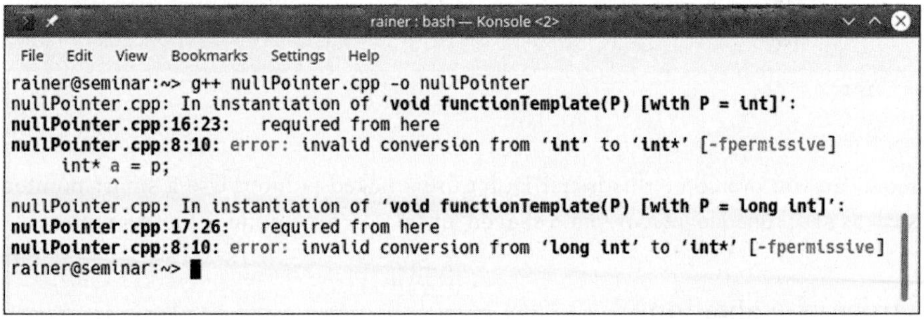

Figure 8.8 *The null pointers* 0, NULL, *and* nullptr

The compiler deduces 0 in the function template to type int; it deduces NULL to the type long int. This observation does not hold for nullptr. nullptr preserves its type std::nullptr_t through template argument deduction.

ES.61	Delete arrays using `delete[]` and non-arrays using `delete`

Explicit memory management and not using a container of the STL or a smart pointer such as `std::unique_ptr<X[]>` is very error prone:

```
void f(int n) {
    auto p = new X[n];   // n default constructed Xs
    // ...
    delete p;   // error: just delete the object p,
                // rather than deleting the array p[]
}
```

Deleting a C-array with an *nonarray* `delete` is undefined behavior.

If you have to manage raw memory, read the rules in the Allocation and Deallocation section of Chapter 7.

ES.65	Don't dereference an invalid pointer

If you dereference an invalid pointer, your program has undefined behavior. The only way to avoid this behavior is to check your pointer before its usage.

```
void func(int* p) {
    if (!p) {
        // do something special
    }
    int x = *p;
}
```

How can you overcome this issue? Don't use a naked pointer. Use a smart pointer such as `std::unique_ptr` or `std::shared_ptr` if you need pointer-like semantics.

Order of evaluation

If you don't apply the right order of evaluation in an expression, your program may end in undefined behavior.

ES.43	Avoid expressions with undefined order of evaluation

In C++14, the following expression has undefined behavior.

```
v[i] = ++i;   // the result is undefined
```

This undefined behavior has been addressed in C++17. With C++17, the order of evaluation of the last code snippet is right to left; therefore, the expression has well-defined behavior.

Here are the additional guarantees we have with C++17:

- Postfix expressions are evaluated from left to right. This includes function calls and member selection expressions.

- Assignment expressions are evaluated from right to left. This includes compound assignments such as +=.

- Operands to shift operators are evaluated from left to right.

Here are a few examples:

```
a.b
a->b
a->*b
a(b1, b2, b3)
b @= a
a[b]
a << b
a >> b
```

How should you read these examples? First, a is evaluated and then b.

The function call a(b1, b2, b3) is tricky. With C++17, we have the guarantee that each function argument is entirely evaluated before each of the other function arguments, but the order of the evaluation of the arguments is still unspecified.

Let me elaborate a little bit more on the last sentence.

ES.44   Don't depend on order of evaluation of function arguments

In the last few years, I have seen many errors because developers assumed that the order of the evaluation of function arguments is left to right. Wrong! There is no such guarantee!

```
// unspecified.cpp

#include <iostream>
```

```
void func(int fir, int sec) {
    std::cout << "(" << fir << "," << sec << ")" << '\n';
}

int main(){
    int i = 0;
    func(i++, i++);
}
```

The order of the evaluation of the function arguments is unspecified. Unspecified behavior means that the behavior of the program may vary between implementations and the conforming implementation is not required to document the effects of each behavior.

Consequently, the output from GCC and Clang differs even if both compilers conform to the C++ standard (see Figure 8.9).

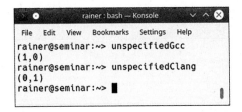

Figure 8.9 *Unspecified behavior*

Guaranteed order of evaluation in expressions with C++17

With C++17, the order of evaluation of the following expressions is specified:

```
f1()->m(f2());          // evaluation left to right
std::cout << f1() << f2();   // evaluation left to right

f1() = f(2);            // evaluation right to left
```

Here is the reason why:

- **f1()->m(f2())**: Postfix expressions are evaluated from left to right. This includes function calls and member selection expressions.

- **std::cout << f1() << f2()**: Operands to shift operators are evaluated from left to right.

- **f1() = f(2)**: Assignment expressions are evaluated from right to left.

Conversions

Casting types is a common cause of undefined behavior. If necessary, use explicit casts.

ES.48	Avoid casts

Let's see what happens if I screw up the type system and cast a `double` to a `long int` and to a `long long int`.

```cpp
// casts.cpp

#include <iostream>

int main() {

    double d = 2;
    auto p = (long*)&d;
    auto q = (long long*)&d;
    std::cout << d << ' ' << *p << ' ' << *q << '\n';

}
```

The result with the Visual Studio compiler is not promising (see Figure 8.10).

Figure 8.10 *Wrong casts with the Visual Studio compiler*

Nor is the result with the GCC or Clang compiler promising (see Figure 8.11).

Figure 8.11 *Wrong casts with the GCC or Clang compiler*

What is terrible about the C-cast? You don't see which cast is actually performed. If you perform a C-cast, a combination of casts is applied if necessary.

Roughly speaking, a C-cast starts with a `static_cast`, continues with a `const_cast`, and finally performs a `reinterpret_cast`.

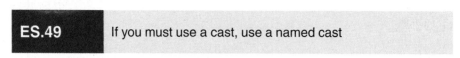

The principle from The Zen of Python, "explicit is better than implicit," also applies to casts in C++: Use a named cast if necessary.

With C++11, we have the following six casts:

- `static_cast`: converts between similar types such as pointer types or numeric types
- `const_cast`: adds or removes `const` or `volatile`
- `reinterpret_cast`: converts between pointers or between integral types and pointers
- `dynamic_cast`: converts between polymorphic pointers or references in the same class hierarchy
- `std::move`: converts to an rvalue reference
- `std::forward`: converts an lvalue to an lvalue reference and an rvalue to an rvalue reference

I assume you are surprised that I presented `std::move` and `std::forward` as casts. Let's have a closer look at the internals of `std::move`:

```
static_cast<std::remove_reference<decltype(arg)>::type&&>(arg)
```

What's happening here? First, the type of the argument `arg` is deduced by `decltype(arg)`. Afterward, all references are removed, and two new references are added. The function `std::remove_reference` is from the type-traits library. In the end, we always get an rvalue reference.

ES.50	Don't cast away `const`

Casting away `const` is undefined behavior if the underlying object such as `constInt` is `const` and you try to modify the underlying object.

```
const int constInt = 10;
const int* pToConstInt = &constInt;

int* pToInt = const_cast<int*>(pToConstInt);
*pToInt = 12;            // undefined behavior
```

You can find the rationale for this rule in the C standard, which is also relevant for the C++ standard: "The implementation may place a const object that is not volatile in a read-only region of storage" (International Organization for Standardization (ISO)/International Electrotechnical Commission (IEC) 9899:2011, subclause 6.7.3, paragraph 4).

Statements

Statements fall mainly into two categories: iteration statements and selection statements. The rules for both kinds of statements are quite clear. Consequently, I quote the rule of the C++ Core Guidelines and add a few pieces of information when necessary.

Iteration statements

C++ implements three iteration statements: `while`, `do while`, and `for`. With C++11, syntactic sugar is added to the for loop: range-based for loop.

```
std::vector<int> vec = {0, 1, 2, 3, 4, 5};

            // for loop
for(std::size_t i = 0; i < vec.size(); ++i) {
    std::cout << vec[i] << ' ';
}

            // range-based for loop
for (auto ele : vec) std::cout << ele << ' ';
```

- A range-based for loop is easier to read, and you cannot make an index error or change the index while looping ("ES.71: Prefer a range-for-statement to a for-statement when there is a choice" and "ES.86: Avoid modifying loop control variables inside the body of raw for loops").

- When you have an obvious loop variable, you should use a for loop instead of a while statement ("ES.72: Prefer a for-statement to a while-statement when there is an obvious loop variable"); if not, you should use a while statement ("ES.73: Prefer a while-statement to a for-statement when there is no obvious loop variable").

```
for (auto i = 0; i < vec.size(); ++i) {
    // do work
}
```

```
int events = 0;
while (wait_for_event()) {
    ++events;
    // do work
}
```

- You should declare a loop variable in a for loop ("ES.74: Prefer to declare a loop variable in the initializer part of a for-statement"). To remind you, since C++17, declaring a variable such as result can also be done in the initialization part of an if or a switch statement.

```
std::map<int,std::string> myMap;
```

```
if (auto result = myMap.insert(value); result.second){
    useResult(result.first);
    // ...
}
else{
    // ...
} // result is automatically destroyed
```

- Avoid do while statements ("ES.75: Avoid do-statements") and goto statements ("ES.76: Avoid goto"), and minimize the use of break and continue in iteration statements ("ES.77: Minimize the use of break and continue in loops") because they are difficult to read. If something is difficult to read, it's error prone and makes refactoring of your code challenging. A break statement ends the iteration statement, and a continue statement ends the current iteration step.

Prefer an algorithm to a raw loop

There is one meta-rule missing in this section: "Prefer an algorithm to a raw loop provided there is a suitable named algorithm for the purpose" (Bjarne Stroustrup during his proofread). The more than 100 algorithms of the STL provide implicit operations on containers. This operation can often be adapted by a lambda expression or performed in a parallel or parallel and vectorized version.

```
std::vector<int> vec = {-10, 5, 0, 3, -20, 31};

            // permitting parallel execution
std::sort(std::execution::par, vec.begin(), vec.end());

            // permitting parallel and vectorized execution
std::sort(std::execution::par_unseq, vec.begin(), vec.end())
```

Selection statements

if and switch are the selection statements of C++ that we inherited from C.

- You should prefer a switch statement to an if statement when there is a choice ("ES.70: Prefer a switch statement to an if-statement when there is a choice") because a switch statement may be more readable and can be better optimized than an if statement.

The next two rules related to switch statements need more attention than the ones before.

ES.78	Don't rely on implicit fallthrough in switch statements

I saw switch statements in legacy code, which had more than 100 case labels. If you use non-empty cases without a break, the maintenance of these switch statements becomes a nightmare. Here is an example from the C++ Core Guidelines:

```
switch (eventType) {
case Information:
    update_status_bar();
    break;
case Warning:
    write_event_log();
    // Bad - implicit fallthrough
```

```
case Error:
    display_error_window();
    break;
}
```

Maybe you overlooked it. The Warning case has no break statement; therefore, the Error case is automatically executed.

Since C++17, we have a cure with the attribute [[fallthrough]]. Now you can explicitly express your intention. [[fallthrough]] has to be in its own statement line and immediately before a case label. [[fallthrough]] indicates to the compiler that a fallthrough is intentional. Consequently, the compiler may not diagnose a warning.

```
void f(int n) {
    void g(), h(), i();
    switch (n) {
        case 1:
        case 2:
            g();
            [[fallthrough]];  // (1)
        case 3:
            h();              // (2)
        case 4:
            i();
            [[fallthrough]];  // (3)
    }
}
```

The [[fallthrough]] attribute in (1) suppresses a compiler warning. That does not hold for (2). The compiler may warn. (3) is ill formed because no case label follows.

ES.79   Use default to handle common cases (only)

The program switch.cpp should exemplify this rule.

```
// switch.cpp

#include <iostream>

enum class Message{
    information,
```

```cpp
    warning,
    error,
    fatal
};

void writeMessage() { std::cerr << "message" << '\n'; }
void writeWarning() { std::cerr << "warning" << '\n'; }
void writeUnexpected() { std::cerr << "unexpected" << '\n'; }

void withDefault(Message message) {
    switch(message) {
        case Message::information:
            writeMessage();
            break;
        case Message:: warning:
            writeWarning();
            break;
        default:
            writeUnexpected();
            break;
    }
}

void withoutDefaultGood(Message message) {
    switch(message) {
        case Message::information:
            writeMessage();
            break;
        case Message:: warning:
            writeWarning();
            break;
        default:
            // nothing can be done
            break;
    }
}

void withoutDefaultBad(Message message) {
    switch(message) {
        case Message::information:
            writeMessage();
            break;
```

```
        case Message::warning:
            writeWarning();
            break;
    }
}

int main() {

    withDefault(Message::fatal);
    withoutDefaultGood(Message::information);
    withoutDefaultBad(Message::warning);

}
```

The implementation of the functions `withDefault` and `withoutDefaultGood` are expressive enough. The maintainer of the function `withoutDefaultGood` knows because of the comment that there is no default case for this `switch` statement. Compare the functions `withoutDefaultGood` and `withoutDefaultBad` from a maintenance point of view. Do you know if the implementer of the function `withoutDefaultBad` forgot the default case or if the enumerator's `Message::error` and `Message::fatal` were later added? To make sure, you have to study the source code or ask the original author of the code, if possible.

Arithmetic

The seven arithmetic rules provide a significant surprise potential. They focus on two topics: arithmetic with signed and unsigned integers, and typical arithmetic errors such as overflow/underflow and division by zero.

Arithmetic with signed/unsigned integers

Breaking these arithmetic rules often ends in unexpected results.

ES.100	Don't mix signed and unsigned arithmetic

If you mix signed and unsigned arithmetic, you may not get the expected result.

```cpp
// mixSignedUnsigned.cpp

#include <iostream>

int main() {

    int x = -3;
    unsigned int y = 7;

    std::cout << x - y << '\n';  // 4294967286
    std::cout << x + y << '\n';  // 4
    std::cout << x * y << '\n';  // 4294967275
    std::cout << x / y << '\n';  // 613566756

}
```

GCC, Clang, and the Microsoft compiler produce the same result.

ES.101   Use unsigned types for bit manipulation

Bit manipulations with bitwise operators (~, >>, >>=, <<, , &, &=, ^, ^=, |, and |=) have implementation-defined behavior when performed on signed operands. Implementation-defined behavior means that the behavior varies between implementations, and the implementation must document the effects of each behavior. Consequently, don't perform bit manipulations on signed types, but use unsigned types instead:

```cpp
unsigned char x = 0b00110010;
unsigned char y = ~x;   // y == 0b11001101
```

ES.102   Use signed types for arithmetic

First, you should not do arithmetic with unsigned types because subtraction of two values often gives a negative value. Second, you should not mix signed and unsigned arithmetic according to the previous rule: "ES.100: Don't mix signed and unsigned arithmetic." Let's see what happens when I break the rule.

GCC, Clang, and the Microsoft compiler produce the same result.

```cpp
// signedTypes.cpp

#include <iostream>

template<typename T, typename T2>
T subtract(T x, T2 y) {
    return x - y;
}

int main() {

    int s = 5;
    unsigned int us = 5;
    std::cout << subtract(s, 7) << '\n';         // -2
    std::cout << subtract(us, 7u) << '\n';       // 4294967294
    std::cout << subtract(s, 7u) << '\n';        // -2
    std::cout << subtract(us, 7) << '\n';        // 4294967294
    std::cout << subtract(s, us + 2) << '\n';    // -2
    std::cout << subtract(us, s + 2) << '\n';    // 4294967294


}
```

ES.106   Don't try to avoid negative values by using `unsigned`

There is an interesting relation. When you assign a -1 to an unsigned int, you get the largest unsigned int.

The behavior of arithmetic expression may differ between signed and unsigned types.

Let's start with a simple program.

```cpp
// modulo.cpp

#include <cstddef>
#include <iostream>

int main(){
```

```
    std::cout << '\n';

    unsigned int max{100000};
    unsigned short x{0};
    std::size_t count{0};
    while (x < max && count < 20) {
        std::cout << x << " ";
        x += 10000;        // (1)
        ++count;
    }

    std::cout << "\n\n";

}
```

The crucial point of the program is that the successive addition to x in (1) does not trigger an overflow but a modulo operation if the value range of x ends. The reason is that x is of type unsigned short.

Making x signed changes the behavior of the program drastically.

```
// overflow.cpp

#include <cstddef>
#include <iostream>

int main() {

    std::cout << '\n';

    int max{100000};
    short x{0};
    std::size_t count{0};
    while (x < max && count < 20) {
        std::cout << x << " ";
        x += 10000;
        ++count;
    }

    std::cout << "\n\n";

}
```

The addition now triggers an overflow. In Figure 8.12, I marked the key points with red circles.

Figure 8.12 *Modulo versus overflow with* unsigneds *and* signeds

Detecting overflow

You may have a burning question: How can you detect an overflow? Quite easily! Replace the erroneous assignment x += 1000 with an expression using curly braces: x = {x + 1000}. The difference is that the compiler checks for narrowing conversions and, therefore, detects the overflow. Figure 8.13 shows the output from GCC.

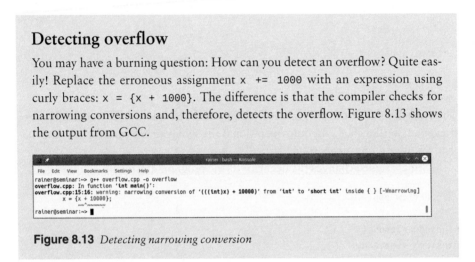

Figure 8.13 *Detecting narrowing conversion*

Typical arithmetic errors

The following three rules always result in undefined behavior.

ES.103   Don't overflow

and

ES.104   Don't underflow

Let me combine both rules. The effect of an overflow or an underflow is the same: memory corruption and, therefore, undefined behavior. Let's make a simple test with an int array. How long will the following program run when I compile it with GCC?

```
// overUnderflow.cpp

#include <cstddef>
```

```
#include <iostream>

int main() {

    int a[0];
    int n = 0;

    while (true){
        if (!(n % 100)){
            std::cout << "a[" << n << "] = " << a[n]
        }
        a[n] = n;
        a[-n] = -n;
        ++n;
    }


}
```

Disturbingly long. The program writes each one-hundredth array entry to std::cout. See Figure 8.14.

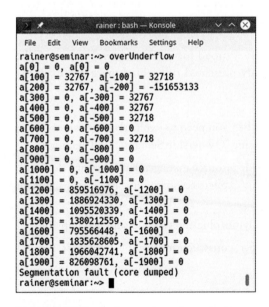

Figure 8.14 *Underflow and overflow of a C-array*

ES.105   Don't divide by zero

Dividing by zero crashes with high probability the execution of your program.

```
auto res = 5 / 0;   // crash
```

Dividing by zero may be fine in a logical expression.

```
auto res = false and (5 / 0);  // fine
```

The result of the expression (5 / 0) is not necessary for the overall result and is thus not evaluated. This technique is called short circuit evaluation and is a special case of lazy evaluation.

Related rules

I write about the rule "ES.25: Declare an object `const` or `constexpr` unless you want to modify its value later on" in Chapter 12, Constants and Immutability.

The section Metaprogramming in Chapter 13 provides an introduction to template metaprogramming and `constexpr` functions as a replacement for a function-like macro.

The rules related to expressions have a broad focus. Consequently, some of the rules have a strong overlap with already presented rules. Find more details in the referenced rules:

- ES.56: Write `std::move()` only when you need to explicitly move an object to another scope (see Parameter Passing: Ownership Semantics in Chapter 4)

- ES.60: Avoid new and delete outside resource management functions (see R.12: Immediately give the result of an explicit resource allocation to a manager object)

- ES.63: Don't slice (see C.67: A polymorphic class should suppress copying)

- ES.64: Use the `T{e}` notation for construction (see ES.23: Prefer the {}-initializer syntax)

Distilled

Important

- If you write a loop, you probably don't know the algorithms of the Standard Template Library (STL) well enough. The STL has more than 100 algorithms.

- Good names are probably the most important rule for good software. Good names means that your names should be self-explanatory, should be as local as possible, should not be similar to existing names, should not be written in `ALL_CAPS`, and should not be reused in nested scopes.

- Always initialize a variable. Prefer {}-initialization to prevent narrowing conversion. For complex initialization of `const` variables, use in-place invoked lambda expressions.

- Don't use macros for constants or functions. If you have to use them or to maintain existing ones, use unique `ALL_CAPS` names.

- You should prefer a range-based for loop to a `for` loop if possible. Range-based for loops are easier to read and cannot cause an index error.

- You should prefer a `switch` statement to an `if` statement. `switch` statements are easier to read and have more optimization potential.

- Unless there is a specific reason, use signed integers and don't mix signed and unsigned arithmetic.

- Be aware that overflow or underflow is undefined behavior and ends typically in a crash at run time of your program.

Chapter 9

Performance

Cippi's performance test

Performance or low latency is the sweet spot for C++, right? Therefore, I'm quite surprised that only a quarter of the 20 rules to performance have substantial content. Hence, I have to improvise a little to make a story out of the existing guidelines. The performance rules of the C++ Core Guidelines start with rules for wrong optimizations, continue with rules about wrong assumptions, and end with rules to enable optimization.

Wrong optimizations

- Per.1: Don't optimize without reason
- Per.2: Don't optimize prematurely
- Per.3: Don't optimize something that's not performance critical

A famous quote can nicely summarize the first three rules.

The real problem is that programmers have spent far too much time worrying about efficiency in the wrong places and at the wrong times; premature optimization is the root of all evil (or at least most of it) in programming.

—Donald Knuth, *The Art of Computer Programming* (1974)

To make it short, keep the phrase "premature optimization is the root of all evil" in mind. Before you make any performance assumption, apply the most critical rule to performance analysis: *Measure the performance of your program.*

Without performance numbers, you don't know the following:

- Which part of your program is the bottleneck?
- How fast is good enough for your user?
- How fast could the program potentially be?

Make the performance test with real-world data and test under version control. Rerun those performance tests each time you change something in your infrastructure such as the hardware or the compiler.

Applying substantial optimization based on wrong assumptions is a typical antipattern.

Wrong assumptions

- Per.4: Don't assume that complicated code is necessarily faster than simple code
- Per.5: Don't assume that low-level code is necessarily faster than high-level code
- Per.6: Don't make claims about performance without measurements

Before I continue, I have to make a disclaimer: I do not recommend using the infamous singleton pattern. The singleton has many drawbacks. You can read more about them in the section dedicated to singletons in Chapter 3. I use the singleton pattern in this section because the following example is based on a real-world example.

Let me show you that complicated and low-level code does not always pay off. To prove my point, I have to measure the performance of various singleton implementations.

The key idea of the performance test is to invoke the singleton pattern 40 million times from four threads, measure the execution time of each thread, and sum the numbers up. Four threads seem to be the right choice due to my four-core machine. The singleton pattern is initialized lazily; therefore, the first call has to initialize it.

Don't take the performance numbers too seriously. They should only give a ballpark feeling.

My first implementation is based on the so-called Meyers singleton. It is thread safe because of the C++11 standard guarantees that a static variable with block scope is initialized in a thread-safe way.

```cpp
// singletonMeyers.cpp

#include <chrono>
#include <iostream>
#include <future>

constexpr auto tenMill = 10'000'000;

class MySingleton {
public:
    static MySingleton& getInstance() {
        static MySingleton instance;
        volatile int dummy{};
        return instance;
    }
private:
    MySingleton()= default;
    ~MySingleton()= default;
    MySingleton(const MySingleton&)= delete;
    MySingleton& operator = (const MySingleton&)= delete;
};

std::chrono::duration<double> getTime() {

    auto begin= std::chrono::system_clock::now();
```

```
    for (size_t i = 0; i < tenMill; ++i) {
        MySingleton::getInstance();
    }
    return std::chrono::system_clock::now() - begin;

};


int main() {

    auto fut1 = std::async(std::launch::async,getTime);
    auto fut2 = std::async(std::launch::async,getTime);
    auto fut3 = std::async(std::launch::async,getTime);
    auto fut4 = std::async(std::launch::async,getTime);

    auto total = fut1.get() + fut2.get() +
                 fut3.get() + fut4.get();

    std::cout << total.count() << '\n';

}
```

Line 12 uses the guarantee of the C++11 run time that the singleton is initialized in a thread-safe way. Each of the four threads in the main function invokes ten million times the singleton in line 27. In total, this makes 40 million calls. The volatile variable dummy at line 13 is necessary. Without the variable dummy, the optimizer would do a perfect job and remove the loop in lines 26–28. Of course, the performance numbers would be impressive.

Let's try to do better. This time I use atomics to make the singleton pattern thread safe. My implementation is based on the infamous double-checked locking pattern. For the sake of simplicity, I will show only the implementation of the class MySingleton.

```
class MySingleton {
public:
    static MySingleton* getInstance() {
        MySingleton* sin= instance.load(std::memory_order_acquire);
        if ( !sin ) {
            std::lock_guard<std::mutex> myLock(myMutex);
            sin = instance.load(std::memory_order_relaxed);
            if( !sin ){
                sin = new MySingleton();
                instance.store(sin,std::memory_order_release);
            }
        }
```

```
            volatile int dummy{};
            return sin;
        }
private:
    MySingleton()= default;
    ~MySingleton()= default;
    MySingleton(const MySingleton&)= delete;
    MySingleton& operator = (const MySingleton&)= delete;

    static std::atomic<MySingleton*> instance;
    static std::mutex myMutex;
};


std::atomic<MySingleton*> MySingleton::instance;
std::mutex MySingleton::myMutex;
```

To understand the implementation, you have to study the memory orderings, think about the acquire-release semantics, and think about the synchronization and ordering constraint. This is not an easy job, and it may take days.

But you know, highly sophisticated code pays off.

Darn. I forgot to apply the critical rule of performance optimization: "Per.6: Don't make claims about performance without measurements". Figure 9.1 shows the performance numbers for the Meyers singleton on Linux. I compiled the program, as always, with maximum optimization.

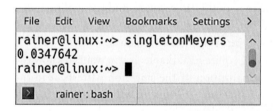

Figure 9.1 *Performance of the Meyers singleton*

Now I'm curious. What are the numbers for my highly sophisticated code? See Figure 9.2.

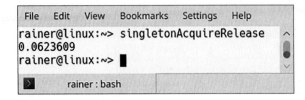

Figure 9.2 *Performance of the singleton based on acquire-release semantics*

80% percent slower! 80% percent slower, and we cannot even prove that the implementation is correct.

Are we done? No! I don't have a baseline. The baseline should be your starting, not your ending, point for a performance test. How fast can 40 million invocations of a singleton be? Invoking 40 million times the singleton from a single-threaded implementation with no synchronization overhead provides me a good baseline. See Figure 9.3.

Figure 9.3 *Performance of the singleton in the single-threaded case*

The single-threaded execution takes about 0.024 seconds, and the mulithreaded execution based on the Meyers singleton about 0.035 seconds. This means that the synchronization overhead makes the Meyers singleton 45% slower.

This small synchronization overhead is quite remarkable. If you want to know the entire story behind the thread-safe initialization of the singleton pattern, read the post "Thread-Safe Initialization of a Singleton" at https://www.modernescpp.com/index.php/thread-safe-initialization-of-a-singleton. This story includes additional implementations based on the function `std::call_once` and the `std::once_flag`, the lock `std::lock_guard`, and atomics using sequential consistency. The performance numbers provided are for Linux (GCC) and the Microsoft platform (cl.exe).

Enable optimization

The last section is about wrong assumptions. Now, I want to take an optimistic approach.

Get the ultimate truth with Compiler Explorer

If you want to know which code is better optimized, you have to study the generated assembler instructions. Compiler Explorer generates the assembler instructions for various compilers including GCC, Clang, and the Microsoft compiler. Various versions of the compilers are available. Additionally, you can specify the compiler flags such as -O3 or /Ox for maximum optimization.

Per.7	Design to enable optimization

This rule applies, in particular, to move semantics because you should write your algorithms using move semantics and not copy semantics. Using move semantics automatically provides a few benefits.

1. Instead of an expensive copy operation, your algorithm uses a cheap move operation.

2. Your algorithm is a lot more stable because it requires no memory allocation, and therefore, `std::bad_alloc` exceptions are not possible.

3. You can use your algorithm with move-only types such as `std::unique_ptr`.

You may see a loophole in my argumentation. What happens when I use a copy-only type in an algorithm requiring move semantics?

```cpp
// swap.cpp

#include <algorithm>
#include <iostream>
#include <utility>

template <typename T>
void swap(T& a, T& b) noexcept {  // (2)
  T tmp(std::move(a));
  a = std::move(b);
  b = std::move(tmp);
}
```

```cpp
class BigArray {

public:
  explicit BigArray(std::size_t sz): size(sz), data(new int[size]) {}

  BigArray(const BigArray& other): size(other.size),
                                   data(new int[other.size]) {
    std::cout << "Copy constructor" << '\n';
    std::copy(other.data, other.data + size, data);
    }

    BigArray& operator = (const BigArray& other) {
      std::cout << "Copy assignment" << '\n';
      if (this != &other){
          delete [] data;
          data = nullptr;
          size = other.size;
          data = new int[size];
          std::copy(other.data, other.data + size, data);
      }
      return *this;
  }

    ~BigArray() {
       delete[] data;
  }
private:
  std::size_t size;
  int* data;
};

int main(){

  std::cout << '\n';

  BigArray bigArr1(2011);
  BigArray bigArr2(2017);
  swap(bigArr1, bigArr2);    // (1)

  std::cout << '\n';

}
```

BigArray does not support move semantics, only copy semantics. What happens if I swap the BigArrays in (1)? My swap algorithm uses move semantics (2) internally. Let's try it out (see Figure 9.4).

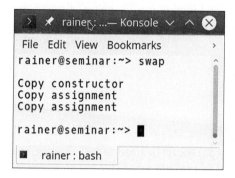

Figure 9.4 *Move semantics on a copy-only type*

Applying move operations on a copy-only type triggers copy operations. Copy semantics is a kind of fallback to move semantics. You can see it the other way around. Move is an optimized copy. How is this possible? I asked for a move operation in my swap algorithm. The reason is that std::move returns an rvalue. A const lvalue reference can bind to an rvalue, and the copy constructor or the copy-assignment operator takes a const lvalue reference. If BigArray would have a move-constructor or a move-assignment operator taking rvalue references, both would have higher priority than the copy constructor or the move-assignment operator. Implementing your algorithms with move semantics means that move semantics automatically kicks in if your data types support it. If not, copy semantics is used as a fallback. In the worst case, you get the classical behavior.

When you study the copy-assignment operator, you see that it has a number of flaws. Here they are:

1. The expression (if(this != &other)) checks for self-assignment. Most of the time self-assignment does not happen, but the check is always performed.

2. If the allocation (data = new int[size]) fails, this is already modified. The size is wrong, and data is already deleted. This behavior means the copy constructor guarantees only that there is no leak after an exception.

3. The expression (std::copy(other.data, other.data + size,data)) is used in the copy constructor and in the copy-assignment operator.

Implementing a swap function for BigArray and implementing the copy-assignment operator with the help of the swap function would solve all flaws. Here is the copy-assignment operator, which takes its argument by value. Consequently, a test for self-assignment is not necessary.

```
BigArray& operator = (BigArray other) {
    swap(*this, other);
    return *this;
}
```

BigArray still has a few flaws. Using a std::vector instead of a C-array solves them. The definition of BigArray boils down to a few lines:

```
class BigArray {
public:
    BigArray(std::size_t sz): vec(std::vector<int>(sz)) {}
private:
    std::vector<int> vec;
};
```

The compiler can autogenerate the big six if all members of the class support them. The big six include the default constructor, destructor, copy- and move-assignment operator, and copy and move constructor. std::vector supports the big six, and therefore, BigArray does support the big six with one exception. Due to the user-defined constructor, BigArray does not have a default constructor.

Per.10   Rely on the static type system

There are many ways that you can help the compiler to generate more optimized code.

- **Write local code:** Using an in-place invoked lambda instead of a function to adjust the behavior of std::sort is in general the faster variant. The compiler has all the information available to generate the most optimized code. On the contrary, a function could be defined in another translation unit, which is a hard boundary for the optimizer.

```cpp
bool lessLength(const std::string& f, const std::string& s){
    return f.size() < s.size();
}

int main() {

    std::vector<std::string> vec = {"12345", "123456", "1234",
                                    "1", "12", "123", "12345"};

    // a function as predicate
    std::sort(vec.begin(), vec.end(), lessLength);

    // a lambda as predicate
    std::sort(vec.begin(), vec.end(),
            [](const std::string& f, const std::string& s) {
                return f.size() < s.size();
            });
}
```

- **Write simple code:** The optimizer looks for known patterns that could be optimized. If your code is very handcrafted and complicated, you make the job of the optimizer to find known patterns harder. In the end, you often get less optimized code.

- **Give the compiler additional hints:** When your function cannot throw, or you don't care, declare it as `noexcept`. It is equally valuable to the optimizer to declare a virtual function as `final` if it should not be overridden.

Per.11	Move computation from run time to compile-time

The following example shows the gcd algorithm, which calculates the greatest common division at run time. gcd is implemented using the Euclidean algorithm.

```cpp
int gcd(int a, int b) {
    while (b != 0) {
        auto t = b;
        b = a % b;
        a = t;
    }
    return a;
}
```

By declaring gcd as constexpr, gcd becomes a function that can be executed at compile time. There are a few restrictions on constexpr functions. gcd must not use static or thread_local variables, exception handling, or goto statements, and all variables have to be initialized and have a literal type. A literal type is essentially a built-in type, or a reference, or an array of literal types, or a class with a constexpr constructor.

Let's try it out.

```cpp
// gcd.cpp

#include <iostream>

constexpr int gcd(int a, int b) {
    while (b != 0){
        auto t = b;
        b = a % b;
        a = t;
    }
    return a;
}

int main() {

    std::cout << '\n';

    constexpr auto res1 = gcd(121, 11);              // (1)
    std::cout << "gcd(121, 11) = " << res1 << '\n';

    auto val = 121;                                  // (3)
    auto res2 = gcd(val, 11);                        // (2)
    std::cout << "gcd(val, 11) = " << res2 << '\n';

    std::cout << '\n';

}
```

Declaring gcd as a constexpr function does not mean that it has to run at compile time. It means that gcd has the potential to run at compile time. A constexpr function has to be executed at compile time if used in a constant expression. res1 in (1) is a constant expression because I ask for the result with a constexpr variable res1. res2 in (2) is not a constant expression because val in (3) is not a constant expression. When I change res2 to `constexpr auto res2`, I get an error: `val` is not a constant expression. Figure 9.5 shows the output of the program.

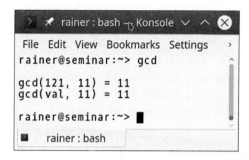

Figure 9.5 *Invoking gcd at compile time and run time*

Once more, here is the key observation. You can use a `constexpr` function at run time and compile time. To use it at compile time, its arguments have to be constant expressions.

Thanks to Compiler Explorer, I can show the relevant assembler instructions for this program. The invocation of the function `gcd(121, 11)` in line 18 boils down to its result as a constant. See Figure 9.6.

```
mov esi, 11
mov edi, OFFSET FLAT:std::cout
call std::basic_ostream<char, std::char_traits<char> >::operator<<(int)
```

Figure 9.6 *The relevant assembler instructions to the algorithm gcd*

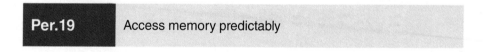

Per.19   Access memory predictably

What does predictably mean? For example, you read an `int` from memory more than the size of this one `int` is read from memory. An entire cache line is read from memory and stored in a CPU's cache. On modern architectures, a cache line typically has

64 bytes. If you now request an additional variable from memory and this variable is already cached, the read directly uses this cache, and the operation is much faster.

A data structure such as std::vector, which stores its data in a contiguous memory block, is a cache-line-friendly data structure because each element in the cache line is typically used. This cache-line friendliness also holds for a std::array and std::string.

std::deque is in its structure similar to std::vector, but the elements of std::deque are not stored in a contiguous memory block. The elements of a std::deque are typically stored in a sequence of fixed-size arrays. The fixed-sized arrays are filled before new arrays are added to the std::deque. See Figure 9.7.

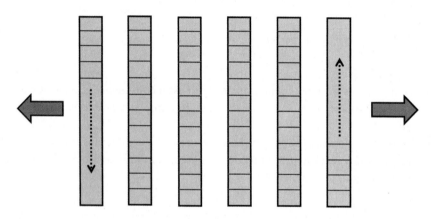

Figure 9.7 *std::deque*

In contrast, std::list and std::forward_list are doubly or singly linked containers. A std::list increases in both directions, a std::forward_list in one direction. See Figures 9.8 and 9.9.

Figure 9.8 *std::list*

Figure 9.9 *std::forward_list*

This was the theory of cache lines. Now I'm curious. Does it make a performance difference to read and accumulate all elements of a std::vector, a std::deque, a std::list, and a std::forward_list? This small program gives an answer.

```cpp
1 // memoryAccess.cpp
2
3 #include <forward_list>
4 #include <chrono>
5 #include <deque>
6 #include <iomanip>
7 #include <iostream>
8 #include <list>
9 #include <string>
10 #include <vector>
11 #include <numeric>
12 #include <random>
13
14 const int SIZE = 100'000'000;
15
16 template <typename T>
17 void sumUp(T& t, const std::string& cont) {
18
19    std::cout << std::fixed << std::setprecision(10);
20
21   auto begin = std::chrono::steady_clock::now();
22    std::size_t res = std::accumulate(t.begin(), t.end(), 0LL);
23    std::chrono::duration<double> last =
24        std::chrono::steady_clock::now() - begin;
25    std::cout << cont <<  '\n';
26    std::cout << "time: " << last.count() << '\n';
27    std::cout << "res: " << res << '\n';
28    std::cout << '\n';
29
30    std::cout << '\n';
31
32 }
33
34 int main() {
35
36    std::cout << '\n';
37
38    std::random_device seed;
39    std::mt19937 engine(seed());
40    std::uniform_int_distribution<int> dist(0, 100);
41
```

```
42    std::vector<int> randNum;
43    randNum.reserve(SIZE);
44    for (int i = 0; i < SIZE; ++i){
45        randNum.push_back(dist(engine));
46    }
47
48    {
49        std::vector<int> vec(randNum.begin(), randNum.end());
50        sumUp(vec,"std::vector<int>");
51    }
52
53
54    {
55        std::deque<int>deq(randNum.begin(), randNum.end());
56        sumUp(deq,"std::deque<int>");
57    }
58
59    {
60        std::list<int>lst(randNum.begin(), randNum.end());
61        sumUp(lst,"std::list<int>");
62    }
63
64    {
65        std::forward_list<int>forwardLst(randNum.begin(),
66                                         randNum.end());
67        sumUp(forwardLst,"std::forward_list<int>");
68    }
69
70 }
```

The program `memoryAccess.cpp` creates first 100 million random numbers between 0 and 100 (line 38). Then it accumulates the elements using a `std::vector` (line 50), a `std::deque` (line 56), a `std::list` (line 61), and a `std::forward_list` (line 67). The actual work is done in the function `sumUp` (lines 16–32). My educated guess is that GCC, Clang, and the Microsoft Visual Studio compiler use a quite similar implementation of `std::accumulate`.

```
template<class InputIt, class T>
T accumulate(InputIt first, InputIt last, T init) {
    for (; first != last; ++first) {
        init = init + *first;
    }
    return init;
}
```

Consequently, the access time of the elements is the dominant factor for the overall performance. See Figure 9.10.

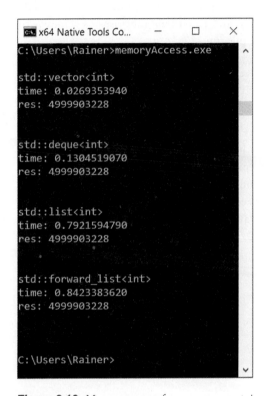

Figure 9.10 *Memory access for sequence containers on Windows*

Here are a few observations:

- `std::vector` is 30 times faster than `std::list` or `std::forward_list`.
- `std::vector` is 5 times faster than `std::deque`.
- `std::deque` is 6 times faster than `std::list` and `std::forward_list`.
- `std::list` and `std::forward_list` are in the same ballpark.

Although I got similar relative numbers on Linux with the GCC compiler, don't take the performance numbers too seriously. The performance numbers give a solid indication that the access time to the elements heavily depends on the cache-line friendliness of the container.

Related rules

The section Metaprogramming in Chapter 13 provides an introduction to template metaprogramming, the type-traits library, and `constexpr` functions as a means to move computation from run time to compile time.

Distilled

Important

- Before you make any supposed optimization based on wrong assumptions, measure the performance of your program.
- Help the compiler to optimize your program. Implement your functions with move semantics, and make them `constexpr` if possible.
- Modern computer architectures are optimized for the contiguous reading of memory. Consequently, `std::vector`, `std::array`, or `std::string` should be your first choice.

Chapter 10

Concurrency

Cippi's challenges with threads

The C++ Core Guidelines list about thirty rules for concurrency that focus on three main goals:

- To help in writing code that is amenable to being used in a multithreaded environment

- To show clean, safe ways to use the threading primitives offered by the standard library

- To offer guidance on what to do when concurrency and parallelism aren't giving the performance gains needed

The rules consist of general guidelines, targeted to a non-expert audience, applied to concurrency, parallelism, message passing, and lock-free programming.

Concurrency versus parallelism

- **Concurrency:** The execution of several tasks overlaps. Concurrency is a superset of parallelism.

- **Parallelism:** Several tasks are run at the same time. Parallelism is a subset of concurrency.

General guidelines

Although the rules of this section have a general focus, all of them are important.

 CP.1   Assume that your code will run as part of a multi-threaded program

Maybe you are surprised to read this rule. Why should I optimize for a special case? To make it clear, this rule is mainly about code used in libraries. And experience shows that library code is often reused. This reuse means that the code is likely to end up being exercised in a multithreaded program.

The code snippet shows an example from the guidelines.

```
1   double cached_computation(double x) {
2     static double cached_x = 0.0;
3     static double cached_result = COMPUTATION_OF_ZERO;
4     double result;
5
```

```
6        if (cached_x == x) return cached_result;
7        result = computation(x);
8        cached_x = x;
9        cached_result = result;
10       return result;
11   }
```

The function `cached_computation` is fine if it runs in a single-threaded environment. This observation does not hold for a multithreading environment because the static variables `cached_x` (lines 2, 6, and 9) and `cached_result` (lines 3, 6, and 9) can be modified simultaneously by various threads.

Unsynchronized reading and writing of a shared non-atomic variable is a data race. Consequently, your program has undefined behavior.

What are your options to get rid of the data race?

1. Use one lock to protect the entire critical region.

2. Protect the call to the function `cached_computation` by a lock.

3. Make both `static` variables `thread_local`. `thread_local` guarantees that each thread gets its variable `cached_x` and `cached_result`. Such a static variable is bound to the lifetime of the main thread; a `thread_local` variable is bound to the lifetime of its thread.

```
std::mutex m;
double cached_computation(double x) {              // (1)
   static double cached_x = 0.0;
   static double cached_result = COMPUTATION_OF_ZERO;
   double result;
   {
       std::lock_guard<std::mutex> lck(m);
   if (cached_x == x) return cached_result;
   result = computation(x);
   cached_x = x;
   cached_result = result;
   }
   return result;
}

std::mutex cachedComputationMutex;                 // (2)
{
```

```
    std::lock_guard<std::mutex> lck(cachedComputationMutex);
    auto cached = cached_computation(3.33);
}


double cached_computation(double x) {                    // (3)
    thread_local double cached_x = 0.0;
    thread_local double cached_result = COMPUTATION_OF_ZERO;
    double result;

    if (cached_x == x) return cached_result;
    result = computation(x);
    cached_x = x;
    cached_result = result;
    return result;
}
```

First, the C++11 standard guarantees that the C++ run time initializes static variables in a thread-safe way; therefore, you do not need to protect their initialization.

1. This version uses a coarse-grained locking approach. Usually, you should not use coarse-grained locking such as in this version, but maybe in this use case, it is acceptable.

2. This version is the most coarse-grained solution because the entire function is locked. Of course, the downside is that the user of the function is responsible for the synchronization. In general, that is a bad idea.

3. Just make the static variables thread_local, and you are done.

CP.2	Avoid data races

First of all, what is a data race?

- A **data race** is a situation in which at least two threads access a non-atomic shared variable without synchronization and at least one thread tries to modify the variable.

The rest is simple. If you have a data race in your program, your program has undefined behavior.

If you read the definition of data race carefully, you will notice that a shared, mutable state is necessary for having a data race. Figure 10.1 displays this critical observation. You should avoid the bottom right quadrant, in particular, in a concurrent environment.

Mutable?

	No	Yes
No	OK	OK
Yes	OK	Data race

(Row label: **Shared?**)

Figure 10.1 *Four categories of variables*

Let me show you a simple data race.

```cpp
// dataRace.cpp

#include <future>

int getUniqueId() {
  static int id = 1;
  return id++;
}

int main() {

    auto fut1 = std::async([]{ return getUniqueId(); });
    auto fut2 = std::async([]{ return getUniqueId(); });

    auto id = fut1.get();
    auto id2= fut2.get();

}
```

What can go wrong? For example id++ is a read-modify-write operation. Even if each of the three operations read, modify, and write were atomic, the read-modify-write operation is not atomic. The effect of this data race would be with high probability that ids would not be unique.

CP.3   Minimize explicit sharing of writable data

Based on the previous rule related to data races, your shared data should be constant.

Now the only challenge left to solve is how to initialize the constant shared data in a thread-safe way. C++11 supports a few ways to achieve this.

1. Initialize your data before you start a thread. This is not due to C++11 but is often quite easy to apply.

```cpp
const std::unordered_map<std::string, int> val = {
        {"Grimm",1966},
        {"Smith",1968},
        {"Blac",1930} };
std::thread t1([&tele] { .... });
std::thread t2([&tele] { .... });
```

2. Use constant expressions because they are initialized at compile time.

```cpp
constexpr auto doub = 5.1;
```

3. Use the function `std::call_once` in combination with the `std::once_flag`. You can put the important initialization stuff into the function `onlyOnceFunc`. The C++ run time guarantees that this function runs exactly once successfully.

```cpp
std::once_flag onceFlag;

void do_once() {
    std::call_once(onceFlag, []{
        std::cout << "Important initialization" << '\n';
    };
}
...
std::thread t1(do_once);
std::thread t2(do_once);
std::thread t3(do_once);
std::thread t4(do_once);
```

4. Use `static` variables with block scope because the C++11 run time guarantees that they are initialized in a thread-safe way.

```cpp
void func() {
    ....
    static int val = 2011;
```

```
    ....
}
...

std::thread t1{ func() };
std::thread t2{ func() };
```

CP.4	Think in terms of tasks, rather than threads

What is a task? "Task" is a general term for a unit of execution. Since C++11, we have used task as a special term, which stands for two components: a promise and a future. A promise produces a value that the future can asynchronously pick up. Promise and future can run in different threads and are connected by a secure data channel.

Promise exists in three variations in C++: `std::async`, `std::packaged_task`, and `std::promise`. To get more details on tasks, consult the blog posts I've written here: https://www.modernescpp.com/index.php/tag/tasks.

A `std::packaged_task` and a `std::promise` have in common that they are quite low level; therefore, I present `std::async`.

Here are a thread and a future/promise pair that calculate the sum of 3 + 4.

```
// thread
int res;
std::thread t([&]{ res = 3 + 4; });
t.join();
std::cout << res << '\n';

// task
auto fut = std::async([]{ return 3 + 4; });
std::cout << fut.get() << '\n';
```

What is the fundamental difference between a thread and a future/promise pair? *A thread is about how something should be calculated; a task is about what should be calculated.*

Let me be more specific.

- The thread t uses the shared variable res to provide its results. In contrast, the promise `std::async` uses a secure data channel established by the promise to communicate its result to the future `fut`. This sharing means for the thread t that you have to protect res.

- In case of a thread, you explicitly create a thread. This creation of a thread does not hold automatically for the promise std::async. You specify what should be calculated and not how it should be calculated. The C++ run time decides to create a thread, if necessary.

CP.8	Don't try to use `volatile` for synchronization

If you want to have an atomic in Java or C#, you declare it as `volatile`. You may think that you could do the same in C++. That is wrong. `volatile` has no multi-threading semantics in C++. Atomics are called `std::atomic` in C++11.

Now, you may be curious: What is the meaning of `volatile` in C++?

`volatile` is meant to be used for special objects, on which optimized read or write operations are not allowed. `volatile` is typically used in embedded programming domains to denote objects that can change independently of the regular program flow. These are, for example, objects that represent an external device (memory-mapped I/O). Because these objects can change independently of the regular program flow, their value is directly written to main memory. Consequently, there is no optimized storing of values in hardware caches.

CP.9	Whenever feasible use tools to validate your concurrent code

This rule is probably one of the most important ones, and I fully agree.

My students write lots of bugs; in fact, even many of my own programs contain bugs! How can I be sure? Because of the dynamic code analysis tool ThreadSanitizer and the static code analysis tool CppMem. The use cases for ThreadSanitizer and CppMem are different.

ThreadSanitizer gives you the big picture and detects if the execution of your program has a data race. CppMem gives you detailed insight into small pieces of your code, most of the time including atomics. You get the answer to the question, Which interleavings are possible according to the memory model?

Let's start with ThreadSanitizer.

ThreadSanitizer

Here is the official introduction to ThreadSanitizer from "ThreadSanitizerCpp Manual" (https://github.com/google/sanitizers/wiki/ThreadSanitizerCppManual): "ThreadSanitizer (aka TSan) is a data race detector for C/C++. Data races are one of the most common and hardest bugs in concurrent systems. A data race occurs when two threads access the same non-atomic variable concurrently, and at least one of the accesses is a write. C++11 standard officially bans data races as undefined behavior."

ThreadSanitizer is part of Clang 3.2 and GCC 4.8. To use it, you have to compile and link using the -fsanitize=thread option and use at least optimization level -O2 and the flag -g for producing debugging information: -fsanitize=thread -O2 -g.

The run-time overhead is significant: The memory usage may increase 5 to 10 times and the execution time 2 to 20 times. Of course, you know the outstanding law of software development: *First, make your program correct; then, make it fast.*

Now let's see ThreadSanitizer in action. Here is a typical exercise I have often given in my multithreading classes to condition variables:

Write a small ping-pong game.

Two threads should alternatively set a `bool` value to true or false. One thread sets the value to true and notifies the other thread. The other thread sets the value to false and notifies the original thread. That play should end after a fixed amount of iterations.

And this is the typical implementation my students come up with.

```cpp
1   // conditionVariablePingPong.cpp
2
3   #include <condition_variable>
4   #include <iostream>
5   #include <thread>
6
7   bool dataReady= false;
8
9   std::mutex mut;
10  std::condition_variable condVar1;
11  std::condition_variable condVar2;
12
13  int counter = 0;
14  int COUNTLIMIT = 50;
15
16  void setTrue() {
17
18      while(counter <= COUNTLIMIT) {
```

```
19              std::unique_lock<std::mutex> lck(mut);
20              condVar1.wait(lck, []{return dataReady == false;});
21              dataReady = true;
22              ++counter;
23              std::cout << dataReady << '\n';
24              condVar2.notify_one();
25          }
26      }
27
28      void setFalse() {
29
30          while(counter < COUNTLIMIT) {
31              std::unique_lock<std::mutex> lck(mut);
32              condVar2.wait(lck, []{return dataReady == true;});
33              dataReady = false;
34              std::cout << dataReady << '\n';
35              condVar1.notify_one();
36          }
37      }
38
39      int main() {
40
41          std::cout << std::boolalpha << '\n';
42
43          std::cout << "Begin: " << dataReady << '\n';
44
45          std::thread t1(setTrue);
46          std::thread t2(setFalse);
47
48          t1.join();
49          t2.join();
50
51          dataReady = false;
52          std::cout << "End: " << dataReady << '\n';
53
54          std::cout << '\n';
55
56      }
```

Function setTrue (line 16) sets the boolean value dataReady (line 21) to true, and function setFalse (line 28) sets it to false. The play starts with setTrue. The condition variable in the function waits for the notification and therefore first checks the boolean dataReady (line 20). Afterward, the function increments the counter (line 22) and notifies the other thread with the help of the condition variable condVar2 (line 24). The function `setFalse` follows the same workflow. If the counter becomes equal to `COUNTLIMIT` (line 18), the game ends. Fine? No!

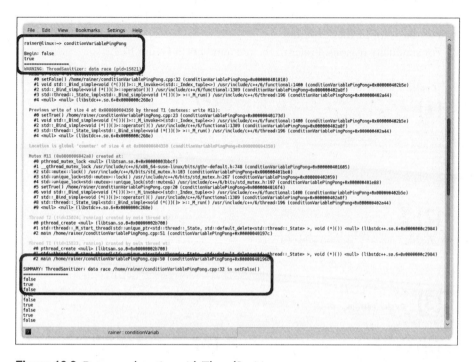

Figure 10.2 *Data race detection with ThreadSanitizer*

There is a data race on the counter. It is read (line 30) and written (line 22) without synchronization. ThreadSanitizer shows the data race (see Figure 10.2).

ThreadSanitizer detects data races during run time; CppMem lets you analyze small code snippets.

CppMem

Here is a short overview of CppMem.

The online tool, which you can also install on your PC, provides very valuable services.

1. CppMem validates small code snippets, typically including atomics.

2. The very accurate analysis of CppMem gives you deep insight into the C++ memory model.

For more in-depth insight, read my blog posts about CppMem at http://www.modernescpp.com/index.php/tag/cppmem. For now, I refer to the first point and provide you a thousand-foot view of CppMem.

My overview uses the default configuration of the tool. This overview should give you the basis for further experiments.

For simplicity reasons, I refer to the red numbers in Figure 10.3.

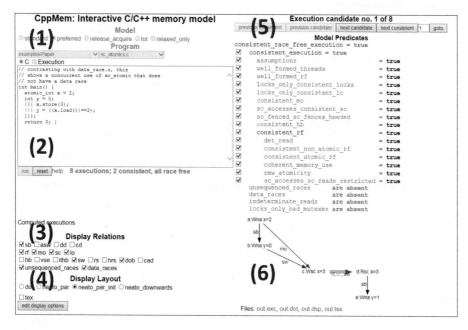

Figure 10.3 *Overview of CppMem*

1. Model

- This specifies the C++ memory model. The C++ memory model is *preferred*.

2. Program

- This is the executable program in C or C++ – like syntax.

- CppMem offers you a bunch of typical interleavings of atomics. To get the details of these programs, read the very well-written article "Mathematizing C++ Concurrency" by Mark Batty et al. at http://www.cl.cam.ac.uk/~pes20/cpp/popl085ap-sewell.pdf. Of course, you can also use your code.

- CppMem is about multithreading, so there are a few simplifications.
  - You can easily define two threads by the symbols {{{ ... ||| ... }}}. The three dots (...) stand for the work package of the thread.

3. **Display Relations**

- This describes the relations between the read, write, and read-write modifications on atomic operations, fences, and locks.

- If the relation is enabled, it is displayed in the annotated graph (see point 6).

  - **sb:** sequenced-before

  - **rf:** read from

  - **mo:** modification order

  - **sc:** sequential consistency

  - **lo:** lock order

  - **sw:** synchronizes-with

  - **dob:** dependency-ordered-before

  - data_races

4. **Display Layout**

- You can choose with this switch which Doxygraph graph is used.

5. **Choose the Executions**

- Switch between the various consistent executions.

6. **Annotated Graph**

- This displays the annotated graph.

Now, let's try it out.

The program `dataRaceOnX.cpp` has a data race on the `int` variable x. y is an atomic and, therefore, fine from a concurrency perspective.

```
// dataRaceOnX.cpp

#include <atomic>
#include <iostream>
#include <thread>
```

```
int x = 0;
std::atomic<int> y{0};

void writing() {
    x = 2000;
    y.store(11);
}

void reading(){
    std::cout << y.load() << " ";
    std::cout << x << '\n';
}

int main() {

    std::thread thread1(writing);
    std::thread thread2(reading);

    thread1.join();
    thread2.join();

}
```

In order to use CppMem, you *must* rewrite your C++ program in the dialect of C expected by CppMem's parser. Cutting and pasting standard C++ code fails with a cryptic "Frontc.ParseError." Here is the equivalent program written in the more concise CppMem syntax.

```
// dataRaceOnXCppMem.txt

int main(){
  int x = 0;
  atomic_int y = 0;

  {{{
    {
      x = 2000;
      y.store(11);
    }
  |||
```

```
    {
      y.load();
      x;
    }
  }}}
}
```

CppMem shows it immediately. The first consistent execution has a data race on x. See Figure 10.4.

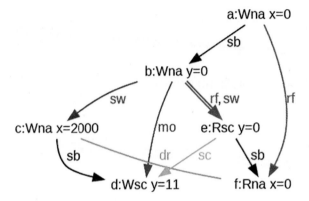

Figure 10.4 *A data race in CppMem*

You can observe the data race in the graph. It is the yellow edge (dr) between the write operation (x=2000) and the read operation (x=0).

To get more details on CppMem, read the blog posts I've written at https://www.modernescpp.com/index.php/tag/cppmem.

Concurrency

Concurrency is a challenging topic. This challenge is due, in particular, to the low-level abstraction we have now at our disposal. Knowing and applying the rules of this section is, therefore, crucial to get a well-defined multithreading program.

Let me classify about fifteen rules into categories related to locks, threads, and condition variables, but also data sharing between threads, resource considerations, and a sometimes overlooked danger.

Locks

NNN stands for No Naked New and means that memory allocation should not be done as a standalone operation but inside a manager object ("R.12: Immediately give the result of an explicit resource allocation to a manager object"). The same observation holds for mutexes. Mutexes should immediately be given to a manager object, which is, in this case, a lock. In modern C++, we have a `std::lock_guard`, `std::unique_lock`, `std::shared_lock` (C++14), or `std::scoped_lock` (C++17). Consequently, keep the acronym NNM, which stands for No Naked Mutex, in mind. Locks implement the RAII idiom. The crucial idea behind the RAII idiom is to bind the lifetime of a resource to the lifetime of a local variable. C++ automatically manages the lifetime of locals.

CP.20	Use RAII, never plain `lock()`/`unlock()`

The small code snippet should make the value of a lock immediately clear.

```
std::mutex mtx;

void do_stuff() {
    mtx.lock();
    // ... do stuff ... (1)
    mtx.unlock();
}
```

It doesn't matter if an exception occurs in (1) or you just forgot to unlock the `mtx`; in both cases, you will get a deadlock if another thread wants to acquire (lock) the `std::mutex mtx`. Locks come to the rescue.

```
std::mutex mtx;

void do_stuff() {
    std::lock_guard<std::mutex> lck {mtx};
    // ... do stuff ...
}
```

Put the mutex into a lock, and the mutex is automatically locked in the constructor of the `std::lock_guard` and unlocked when `lck` goes out of scope.

<table>
<tr><td>CP.21</td><td>Use std::lock() or std::scoped_lock to acquire multiple mutexes</td></tr>
</table>

If a thread needs more than one mutex at a time, you have to be extremely careful that you always lock the mutexes in the same sequence. If not, a bad interleaving of threads may cause a deadlock. The following program causes a deadlock.

```cpp
// lockGuardDeadlock.cpp

#include <iostream>
#include <chrono>
#include <mutex>
#include <thread>

struct CriticalData {
  std::mutex mut;
};

void deadLock(CriticalData& a, CriticalData& b) {

    std::lock_guard<std::mutex> guard1(a.mut);        // (1)
    std::cout << "Thread: " << std::this_thread::get_id() << '\n';

    std::this_thread::sleep_for(std::chrono::milliseconds(1));

    std::lock_guard<std::mutex> guard2(b.mut);        // (1)
    std::cout << "Thread: " << std::this_thread::get_id() <<  '\n';

    // do something with a and b (critical region)        (2)
}

int main() {

    std::cout << '\n';

    CriticalData c1;
    CriticalData c2;

    std::thread t1([&]{deadLock(c1, c2);});
    std::thread t2([&]{deadLock(c2, c1);});
```

```
    t1.join();
    t2.join();

    std::cout << '\n';

}
```

Threads t1 and t2 need two CriticalDatas, to perform their jobs in (2). Critical-Data has its mutex mut to synchronize the access. Unfortunately, both invoke the function deadlock with the arguments c1 and c2 in a different sequence (1). Now we have a race condition that could end up in a deadlock. Thread t1 can lock the first mutex a.mut but not the second one b.mut because, in the meantime, thread t2 locked the second one. See Figure 10.5.

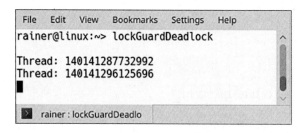

Figure 10.5 *A deadlock due to multiple locked mutexes*

The easiest way to solve the deadlock is to lock both mutexes atomically.

With C++11, you can use a std::unique_lock together with std::lock. Thanks to the tag std::defer_lock, the std::unique_lock takes the mutex without locking it. The locking finally takes place in the std::lock call. std::lock can take an arbitrary number of arguments.

```
void deadLock(CriticalData& a, CriticalData& b) {
    std::unique_lock<mutex> guard1(a.mut, std::defer_lock);
    std::unique_lock<mutex> guard2(b.mut, std::defer_lock);
    std::lock(guard1, guard2);
    // do something with a and b (critical region)
}
```

With C++17, a std::scoped_lock can lock an arbitrary number of mutexes in an atomic operation.

```
void deadLock(CriticalData& a, CriticalData& b) {
    std::scoped_lock scoLock(a.mut, b.mut);
```

```
    // do something with a and b (critical region)
}
```

CP.22	Never call unknown code while holding a lock (e.g., a callback)

Why is this code snippet bad, and why should it not pass a code review?

```
std::mutex m;
{
    std::lock_guard<std::mutex> lockGuard(m);
    sharedVariable = unknownFunction();
}
```

I can only speculate about the unknownFunction. If unknownFunction

- Tries to lock the mutex m, you get undefined behavior. Most of the time, the result of this undefined behavior is a deadlock.

- Starts a new thread that tries to lock the mutex m, you get a deadlock.

- Locks another mutex m2, you may get a deadlock because you lock the two mutexes m and m2 at the same time. Another thread may lock the same mutexes in a different sequence.

- Does not directly or indirectly try to lock the mutex m, all seems to be fine. "Seems" because a coworker can modify the function, and you get a changed version of the function unknownFunction. Now all bets are off.

- Works as expected, you still may have a performance issue because the unknownFunction takes quite a while. What was meant to be a multithreaded program behaves similarly to a single-threaded program.

To overcome the issues, use a local variable and invoke the unknown function outside of the critical region.

```
std::mutex m;
auto tempVar = unknownFunction();
{
    std::lock_guard<std::mutex> lockGuard(m);
    sharedVariable = tempVar;
}
```

This additional indirection solves all issues. `tempVar` is a local variable and can, therefore, not be a victim of a data race. No victim means that you can invoke `unknownFunction` without a synchronization mechanism. Additionally, the time for holding the lock is reduced to its bare minimum: assigning the value of `tempVar` to `sharedVariable`.

Threads

Threads are the basic building block for concurrent and parallel programming. With each new C++ standard, threads become more and more an implementation detail for concurrency. For example, with C++17, we got the parallel STL, which allows us to specify the execution policy; with C++20, coroutines; and with C++23, we can hope for transactional memory.

CP.23	Think of a joining `thread` as a scoped container

and

CP.24	Think of a `thread` as a global container

The slight variation of the code snippet from the C++ Core Guidelines should make both rules clear:

```
void f(int* p) {
    // ...
    *p = 99;
    // ...
}

int glob = 33;

void some_fct(int* p) {              // (1)
    int x = 77;
    std::thread t0(f, &x);           // OK
    std::thread t1(f, p);            // OK
    std::thread t2(f, &glob);        // OK
    auto q = make_unique<int>(99);
    std::thread t3(f, q.get());      // OK
    // ...
    t0.join();
```

```
      t1.join();
      t2.join();
      t3.join();
      // ...
  }

  void some_fct2(int* p) {              // (2)
      int x = 77;
      std::thread t0(f, &x);            // bad
      std::thread t1(f, p);             // bad
      std::thread t2(f, &glob);         // OK
      auto q = make_unique<int>(99);
      std::thread t3(f, q.get());       // bad
      // ...
      t0.detach();
      t1.detach();
      t2.detach();
      t3.detach();
      // ...
  }
```

The only difference between the functions some_fct (1) and some_fct2 (2) is that the first variation joins its created threads, but the second variation detaches all created threads.

First of all, you have to join or detach the children threads. If you don't, you get a std::terminate in the destructor of the child thread (see rule "CP.25: Prefer gsl::joining_thread over std::thread").

The difference between joining or detaching a created thread is the following: When the creator calls a thr.join() call on the created thread thr, it waits until the created thread is done. thr.join() is a synchronization point. To put it the other way around, the child thread thr can use all variables (state) of the enclosing scope in which it was created. Consequently, all calls of the function f are well-defined.

On the contrary, a thr.detach() call does not wait and is, therefore, not a synchronization point. This means that the created thread can outlive its creator. Consequently, using variables of the enclosing scope may not be valid anymore. This is precisely the issue in the function some_fct2. The variable x, the pointer p, or the resource of the std::unique_ptr q may not be valid anymore.

A thread can be seen as a global container using variables from outside. Additionally, in case of a joining thread, the lifetime of the container is scoped.

CP.25 Prefer std::jthread over std::thread

The original title of this rule is "CP.25: Prefer gsl::joining_thread over std::thread." I replaced gsl::joining_thread from the Guidelines Support Library with std::jthread from C++20.

In the following program, I forgot to join the thread t.

```cpp
// threadWithoutJoin.cpp

#include <iostream>
#include <thread>

int main() {

    std::thread t([]{
        std::cout << std::this_thread::get_id() << '\n';
    });

}
```

The execution of the program ends abruptly. See Figure 10.6.

Figure 10.6 *Forgot to join a thread*

The lifetime of the created thread t ends with its callable. The creator has two choices. First, it waits until its child is done (t.join()). Second, it detaches itself from its child (t.detach()). A thread t with a callable unit—you can create threads without callable units—is called joinable if neither a t.join() nor t.detach() call happened. The destructor of a joinable thread throws a std::terminate exception, which ends in std::abort. In our case, the program terminated before the child thread had time to display its id.

In addition to a std::thread, a std::jthread automatically joins on destruction. Replacing the std::thread with a std::jthread, therefore, solves the issue.

```cpp
// threadWithJoin.cpp; C++20

#include <iostream>
#include <thread>
```

```cpp
int main() {

    std::jthread t([]{
        std::cout << std::this_thread::get_id() << '\n';
    });

}
```

CP.26	Don't detach() a thread

This rule sounds strange. The C++11 standard supports detaching a thread, but we should not do it! The reason is that detaching a thread can be quite challenging. For example, have a look at this small program that has undefined behavior. Even objects with static duration can be critical.

```cpp
// threadDetach.cpp

#include <iostream>
#include <string>
#include <thread>

void func() {
    std::string s{"C++11"};
    std::thread t([&s]{ std::cout << s << '\n';});
    t.detach();
}

int main() {
    func();
}
```

The lambda takes s by reference. This is undefined behavior because the child thread t uses the variable s, which goes out of scope. Stop! This is the obvious problem, but the hidden issue that many programmers overlook is std::cout. std::cout has static duration. Static duration means the lifetime of std::cout ends with the end of the process, and we have, additionally, a race condition: Thread t may use std::cout at this time.

> **Race condition:** A race condition is a situation in which the result of an operation depends on the interleaving of certain individual operations.

Condition variables

CP.42	Don't wait without a condition

Condition variables support a quite simple concept. One thread prepares something and sends a notification to another thread that is waiting for it.

Here is the rationale for the rule: "A wait without a condition can miss a wakeup or wake up simply to find that there is no work to do." What does that mean? Condition variables are subject to two very serious issues: lost wakeups and spurious wakeups. The key concern about condition variables is that they have no memory.

Before I present you with this issue, let me first present the correct way to use condition variables.

```cpp
// conditionVariable.cpp

#include <condition_variable>
#include <iostream>
#include <mutex>
#include <thread>

std::mutex mut;
std::condition_variable condVar;

bool dataReady{false};

void waitingForWork() {
    std::cout << "Waiting " << '\n';
    std::unique_lock<std::mutex> lck(mut);
    condVar.wait(lck, []{ return dataReady; });   // (4)
    std::cout << "Running " << '\n';
}

void setDataReady() {
    {
        std::lock_guard<std::mutex> lck(mut);
        dataReady = true;
    }
    std::cout << "Data prepared" << '\n';
    condVar.notify_one();                          // (3)
}

int main() {

    std::cout << '\n';
```

```
    std::thread t1(waitingForWork);              // (1)
    std::thread t2(setDataReady);                // (2)

    t1.join();
    t2.join();

    std::cout << '\n';

}
```

How does the synchronization work? The program has two children threads: t1 and t2. They get their work package waitingForWork and setDataReady (1) and (2). setDataReady sends a notification—using the condition variable condVar—that it is done with the preparation of the work: condVar.notify_one()(3). While holding the lock, thread t1 waits for its notification: condVar.wait(lck, []{ return data-Ready; })(4). The sender and receiver need a lock. In the case of the sender, a std::lock_guard is sufficient because it calls lock and unlock only once. In the case of the receiver, a std::unique_lock is necessary because it usually frequently locks and unlocks its mutex.

Figure 10.7 shows the output of the program.

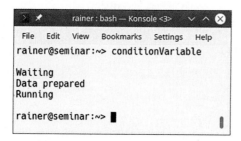

Figure 10.7 *A condition variable in action*

Maybe you are wondering, Why do we need a predicate for the wait call since you can invoke wait without a predicate? This workflow seems too complicated for such a simple synchronization of threads.

Now we are back to the missing memory of condition variables and the two phenomena called lost wakeup and spurious wakeup.

- **Lost wakeup:** The phenomenon of the lost wakeup is that the sender sends its notification before the receiver begins waiting. The consequence is that the notification is lost.

- **Spurious wakeup:** The receiver may wake up even if no notification has been sent. At least POSIX Threads and the Windows API can be victims of these phenomena.

To avoid these two issues, you have to use an additional predicate as memory or, as the rule states it, an additional condition. If you use a condition variable without a predicate, it's possible that you will get a lost wakeup and, therefore, a deadlock because the waiting thread is waiting for something that never happens.

The following program uses a condition variable without an additional predicate. Let's see what happens:

```cpp
// conditionVariableWithoutPredicate.cpp

#include <condition_variable>
#include <iostream>
#include <mutex>
#include <thread>

std::mutex mut;
std::condition_variable condVar;

void waitingForWork() {
    std::cout << "Waiting " << '\n';
    std::unique_lock<std::mutex> lck(mut);
    condVar.wait(lck);
    std::cout << "Running " << '\n';
}

void setDataReady() {
    std::cout << "Data prepared" << '\n';
    condVar.notify_one();
}

int main() {

    std::cout << '\n';

    std::thread t1(waitingForWork);
    std::thread t2(setDataReady);
```

```
    t1.join();
    t2.join();

    std::cout << '\n';

}
```

Whenever the notification thread t2 runs before the waiting thread t1, the notification is lost. The second execution shows this phenomenon that results in a deadlock. See Figure 10.8.

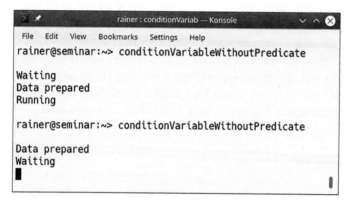

Figure 10.8 *A condition variable without a predicate*

Data sharing

The less you share data, and the more you work with local variables, the better. Sometimes, though, you have no other option but to share data. For example, the child thread wants to communicate its work to its parent thread.

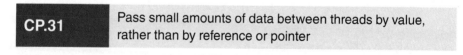

CP.31	Pass small amounts of data between threads by value, rather than by reference or pointer

Passing data to a thread by value immediately gives you two benefits:

1. There is no sharing, and therefore, no data race is possible. The requirement for a data race is a mutable, shared state.

2. You don't have to be concerned about the lifetime of the data. The data stays alive for the lifetime of the created thread.

Of course, the crucial question is, What does a small amount of data mean? The C++ Core Guidelines are not clear about this point. In the rule "F.16: For 'in' parameters, pass cheaply-copied types by value and others by reference to," the C++ Core Guidelines state that 4 * sizeof(int) is a rule of thumb for functions. This means that smaller than 4 * sizeof(int) should be passed by value, bigger than 4 * sizeof(int) by reference or pointer.

In the end, you must measure the performance of your program if necessary.

CP.32	To share ownership between unrelated `threads` use `shared_ptr`

Imagine that you have an object that you want to share between unrelated threads. Unrelated means that there is no data race on that object. The key question is, Who is the owner of the object and, therefore, responsible for releasing the memory? Now you can choose between a memory leak if you don't deallocate the memory or undefined behavior if you invoke delete more than once. Most of the time, the undefined behavior causes a run-time crash.

```cpp
// threadSharesOwnership.cpp

#include <iostream>
#include <thread>

using namespace std::literals::chrono_literals;

struct MyInt {
    int val{2017};
    ~MyInt() {                              // (4)
        std::cout << "Goodbye" << '\n';
    }
};

void showNumber(const MyInt* myInt) {
    std::cout << myInt->val << '\n';
}

void threadCreator() {
    MyInt* tmpInt= new MyInt;               // (1)

    std::thread t1(showNumber, tmpInt);     // (2)
    std::thread t2(showNumber, tmpInt);     // (3)
```

```
        t1.detach();
        t2.detach();
}

int main() {

    std::cout << '\n';

    threadCreator();
    std::this_thread::sleep_for(1s);

    std::cout << '\n';

}
```

The example is intentionally simple. I let the main thread sleep for one second to be sure that it outlived the lifetime of the children threads t1 and t2. This is, of course, not an appropriate synchronization, but it helps to make my point. The vital issue of the program is, Who is responsible for the deletion of tmpInt (1)? Thread t1 (2), thread t2 (3), or the function (main thread) itself? Because I cannot forecast how long each thread runs, I decided to go with a memory leak. Consequently, the destructor of MyInt (4) is never called (see Figure 10.9).

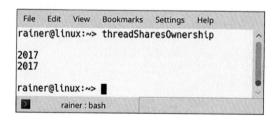

Figure 10.9 *Shared ownership using a pointer*

The lifetime issues are easy to handle if I use a std::shared_ptr.

```
// threadSharesOwnershipSharedPtr.cpp

#include <iostream>
#include <memory>
#include <thread>
```

```
using namespace std::literals::chrono_literals;

struct MyInt {
    int val{2017};
    ~MyInt() {
        std::cout << "Goodbye" << '\n';
    }
};

void showNumber(std::shared_ptr<MyInt> myInt) {
    std::cout << myInt->val << '\n';
}

void threadCreator() {
    auto sharedPtr = std::make_shared<MyInt>();    // (1)

    std::thread t1(showNumber, sharedPtr);
    std::thread t2(showNumber, sharedPtr);

    t1.detach();
    t2.detach();
}

int main() {

    std::cout << '\n';

    threadCreator();
    std::this_thread::sleep_for(1s);

    std::cout << '\n';

}
```

Two small changes to the source code are necessary. First, the pointer in (1) becomes a std::shared_ptr, and second, the function showNumber takes a smart pointer instead of a raw pointer. I assume for simplicity reasons that the threads t1 and t2 are done within a second. See Figure 10.10.

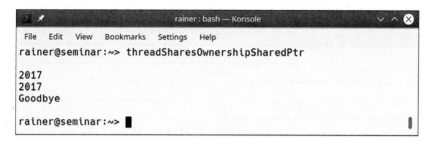

Figure 10.10 *Shared ownership using a smart pointer*

Resources

One of the main reasons for using concurrency is performance. You have to keep in mind that using threads requires resources: time and memory. The resource usage begins with creation, continues with context switching from user space, to kernel space, and ends with the destruction of a thread. Additionally, a thread has its own state that has to be allocated and maintained.

and

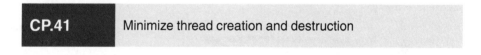

How expensive is a thread? The answer to this question is the reason for this rule. Let me first talk about the usual size of a thread and then about the costs of its creation.

Size

A `std::thread` is a thin wrapper around the native thread, and I'm, therefore, interested in the size of a Windows thread and a POSIX thread.

- **Windows systems:** The blog post "Thread Stack Size" on the Microsoft website (https://msdn.microsoft.com/en-us/library/windows/desktop/ms686774 (v=vs.85).aspx) gave me the answer: 1MB.
- **Linux systems:** The pthread_create man page (http://man7.org/linux/man-pages/man3/pthread_create.3.html) provided me with the answer: 2MB. This number applies to the i386 and x86_64 architectures. If you want to know the sizes for other architectures that support POSIX, see Table 10.1.

Table 10.1 *Typical thread size*

Architecture	Default stack size
i386	2MB
IA-64	32MB
PowerPC	4MB
S/390	2MB
Sparc-32	2MB
Sparc-64	4MB
x86_64	2MB

Creation

I didn't find numbers on how much time it takes to create a thread. To get a gut feeling, I made a simple performance test on Linux and Windows. Don't use the numbers to compare Linux and Windows. This is not the point of this experiment.

I used GCC 6.2.1 on a desktop and Microsoft Visual Studio 2017 on a laptop for my performance tests. I compiled the programs with maximum optimization on both platforms.

Here is the small test program.

```cpp
// threadCreationPerformance.cpp

#include <chrono>
#include <iostream>
#include <thread>

constexpr long long numThreads= 1'000'000;

int main() {

    auto start = std::chrono::system_clock::now();

    for (long long i = 0; i < numThreads; ++i) {     // (1)
        std::thread([]{}).detach();
    }

    std::chrono::duration<double> dur =
        std::chrono::system_clock::now() - start;

    std::cout << "time: " << dur.count()

}
```

The program creates one million threads that execute an empty lambda function (1). Figures 10.11 and 10.12 show the results for Linux and Windows.

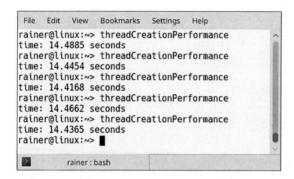

Figure 10.11 *Thread creation on Linux*

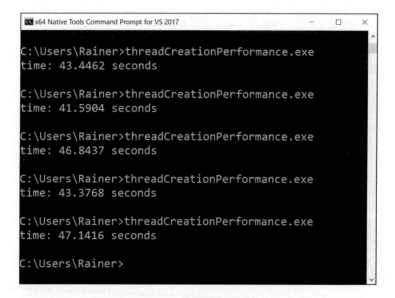

Figure 10.12 *Thread creation on Windows*

This means that the creation of a single thread took about 14.5 seconds / 1000000 = 14.5 microseconds on Linux and about 44 seconds / 1000000 = 44 microseconds on Windows.

To put it another way, in one second, you can create about 69,000 threads on Linux and 23,000 threads on Windows.

CP.43	Minimize time spent in a critical section

The less time you lock a mutex, the more time other threads can run. Let's take the example of the notification of a condition variable.

```
void setDataReady() {
    std::lock_guard<std::mutex> lck(mut);
    dataReady = true;                           // (1)
    std::cout << "Data prepared" << '\n';
    condVar.notify_one();
}
```

The mutex mut is locked at the beginning of the function and unlocked at the end of the function. This locking is not necessary. Only the expression dataReady = true (1) has to be protected.

First, std::cout is thread safe. The C++11 standard guarantees that each character is written in an atomic step and the right sequence. Second, the notification condVar.notify_one() is thread safe.

Here is the improved version of the function setDataReady:

```
void setDataReady() {
    {
        std::lock_guard<std::mutex> lck(mut);
        dataReady = true;
    }
    std::cout << "Data prepared" << '\n';
    condVar.notify_one();
}
```

Overlooked danger

CP.44	Remember to name your lock_guards and unique_locks

When you don't name the std::lock_guard or the std::unique_lock, you just create a temporary that is created and immediately destroyed. The std::lock_guard or std::unique_lock automatically locks its mutex and its constructor and unlocks it in its destructor. This pattern is called RAII.

My small example shows the conceptual behavior of a std::lock_guard. Its big brother std::unique_lock supports more operations.

```cpp
// myGuard.cpp

#include <mutex>
#include <iostream>

template <typename T>
class MyGuard {
public:
    explicit MyGuard(T& m): myMutex(m) {
        std::cout << "lock" << '\n';
        myMutex.lock();
    }
    ~MyGuard() {
        myMutex.unlock();
        std::cout << "unlock" << '\n';
    }
private:
    T& myMutex;
};

int main() {

    std::cout << '\n';

    std::mutex m;
    MyGuard<std::mutex> {m};                    // (1) oops!
    std::cout << "CRITICAL SECTION" << '\n';    // (2)

    std::cout << '\n';

}                                               // (3)
```

MyGuard calls lock and unlock in its constructor and its destructor. Because of the temporary, the call to the constructor and destructor happens in (1) and not, as usual, in line (3). As a consequence, the critical section in line (2) is executed unprotected.

This execution of the program shows that the output of the message unlock happens before the output of the message CRITICAL SECTION. See Figure 10.13.

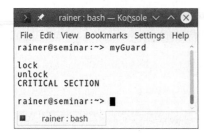

Figure 10.13 *Using a temporary lock* `std::lock_guard`

By giving the unnamed `MyGuard` `MyGuard<std::mutex>` `{m};` (1) a name `MyGuard<std::mutex>` `myGuard{m};`, the critical section becomes protected. See Figure 10.14.

Figure 10.14 *Using a named temporary* `std::lock_guard`

Parallelism

Besides the title, there is no content regarding parallelism in the C++ Core Guidelines. To fill the gap, I have provided a short introduction to the parallel STL and a rule. First of all, here is my rule.

> **Prefer the parallel algorithms of the STL to handcrafted solutions with threads.**

The idea is quite simple. The Standard Template Library has more than 100 algorithms for searching, counting, and manipulating of ranges and their elements. With C++17, 69 of them are overloaded and a few new ones are added. The overloaded and new algorithms can be invoked with a so-called execution policy. By using the execution policy, you can specify whether the algorithm should run sequential, parallel, or parallel and vectorized.

- **std::execution::seq:** runs the algorithm sequentially
- **std::execution::par:** runs the algorithm in parallel on multiple threads
- **std::execution::par_unseq:** runs the algorithm in parallel on multiple threads and allows the interleaving of individual loops

Vectorization (std::execution::par_unseq) stands for the SIMD (Single Instruction, Multiple Data) extensions of the instruction set of a modern processor. SIMD enables your processor to execute one operation in parallel on multiple data.

With the execution policy tag, you can choose which variant of an algorithm should be performed. The tag is not binding but is a strong hint to the C++ run time.

```
std::vector<int> v = {5, -3, 10, -5, -10, 22, 0};

// standard sequential sort
std::sort(v.begin(), v.end());

// sequential execution
std::sort(std::execution::seq, v.begin(), v.end());

// permitting parallel execution
std::sort(std::execution::par, v.begin(), v.end());

// permitting parallel and vectorized execution
std::sort(std::execution::par_unseq, v.begin(), v.end())
```

Sixty-nine of the algorithms of the STL support a parallel or a parallel and vectorized execution. See Table 10.2.

Table 10.2 *Algorithms of the STL for which parallel versions are available (the std namespace is omitted)*

adjacent_difference	is_heap_until	replace_copy_if
adjacent_find	is_partitioned	replace_if
all_of	is_sorted	reverse
any_of	is_sorted_until	reverse_copy
copy	lexicographical_compare	rotate
copy_if	max_element	rotate_copy

copy_n	merge	search
count	min_element	search_n
count_if	minmax_element	set_difference
equal	mismatch	set_intersection
fill	move	set_symmetric_difference
fill_n	none_of	set_union
find	nth_element	sort
find_end	partial_sort	stable_partition
find_first_of	partial_sort_copy	stable_sort
find_if	partition	swap_ranges
find_if_not	partition_copy	transform
generate	remove	uninitialized_copy
generate_n	remove_copy	uninitialized_copy_n
includes	remove_copy_if	uninitialized_fill
inner_product	remove_if	uninitialized_fill_n
inplace_merge	replace	unique
is_heap	replace_copy	unique_copy

Additionally, eight new algorithms are added with C++17.

```
std::for_each
std::for_each_n
std::exclusive_scan
std::inclusive_scan
std::transform_exclusive_scan
std::transform_inclusive_scan
std::reduce
std::transform_reduce
```

The following example shows the usage of the std::transform_exclusive_scan algorithm.

```
// transformExclusiveScan.cpp; C++17 with MSVC

#include <execution>
#include <numeric>
#include <iostream>
#include <vector>

int main() {
```

```
    std::cout << '\n';

    std::vector<int> resVec{1, 2, 3, 4, 5, 6, 7, 8, 9};
    std::vector<int> resVec1(resVec.size());
    std::transform_exclusive_scan(std::execution::par,
                                  resVec.begin(), resVec.end(),
                                  resVec1.begin(), 0,
                                  [](int fir, int sec){ return fir + sec; },
                                  [](int arg){ return arg * arg; });

    std::cout << "transform_exclusive_scan: ";
    for (auto v: resVec1) std::cout << v << " ";

    std::cout << '\n';

}
```

The std::transform_exclusive_scan algorithm is quite challenging to read. Let me try to explain it. In the first step, std::transform_exclusive_scan applies the lambda expression [](int arg){ return arg * arg; } to each element of the range resVec.begin() to resVec.end(). In the second step, the algorithm applies the binary operation [](int fir, int sec){ return fir + sec; } to the intermediate vector. This means the algorithm sums up all elements using 0 as the initial value. The result is placed in resVec1. See Figure 10.15.

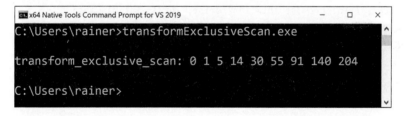

Figure 10.15 *Usage of* std::transform_exclusive_scan

Message passing

The section on message passing has two rules.

- CP.60: Use a future to return a value from a concurrent task
- CP.61: Use an async() to spawn a concurrent task

Both rules lack content. Therefore, I have to improvise.

A task is the C++-ish way to pass messages between threads. The message can be a value, an exception, or a notification. A task consists of the two components promise and future. Promise exists in three variations in C++: `std::async`, `std::packaged_task`, and `std::promise`. The promise creates the message, which the future picks up asynchronously.

I already gave a short example of `std::async` in the rule "CP.4: Think in terms of tasks, rather than threads" to send a value from the promise to the future. In this section, I use a `std::promise` as the sender.

Sending a value, or an exception

In contrast to a thread, the promise and the associated future share a secure channel. In the following example, one promise sends a value, and one promise sends an exception.

```cpp
// promiseFutureException.cpp

#include <exception>
#include <future>
#include <iostream>
#include <thread>
#include <utility>

struct Div {
  void operator()(std::promise<int> intPromise, int a, int b) const {
    try {                                                    // (4)
      if (b == 0) {
        std::string err = "Illegal division by zero: " +
                          std::to_string(a) + "/" + std::to_string(b);
        throw std::runtime_error(err);
      }
      intPromise.set_value(a / b);                           // (2)
    }
    catch ( ... ) {
      intPromise.set_exception(std::current_exception());    // (1)
    }
  }
};

void executeDivision(int nom, int denom) {
  std::promise<int> divPromise;
  std::future<int> divResult= divPromise.get_future();
```

```cpp
  Div div;
  std::thread divThread(div, std::move(divPromise), nom, denom);

  // get the result or the exception                          // (5)
  try {
    std::cout << nom << "/" << denom << " = "
  }
  catch (std::runtime_error& e){
    std::cout << e.what() << '\n';
  }

  divThread.join();
}

int main() {

  std::cout << '\n';

  executeDivision(20, 0);
  executeDivision(20, 10);

  std::cout << '\n';

}
```

If the callable used by `std::promise` throws an error, the exception is stored in the shared state. When the future `divResult` then calls `divResult.get()` (3), the exception is rethrown, and the associated future has to handle it. The `std::promise` prom set the exception via `prom.set_value(std::current_exception())` (1) and the value via `divPromise.set_value` (2) as the shared state. As the promise in (4), the future has to deal with the exception in its try-catch block (5). Dividing a number by 0 is undefined behavior. The function `executeDivision` displays the result of the calculation or the exception. See Figure 10.16.

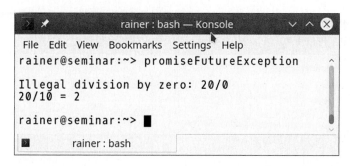

Figure 10.16 *A value and an exception as message*

Sending a notification

If you use promises and futures (in short tasks) to synchronize threads, they have a lot in common with condition variables. Most of the time, promises and futures are the safer choice than condition variables.

Before I present you with an example, Table 10.3 shows the big picture.

Table 10.3 *Condition variables versus tasks*

Criteria	Condition variables	Tasks
Multiple synchronizations	Yes	No
Critical section	Yes	No
Spurious wakeup	Yes	No
Lost wakeup	Yes	No

The advantage of a condition variable with respect to a promise and future is that you can use condition variables to synchronize threads multiple times. In contrast to that, a promise can send its notification only once. If you use a condition variable for only one synchronization, the condition variable is a lot more challenging to use correctly. A promise and future pair needs no locks and is not prone to spurious or lost wakeups, and there are no critical sections or additional conditional.

```cpp
// promiseFutureSynchronize.cpp

#include <future>
#include <iostream>
#include <utility>

void waitingForWork(std::future<void> fut) {
    std::cout << "Waiting " << '\n';
    fut.wait();                                    // (5)
    std::cout << "Running " << '\n';
}

void setDataReady(std::promise<void> prom) {
    std::cout << "Data prepared" << '\n';
    prom.set_value();                              // (6)
}

int main() {

    std::cout << '\n';
```

```
std::promise<void> sendReady;                      // (1)
auto fut = sendReady.get_future();                 // (2)

std::thread t1(waitingForWork, std::move(fut));    // (3)
std::thread t2(setDataReady, std::move(sendReady)); // (4)

t1.join();
t2.join();

std::cout << '\n';

}
```

Thanks to sendReady (1), you get a future fut (2). Both communication endpoints are moved into threads t1 (3) and t2 (4). The future waits using the call fut.wait() (5), and it gets the notification of the associated promise: prom.set_value() (6).

The structure and the output of the program match the corresponding program in the rule for condition variables: "C.42: Don't wait without a condition." See Figure 10.17.

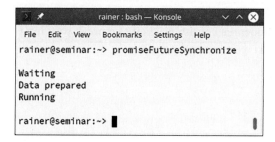

Figure 10.17 *Notifications with a task*

Lock-free programming

The rules on concurrency and parallelism target non-experts. Lock-free programming is an experts-only topic. Consequently, there are only a few short rules to lock-free programming.

CP.100	Don't use lock-free programming unless you absolutely have to

This rule is the most critical meta-rule to lock-free programming. If you don't believe me, here are a few quotes from talks given by worldwide recognized experts in this particular domain.

- **Herb Sutter:** "Lock-free programming is like playing with knives" (CppCon 2014).
- **Anthony Williams:** "Lock-free programming is about how to shoot yourself in the foot" (NDC 2016).
- **Tony Van Eerd:** "Lock-free coding is the last thing you want to do" (NDC 2016).
- **Fedor Pikus:** "Writing lock-free programs is hard. Writing correct lock-free programs is even harder" (NDC 2018).

CP.101   Distrust your hardware/compiler combination

What does "distrust your hardware/compiler combination" mean? Let me put it another way: When you break the sequential consistency, you also break your intuition with high probability. Let me start with a simple program.

```cpp
// sequentialConsistency.cpp

#include <atomic>
#include <iostream>
#include <thread>

std::atomic<int> x{0};
std::atomic<int> y{0};

void writing(){
    x.store(2000);              // (1)
    y.store(11);               // (2)
}

void reading(){
    std::cout << y.load() << " ";     // (3)
    std::cout << x.load() << '\n';    // (4)
}
```

```cpp
int main(){
    std::thread thread1(writing);
    std::thread thread2(reading);
    thread1.join();
    thread2.join();
}
```

I have a question about a short example: Which values for y and x are possible in (3) and (4)? Because y and x are atomic, no data race is possible. I further don't specify the memory ordering; therefore, sequential consistency applies. Sequential consistency means the following:

- Each thread performs its operation in the specified sequence: (1) happens before (2), and (3) happens before (4).

- There is a global order of all operations on all threads. To put it the other way around, each thread sees all operations in the same sequence.

If you combine these two properties of the sequential consistency, there is only one combination of x and y not possible: y == 11 and x == 0. Now let me break the sequential consistency and maybe your intuition.

The relaxed semantics is the weakest of all memory orderings. Relaxed semantics essentially boils down to one guarantee: Operations on atomics only guarantee atomicity.

```cpp
// relaxedSemantic.cpp

#include <atomic>
#include <iostream>
#include <thread>

std::atomic<int> x{0};
std::atomic<int> y{0};

void writing(){
    x.store(2000, std::memory_order_relaxed);
    y.store(11, std::memory_order_relaxed);
}

void reading(){
    std::cout << y.load(std::memory_order_relaxed) << " ";
    std::cout << x.load(std::memory_order_relaxed) << '\n';
}
```

```
int main(){
    std::thread thread1(writing);
    std::thread thread2(reading);
    thread1.join();
    thread2.join();
}
```

Two highly unintuitive phenomena can happen. First, `thread2` can see the operations of `thread1` in a different sequence. Second, `thread1` can reorder its instruction because it is not performed on the same atomic. What does this mean for the possible values of x and y? `y == 11` and `x == 0` is now a possible result. I want to be more specific. Which result is possible depends on your hardware. See Table 10.4.

For example, operation reordering is quite conservative on x86 or AMD64; stores can be reordered after loads, but on Alpha, IA64, or RISC (ARM) architectures, all four possible reorderings of store and load operations are allowed.

Table 10.4 *Operation reordering on various platforms*

Architecture	LoadLoad	LoadStore	StoreLoad	StoreStore
x86, AMD64			Yes	
Alpha, IA64, RISC	Yes	Yes	Yes	Yes

LoadLoad in the table means for one control flow that a load operation on an atomic is followed by a load operation on another atomic. The same argumentation applies to LoadStore, StoreLoad, and StoreStore.

CP.102   Carefully study the literature

Here are a few resources for outstanding literature. Study them first.

- **Anthony Williams:** *C++ Concurrency in Action*, 2nd ed., Manning Publications, 2019, ISBN 9781617294693 (https://www.manning.com/books/c-plus-plus-concurrency-in-action-second-edition)

- **Bartosz Milewski:** Bartosz Milewski's Programming Cafe (https://bartoszmilewski.com/)

- **Herb Sutter:** Effective Concurrency (http://www.gotw.ca/publications/)

- **Jeff Preshing:** Preshing on Programming (https://preshing.com/)

Related rules

- The two rules "CP.110: Do not write your own double-checked locking for initialization" and "CP.111: Use a conventional pattern if you really need double-checked locking" are already covered by the rule about wrong assumptions.

- The rule "CP.200: Use volatile only to talk to non-C++ memory" was already addressed in the rule "CP.8: Don't try to use `volatile` for synchronization."

Distilled

Important

- Distinguish concurrency from parallelism. Concurrency is the overlap of several tasks, but parallelism is when several tasks run at the same time.

- Avoid data races by minimizing the sharing of data, and make your shared data immutable.

- Use tools such as ThreadSanitizer or CppMem to validate your concurrent code.

- Don't lock or unlock a mutex directly. Put your mutexes into a lock such as `std::lock_guard` or `std::unique_lock`.

- Don't call unknown code while holding a lock. Try to acquire not more than one lock at any point in time.

- When you need more than one lock at a given time, acquire them atomically by using `std::lock` or `std::scoped_lock`.

- Use `std::jthread` instead of `std::thread` for automatic rejoining at destruction.

- Don't use a condition variable without an additional predicate to avoid spurious wakeup and lost wakeup.

- If you want to perform a job in parallel, prefer the parallel algorithms of the STL over handcrafted solutions with threads.

- Use tasks to pass messages or exceptions between threads. Use tasks and not condition variables to synchronize threads.

- Use lock-free programming techniques only if you have to. Study the literature carefully beforehand.

Chapter 11

Error Handling

Cippi handles errors.

First of all, according to the C++ Core Guidelines, the following actions are involved in error handling:

- Detect an error.
- Transmit information about an error to some handler code.
- Preserve the valid state of a program.
- Avoid resource leaks.

You should use exceptions for error handling. David Abrahams, one of the founders of the Boost C++ Library and former member of the ISO C++ standardization committee, formalized in the document "Exception Safety in Generic Components" what exception safety means. "Abrahams guarantees" describe a contract that is fundamental if you think about exception safety. Here are the four levels of the contract[1]:

1. **No-throw guarantee**, also known as **failure transparency**: Operations are guaranteed to succeed and satisfy all requirements, even in exceptional situations. If an exception occurs, it is handled internally and cannot be observed by clients.

2. **Strong exception safety**, also known as **commit or rollback semantics**: Operations can fail, but failed operations are guaranteed to have no side effects, so all data retain their original values.

3. **Basic exception safety**, also known as a **no-leak guarantee**: Partial execution of failed operations can cause side effects, but all invariants are preserved, and there are no resource leaks (including memory leaks). Any stored data contains valid values, even if they differ from what they were before the exception.

4. **No exception safety**: No guarantees are made.

The rules from the guidelines should help you to avoid the following kinds of errors. I added typical examples in parentheses:

- Type violations (casts)
- Resource leaks (memory leaks)
- Bounds errors (accessing a container outside the boundaries)
- Lifetime errors (accessing an object after deletion)
- Logical errors (logical expressions)
- Interface errors (passing wrong values in interfaces)

---

1. Source: Bjarne Stroustrup, *The C++ Programming Language*, Third Edition. Addison-Wesley, 1997.

There are more than 20 rules divided into three categories. The first two categories are about the design of the error-handling strategy and its concrete implementation. The third category discusses situations where you can't throw an exception.

This section on error handling has a massive overlap with the sections for functions and classes and class hierarchies. I intentionally skipped all rules that I already presented in those sections. The "Related rules" section provides you with the details on the skipped rules.

Design

Each software unit has two communication channels to its client: one for the regular case and one for the irregular case. The software units should be designed around invariants.

Communication

- E.1: Develop an error handling strategy early in a design
- E.17: Don't try to catch every exception in every function
- E.18: Minimize the use of explicit `try/catch`

First of all, what is a software unit? A software unit may be a function, an object, a subsystem, or the entire system. The software units communicate with their clients. Designing the communication should, therefore, occur early in the design of your system. At the boundary level, you have two ways to communicate: regularly and irregularly. The regular communication is the functional aspect of the interface or, to say it differently, what the software unit should do. The irregular communication stands for the nonfunctional aspects. The nonfunctional aspects specify how a system should operate. A big part of the nonfunctional aspects is error handling, or what can go wrong. Often the nonfunctional aspects are just called "quality attributes."

From the control-flow perspective, explicit `try/catch` has a lot in common with the `goto` statement. This means that if an exception is thrown, the control flow directly jumps to the exception handler, which might be in a different software unit. In the end, you may get spaghetti code, meaning code with control flow that is difficult to predict and maintain.

Now, the question is, How should you structure your exception handling? I think you should ask yourself the question, Is it possible to handle the exception locally?

If yes, do it. If not, let the exception propagate until you have sufficient context to handle it. Handling an exception can also mean catching it and then rethrowing a different exception more convenient to the client. This translation of an exception may serve the purpose that the client of the software unit has only to deal with a limited number of different exceptions.

Often boundaries are the appropriate place to handle exceptions because you want to protect the client from arbitrary exceptions. Consequently, boundaries are also the appropriate place to test regular and irregular communication.

Invariants

- E.2: Throw an exception to signal that a function can't perform its assigned task
- E.4: Design your error handling strategy around invariants
- E.5: Let a constructor establish an invariant, and throw if it cannot

According to the C++ Core Guidelines, "An invariant is a logical condition for the members of an object that a constructor must establish for the public member functions to assume. After the invariant is established (typically by a constructor) every member function can be called for the object." This definition is too narrow for me. An invariant can also be established by a function using concepts or contracts.

There are more rules about invariants and how to establish an invariant that complement the discussion at the beginning of this chapter:

- C.2: Use `class` if the class has an invariant; use `struct` if the data members can vary independently
- C.41: A constructor should create a fully initialized object
- C.45: Don't define a default constructor that only initializes data members; use member initializers instead

The Core Guidelines' definition   essentially says that you should define your error-handling strategy around invariants. If an invariant can't be established, throw an exception.

Implementation

When implementing the error handling, you have to keep a few do's and don'ts in mind.

Do's

Besides the do's referred to in the section "Related rules" at the end of this chapter, there are three additional rules.

> **E.3**   Use exceptions for error handling only

Exceptions are a kind of `goto` statement. Maybe your code guidelines forbid you to use `goto` statements. Therefore, you come up with a clever idea: Use exceptions for the control flow. In the following example, the exception is used in the success case.

```
// don't: exception not used for error handling
int getIndex(std::vector<const std::string>& vec,
             const std::string& x) {
    try {
        for (auto i = 0; i < vec.size(); ++i) {
            if (vec[i] == x) throw i;  // found x
        }
    } catch (int i) {
        return i;
    }
    return -1;   // not found
}
```

In my opinion, this is the worst misuse of exceptions. In this case, the regular control flow is not separated from the exceptional control flow. In the success case, the code uses a throw statement; in the failure case, the code uses a return statement. That is confusing, isn't it?

> **E.14**   Use purpose-designed user-defined types as exceptions (not built-in types)

You should not use built-in types or even the standard exception types. Here are two code snippets from the C++ Core Guidelines exemplifying the don'ts.

```cpp
void my_code()      // Don't
{
    // ...
    throw 7;        // 7 means "moon in the 4th quarter"
    // ...
}

void your_code()   // Don't
{
    try {
        // ...
        my_code();
        // ...
    }
    catch(int i) {  // i == 7 means "input buffer too small"
        // ...
    }
}
```

In this case, the exception is an int without any semantics. What 7 means is described in the comment, but it would be better to use a self-describing type. The comment can be wrong. To be sure, you have to consult the documentation to get an idea. You cannot attach any meaningful information to an exception of kind int. If you have a 7, I assume you use at least the numbers 1 to 6 for your exception handling, 1 probably meaning an unspecific error and so on. This strategy is way too sophisticated, error prone, and quite hard to read and to maintain.

Let's use a standard exception instead of an int.

```cpp
void my_code()   // Don't
{
    // ...
    throw std::runtime_error{"moon in the 4th quarter"};
    // ...
}

void your_code()   // Don't
{
    try {
        // ...
        my_code();
```

```
        // ...
    }
    catch(const std::runtime_error&) {   // std::runtime_error means
                                         // "input buffer too small"
        // ...
    }
}
```

Using a standard exception instead of a built-in type is better because you can attach additional information to an exception or build hierarchies of exceptions. This standard exception is better but not good. Why? The exception is too generic. It's just a std::runtime_error. Imagine that the function my_code is part of an input subsystem. If the client of the function catches the exception by std::runtime_error, it has no idea if it was a generic error such as "input buffer too small" or a subsystem-specific error such as "input device is not connected."

To overcome these issues, derive your specific exception from std::runtime_error. Here is a short example to give you the idea:

```
class InputSubsystemException: public std::runtime_error {
    const char* what() const noexcept override {
        return "Provide more details to the exception";
    }
};
```

Now the client of the input, subsystem can specifically catch the exception via catch(const InputSubsystemException& ex). Additionally, you can refine the exception hierarchy by further deriving from the class InputSubsystemException.

E.15 Catch exceptions from a hierarchy by reference

If you catch an exception from a hierarchy by value, you may become a victim of slicing.

Imagine that you derive a new exception class USBInputException from Input-SubsystemException (previous rule "E.14: Use purpose-designed user-defined types as exceptions [not built-in types]"). You then catch the exception by value of type InputSubsystemException. Now an exception of type USBInputException is thrown.

```
void subsystem() {
    // ...
```

```
        throw USBInputException();
        // ...
}

void clientCode() {
    try {
        subsystem();
    }
    catch(InputSubsystemException e) {    // slicing may happen
        // ...
    }
}
```

By catching the USBInputException by value to InputSubsystemException, slicing kicks in and e has the base type InputSubsystemException. Read the details on slicing in the guideline "C.67: A polymorphic class should suppress copying".

To say it explicitly,

1. Catch your exception by const reference and only by reference if you want to modify the exception.

2. If you rethrow an exception e in the exception handler, just use throw and not throw e. In the second case, e would be copied.

There is a straightforward cure to catch an exception by value: Apply the rule "C.121: If a base class is used as an interface, make it an abstract class." Making the InputSubsystemException an abstract base class makes it impossible to catch InputSubsystemException by value.

Don'ts

In addition to the do's, the C++ Core Guidelines have three don'ts.

| **E.13** | Never throw while being the direct owner of an object |

This is the example of direct ownership from the C++ Core Guidelines:

```
void leak(int x) {         // Bad: may leak
    auto*  p = new int{7};
    auto* pa = new int[100]
```

```
    if (x < 0) throw Get_me_out_of_here{};  // leaks *p, and *pa
    // ...
    delete p;   // we may never get here
    delete [] pa;
}
```

If the throw is fired, the memory is lost and you have a memory leak. The simple solution is to get rid of the ownership and make the C++ run time the direct owner of the object. This means you simply apply RAII: "R.1: Manage resources automatically using resource handles and RAII (Resource Acquisition Is Initialization)."

Just create a local object or at least a guard as a local object. The C++ run time takes care of local objects and, therefore, frees the memory if necessary. Here are three variations of automatic memory management:

```
void leak(int x) {     // Good: does not leak
    auto p1 = int{7};
    auto p = std::make_unique<int>(7);
    auto pa = std::vector<int>(100);
    if (x < 0) throw Get_me_out_of_here{};
    // ...
}
```

`p1` is a local, but `p` and `pa` are a kind of guard for the underlying objects. The `std::vector` uses the heap to manage its data. Additionally, with all three variations, you eliminate the delete call.

E.30   Don't use exception specifications

First, here is an example of an exception specification:

```
int use(int arg) throw(X, Y) {
    // ...
    auto x = f(arg);
    // ...
}
```

This means that the function use may throw an exception of type X or Y. If a different exception is thrown, `std::terminate` is called.

Dynamic exception specifications with argument `throw(X, Y)` and without argument `throw()` were deprecated in C++11. Dynamic exception specifications with arguments were removed with C++17; dynamic exception specifications without arguments were removed with C++20. Until C++20, throw() was equivalent to noexcept.

Read more details on noexcept in the rule "E.12: Use noexcept when exiting a function because of a throw is impossible or unacceptable."

E.31   Properly order your catch-clauses

An exception is caught according to the first match strategy. This means that the first exception handler that fits for an exception is used. This is the reason why you should structure your exception handler from specific to general. If not, your specific exception handler may never be invoked. In the following example, the DivisionByZero-Exception is derived from std::exception.

```
try{
    // throw an exception    (1)
}
catch(const DivisionByZeroException& ex) { .... } // (2)
catch(const std::exception& ex) { .... }        // (3)
catch(...) { .... }                             // (4)
```

In this case, the DivisionByZeroException (2) is used first for handling the exception thrown in (1). If the specific handler does not fit, all exceptions derived from std::exception are caught in the following line (3). The last exception handler in line (4) has an ellipsis (...) and can, therefore, catch all other exceptions.

If you can't throw

- E.25: If you can't throw exceptions, simulate RAII for resource management
- E.26: If you can't throw exceptions, consider failing fast
- E.27: If you can't throw exceptions, use error codes systematically

Let me start with the first rule: "E.25: If you can't throw exceptions, simulate RAII for resource management." The idea of RAII is simple. If you have to take care of a resource, put the resource into a class. Use the constructor of the class for the initialization and the destructor for the destruction of the resource. When you create a local instance of the class on the stack, the C++ run time automatically takes care of the resource and you are done. For more information on RAII, read the first rule for resource management: "R.1: Manage resources automatically using resource handles and RAII (Resource Acquisition Is Initialization)."

What does it mean to simulate RAII for resource management? Imagine you have a function `func` that exits with an exception if `Gadget` can't be created.

```
void func(std::string& arg) {
    Gadget g {arg};
    // ...
}
```

If you can't throw an exception, you should simulate RAII by adding a `valid` member function to `Gadget`.

```
error_indicator func(std::string& arg) {
    Gadget g {arg};
    if (!g.valid()) return gadget_construction_error;
    // ...
    return 0;   // zero indicates "good"
}
```

In this case, the caller has to test the return value of `func`.

The rule "E.26: If you can't throw exceptions, consider failing fast" is straight-forward. If there is no way to recover from an error such as memory exhaustion, fail fast. If you can't throw an exception, call `std::abort`, which causes abnormal program termination.

```
void f(int n) {
    // ...
    p = static_cast<X*>(malloc(n, X));
    if (!p) std::abort();   // abort if memory is exhausted
    // ...
}
```

`std::abort` causes an abnormal program termination if you don't install a signal handler that catches the signal SIGABRT.

When you don't install a signal handler, the function `f` behaves like the following one:

```
void f(int n) {
    // ...
    p = new X[n];     // throw if memory is exhausted
    // ...
}
```

Now, I write about the abominable keyword goto in the last rule: "E.27: If you can't throw exceptions, use error codes systematically."

In case of an error, you have a few issues to solve, according to the C++ Core Guidelines:

1. How do you transmit an error indicator out of a function?

2. How do you release all resources from a function before doing an error exit?

3. What do you use as an error indicator?

In general, your function should have two return values, the value and the error indicator. Therefore, std::pair is a good fit. Releasing the resources may easily become a maintenance nightmare, even if you encapsulate the cleanup code in a function.

```
std::pair<int, error_indicator> user() {

    Gadget g1 = make_gadget(17);
    Gadget g2 = make_gadget(17);

    if (!g1.valid()) {
        return {0, g1_error};
    }

    if (!g2.valid()) {
        cleanup(g1);
        return {0, g2_error};
    }

    // ...

    if (all_foobar(g1, g2)) {
        cleanup(g1);
        cleanup(g2);
        return {0, foobar_error};
    // ...

    cleanup(g1);
    cleanup(g2);
    return {res, 0};
}
```

Okay, seems to be correct! Or?

Do you recall what DRY stands for? Don't repeat yourself. Although the cleanup code is encapsulated into functions, the code has a smell of code repetition because the cleanup functions are invoked in various places. How can we get rid of this repetition? Just put the cleanup code at the end of the function and jump to it.

```
std::pair<int, error_indicator> user() {
    error_indicator err = 0;

    Gadget g1 = make_gadget(17);
    Gadget g2 = make_gadget(17);

    if (!g1.valid()) {
        err = g1_error;         // (1)
        goto exit;
    }

    if (!g2.valid()) {
        err = g2_error;         // (1)
        goto exit;
    }

    if (all_foobar(g1, g2)) {
        err = foobar_error;     // (1)
        goto exit;
    }
    // ...

exit:
    if (g1.valid()) cleanup(g1);
    if (g2.valid()) cleanup(g2);
    return {res, err};
}
```

Admittedly, with the help of `goto`, the overall structure of the function is quite clear. In case of an error, just the error indicator (1) is set. Exceptional circumstances require exceptional actions.

Related rules

RAII was already the topic of the first rule to resource management: "R.1: Manage resources automatically using resource handles and RAII (Resource Acquisition Is Initialization)." Consequently, I skipped the rule "E.6: Use RAII to prevent leaks."

The rules "E.7: State your preconditions" and "E.8: State your postconditions" are about contracts, which are not part of C++20. I give a concise introduction to them in Appendix C, Contracts.

The rule "E.12: Use noexcept when exiting a function because of a throw is impossible or unacceptable" is already handled in the rule on functions "F.6: If your function may not throw, declare it noexcept."

Global state is hard to manage and introduces hidden dependencies: "I.2: Avoid non-const global variables." Consequently, rule E.28 applies: "Avoid error handling based on global state (e.g. errno)."

The rule "E.16: Destructors, deallocation, and swap must never fail" is already handled in the rules about classes in the sections Failing Destructors and swap Function in Chapter 5.

Distilled

Important

- Software units communicate their results via a regular and an irregular channel to their clients. Error handling is a main part of the irregular channel and should be developed early in the design.
- Design your error handling around invariants. The job of a constructor is to establish the invariant. If the invariant cannot be established, throw an exception.
- Use user-defined types for exceptions. Catch them by reference, ordered from specific to general.
- Use exceptions only for error handling.
- Never directly own an object. Always use RAII types to manage any resources that will need freeing. RAII helps with resource management, even if you don't use exceptions.

Chapter 12

Constants and Immutability

Cippi admires her diamond.

I have a bit of an issue: On the one hand, pretty much everything in the five rules about constants and immutability has been covered in previous rules. On the other hand, writing your software using as much constant and immutable data as possible solves many challenges by design. Therefore, this section recapitulates the rules on constness and refers to previous rules when they provide additional value. In the end, const, constexpr, and immutability are such essential ideas that they should have an explicit place in this book about the C++ Core Guidelines.

Use **const**

> ### const correctness
>
> When someone speaks or writes about constness and immutability, you often hear the term const correctness. According to the C++ FAQ, "It [const correctness] means using the keyword const to prevent const objects from getting mutated."

Con.1   By default, make objects immutable

This rule is straightforward. You can make a value of a built-in data type or an instance of a user-defined data type const. The effect is the same. If you want to change it, you get a compiler error.

```
struct Immutable {
    int val{12};
};
int main() {
    const int val{12};
    val = 13;      // assignment of read-only variable 'val'

    const Immutable immu;
    immu.val = 13;
    // assignment of member 'Immutable::val'
    // in read-only object
}
```

Casting away const may cause undefined behavior if the underlying object is const: "ES.50: Don't cast away const."

Con.2   By default, make member functions const

Declaring member functions const has two obvious benefits. An immutable object can only invoke const member functions, and const member functions cannot modify the underlying object. Here is a short example that includes the error messages from GCC:

```
struct Immutable {
    int val{12};
    void canNotModify() const {
        val = 13;  // assignment of member 'Immutable::val'
                   // in read-only object
    }
    void modifyVal() {
        val = 13;
    }
};

int main() {
    const Immutable immu;
    immu.modifyVal();  // passing 'const Immutable' as 'this'
                       // argument discards qualifiers
}
```

This was not the full truth. Sometimes you have to distinguish between the logical and the physical constness of an object. Sounds strange, right?

- **Physical constness:** Your object is declared const and cannot, therefore, be changed. Its representation in memory is fixed.

- **Logical constness:** Your object is declared const but could be changed. Its logical value is fixed, but its representation in memory may change at run time.

Physical constness is quite easy to comprehend, but logical constness is more subtle. Let me modify the previous example a bit. Assume I want to change the attribute val in a const member function.

```
// mutable.cpp

#include <iostream>

struct Immutable {
    mutable int val{12};          // (1)
    void canNotModify() const {
        val = 13;
    }
};

int main() {
```

```
    std::cout << '\n';

    const Immutable immu;
    std::cout << "val: " << immu.val << '\n';
    immu.canNotModify();              // (2)
    std::cout << "val: " << immu.val << '\n';

    std::cout << '\n';

}
```

The specifier `mutable` (1) made the magic possible. The `const` object can, therefore, invoke the `const` member function (2), which modifies `val`. See Figure 12.1.

Figure 12.1 *A mutable variable*

Typically, a mutex used in a class member variable is `mutable`. Imagine your class has a read operation, which should be `const`. Because you use the data of the class concurrently, you have to protect the read member function with a mutex. So the class gets a mutex, and you lock the mutex in the read operation. Now you have an issue. Your read member function cannot be `const` because of the locking of the mutex. The solution is to declare the mutex as `mutable`.

Here is a sketch of the presented use case. Without `mutable`, this code would not work.

```
struct Immutable {
    mutable std::mutex m;
    int read() const {
        std::lock_guard<std::mutex> lck(m);
        // critical section
```

```
    . . .
  }
};
```

Con.3   By default, pass pointers and references to `const`s

If you pass pointers or references to `const` to a function, the intention of the function is obvious. The pointed to or referenced object cannot be modified. This observation matches the previous rule covered in the section Parameter Passing: In and Out in Chapter 4.

```
void getCString(const char* cStr);
void getCppString(const std::string& cppStr);
```

Are both declarations equivalent? No! In the case of the function `getCString`, the pointer could be a null pointer. This means you have to check it before its usage: `if (cStr) .... .`

But there is even more. The pointer and the pointee can be `const`.

- **`const char* cStr`:** `cStr` points to a `char` that is `const`; the pointee cannot be modified but the pointer can.

- **`char* const cStr`:** `cStr` is a `const` pointer; the pointer cannot be modified but the pointee can.

- **`const char* const cStr`:** `cStr` is a `const` pointer to a `char` that is `const`; neither the pointer nor the pointee can be modified.

Too complicated? Read the expressions from right to left or use a reference to const.

Con.4   Use `const` to define objects with values that do not change after construction

If you want to share a variable `immutable` between threads and this variable is declared as `const`, you are done. You can use `const` variables without synchronization, and you get the most performance out of your machine. The reason is quite simple. To get a data race, you need to have a mutable, shared state. I already wrote about data races in the section addressing concurrency and parallelism: "CP.2: Avoid data races."

There is an additional problem to solve when using immutable and shared data in a concurrent environment. You have to initialize the shared variable in a thread-safe way. I have at least four ideas in mind.

1. Initialize the shared variable before you start a thread.

2. Use the function `std::call_once` in combination with the flag `std::once_flag`.

3. Use a `static` variable with block scope.

4. Use a `constexpr` variable.

In the rule "CP.3: Minimize explicit sharing of writable data," I addressed these challenges.

Use **constexpr**

Con.5	Use `constexpr` for values that can be computed at compile-time

`constexpr` values give you better performance, are evaluated at compile time, and are never subject to data races. You must initialize a `constexpr` value `constexprValue` at compile time:

```
constexpr double constexprValue = constexprFunction(2);
```

A `constexpr` function `constexprFunction` can be executed at compile time. There is no state at compile time. A `constexpr` function, when executed at compile time, is pure. Pure functions have many advantages:

1. The function call can be replaced by the result.

2. The function can be performed on a different thread.

3. A function call can be reordered.

4. The function can easily be refactored or be tested in isolation.

Read more details about the benefits of `constexpr` functions in previous rules for functions:

- F.4: If a function may have to be evaluated at compile-time, declare it `constexpr`
- F.8: Prefer pure functions

Distilled

Important

- By default, make objects immutable. Immutable objects cannot be subject to data races. Ensure that these objects are initialized in a thread-safe way.

- By default, make member functions `const`. Distinguish if your object should be a physical or logical `const`.

- Don't cast away the constness from an original `const` object. This conversion is undefined behavior if you try to modify the object.

- If possible, make your functions `constexpr`. `constexpr` functions can run at compile time, are pure when they run at compile time, and provide additional optimization opportunities.

Chapter 13

Templates and Generic Programming

Should Cippi use the left or right door?

There are more than 50 rules regarding templates and generic programming that are unique for many reasons.

- Often, they have a very low-level focus. Since they address the experts, they are irrelevant for the novice or need additional information. This observation holds true, in particular, for this section, which gives additional information to get the most out of the rules of the C++ Core Guidelines.

- Often the rules lack content, or sometimes they contradict each other. For example, the rule "T.5: Combine generic and OO techniques to amplify their strengths, not their costs" presents type erasure (read more at https://www.modernescpp.com/index.php/c-core-guidelines-type-erasure) as a solution, but the rule "T.49: Where possible, avoid type-erasure" states the contrary.

- More than ten rules are about concepts in C++20. I provide a short introduction to concepts in Appendix B. In the examples in the C++ Core Guidelines, concepts are often commented out. I follow this convention. If you want to try them out, comment them in. cppreference.com provides details to the current compiler support of concepts.

First of all, I use the terms "templates" and "generic programming," although templates are just one way to write generic code. I assume you know what templates in C++ are, but do you know what generic programming means? Here is my favorite definition from Wikipedia (https://en.wikipedia.org/wiki/Generic_programming).

> **Generic programming** is a style of computer programming in which algorithms are written in terms of types to-be-specified-later that are then instantiated when needed for specific types provided as parameters.

The rules about templates focus on their use, their interfaces, and their definition. Additional rules address hierarchies with templates, variadic templates, metaprogramming, and more.

Use

Concepts are predicates on templates that are evaluated at compile time. They should model semantic categories such as `Arithmetic`, `Callable`, `Iterator`, or `Range` but not syntactic restrictions such as `HasPlus` or `IsInvocable`. Maybe you are puzzled by the difference between semantic categories and syntactic restrictions. The first rule helps to distinguish those terms.

T.1   Use templates to raise the level of abstraction of code

Here is the example from the guidelines, but I renamed the second concept `Addable`.

```
template<typename T>
    // requires Addable<T>
T sum1(const std::vector<T>& v, T s) {
    for (auto x : v) s += x;
    return s;
}


template<typename T>
    // requires Addable<T>
T sum2(const std::vector<T>& v, T s) {
    for (auto x : v) s = s + x;
    return s;
}
```

What is wrong with those concepts? Both concepts are too specific. Both concepts are based on specific operations such as the increment and the + operation. Let's go one step further from the syntactic constraints to the semantic category `Arithmetic`.

```
template<typename T>
    // requires Arithmetic<T>
T sum(const std::vector<T>& v, T s) {
    for (auto x : v) s += x;
    return s;
}
```

Now the algorithm has the adequate requirements. The algorithm is better but not good. It works only on a `std::vector`. It's generic on the element type of the container but not on the container. Let me generalize the sum algorithm further.

```
template<typename Cont, typename T>
    // requires Container<Cont>
    // && Arithmetic<T>
T sum(const Cont& v, T s) {
    for (auto x : v) s += x;
    return s;
}
```

Now, that's better. Maybe you prefer a more concise definition of sum. Instead of the keyword typename, I use the concepts directly.

```
template<Container Cont, Arithmetic T>
T sum(const Cont& cont, T s) {
    for (auto x : cont) s += x;
    return s;
}
```

T.2   **Use templates to express algorithms that apply to many argument types**

When you study the first overload of std::find at cppreference.com, it looks like this:

```
template< class InputIt, class T >
InputIt find( InputIt first, InputIt last, const T& value );
```

The types of the iterators are encoded in their names: InputIt stands for input iterator and essentially means that it is an iterator that can read from the pointed-to element at least once and allows iteration in one direction. An input iterator It supports the following operations:

```
++It, It++
*It
It == It2, It != It2
```

There are two issues with this declaration:

1. The requirements for the iterators are encoded in the name. This encoding reminds me of the infamous Hungarian notation.

2. There is no requirement specifying that the pointed-to element can be compared with the value.

Let me use the iterator concept directly:

```
template<Input_iterator Iter, typename Val>
    // Equality_comparable<Value_type<Iter>, Val>
Iter find(Iter b, Iter e, const Val& v) {
    // ...
}
```

T.3   Use templates to express containers and ranges

Containers need to be generic. Thanks to templates, you can rely on the static type system (Per.10). For example, here is a `Vector`.

```
template<typename T>
    // requires Regular<T>
class Vector {
    // ...
    T* elem;   // points to sz Ts
    int sz;
};


Vector<double> v(10);
v[7] = 9.9;
```

One question remains. When is a type `T` regular? I answer this question later in this chapter in the section "T.46: Require template arguments to be at least Regular or SemiRegular."

Interfaces

An interface is a contract between a user and an implementer. It should, therefore, be written with great care.

T.40   Use function objects to pass operations to algorithms

Often, you can adapt the behavior of the around one hundred algorithms of the Standard Template Library (STL) by providing a callable. Callables are typically functions, function objects, or lambdas.

There are various ways to sort a vector of strings.

```
// functionObjects.cpp

#include <algorithm>
#include <functional>
#include <iostream>
#include <iterator>
```

```cpp
#include <string>
#include <vector>

  bool byLessLength(const std::string& f,
                    const std::string& s) {                    // (4)
    return f.size() < s.size();
}


class ByGreaterLength {
 public:
  bool operator()(const std::string& f, const std::string& s)
                                         const {               // (5)
      return f.size() > s.size();
   }
};


int main() {

    std::vector<std::string> myStrVec = {"523345", "4336893456", "7234",
                                         "564", "199", "433", "2435345"};

    std::cout << '\n';

    std::cout << "Ascending by length with a function \n";
    std::sort(myStrVec.begin(), myStrVec.end(), byLessLength);    // (1)
    for (const auto& str: myStrVec) std::cout << str << " ";
    std::cout << "\n\n";

    std::cout << "Descending by length with a function object \n";
    std::sort(myStrVec.begin(), myStrVec.end(), ByGreaterLength());   // (2)
    for (const auto& str: myStrVec) std::cout << str << " ";
    std::cout << "\n\n";

    std::cout << "Ascending by length with a lambda \n";
    std::sort(myStrVec.begin(), myStrVec.end(),
            [](const std::string& f, const std::string& s){       // (3)
                return f.size() < s.size();
            });
    for (const auto& str: myStrVec) std::cout << str << " ";

    std::cout << "\n\n";


}
```

The program sorts a vector of strings based on the length of the strings. The markers (1), (2), and (3) use a function (4), a function object (5), and a lambda expression (3). A function object is a class (5), for which the call operator (operator()) is overloaded.

For completeness, Figure 13.1 shows the output of the program.

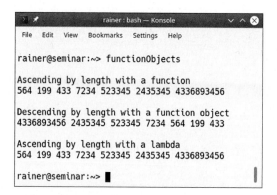

Figure 13.1 *A function, a function object, and a lambda as sorting criteria*

The rule states you should use function objects to pass operations to algorithms.

Advantages of function objects

My argumentation for function objects boils down to three points: performance, expressiveness, and state. It makes my argumentation easier if we consider that lambda functions are function objects under the hood.

Performance

The more the optimizer can reason locally, the better the code becomes. A lambda (3) is compiler generated just in place. Compare this to a function that is defined in a different translation unit. In this case, the optimizer cannot perform all optimization steps.

Expressiveness

Your code should be so expressive that it needs no documentation, and lambdas give you this expressiveness. I can make my argumentation short because I already wrote about the expressiveness of lambdas in the chapter on functions.

State

In contrast to a function, a function object can have state. The code example makes my point.

```cpp
// sumUpFunctionObject.cpp

#include <algorithm>
#include <iostream>
#include <vector>

class SumMe {
  int sum{0};
 public:
  SumMe() = default;

  void operator()(int x) {
    sum += x;
  }

  int getSum() const {
    return sum;
  }
};

int main() {

  std::vector<int> intVec{1, 2, 3, 4, 5, 6, 7, 8, 9, 10};

                                                                    // (1)
  SumMe sumMe = std::for_each(intVec.begin(), intVec.end(), SumMe());

  std::cout << '\n';                                                // (2)
  std::cout << "Sum of intVec= " << sumMe.getSum() << '\n';
  std::cout << '\n';

}
```

The `std::for_each` call in (1) is crucial. `std::for_each` is a unique algorithm of the Standard Template Library because it can return its callable. I invoke `std::for_each` with the function object `SumMe` and can, therefore, store the result of the function call directly in the function object. I ask in (2) for the sum of all calls. See Figure 13.2.

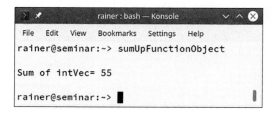

Figure 13.2 *A function object with state*

Just to be complete, lambdas can also have state. You can use a lambda to accumulate values.

```
// sumUpLambda.cpp

#include <algorithm>
#include <iostream>
#include <vector>

int main(){

    std::cout << '\n';

    std::vector<int> intVec{1, 2, 3, 4, 5, 6, 7, 8, 9, 10};

    std::for_each(
        intVec.begin(), intVec.end(),
        [sum = 0](int i) mutable {
            sum += i;
            std::cout << sum << " ";
        }
    );

    std::cout << "\n\n";

}
```

This lambda looks scary. First of all, the variable sum represents the state of the lambda. With C++14, the so-called initialization capture of lambdas is supported. sum = 0 declares and initializes a variable of type int, which is valid only in the scope of the lambda. Lambdas are per default const. By declaring it as mutable, I can add the numbers to sum. See Figure 13.3.

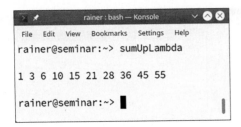

Figure 13.3 *A lambda with state*

A lambda expression is syntactic sugar for a function object that is instantiated in place. Thanks to C++ Insights, you can observe the transformation performed by the compiler (https://cppinsights.io/s/0a702053).

T.42	Use template aliases to simplify notation and hide implementation details

Since C++11, we have had template aliases. A template alias is a name that refers to a family of types. Using them makes your code more readable and helps you to get rid of type traits. The section Metaprogramming later in this chapter provides more information on type traits.

Let's see what the C++ Core Guidelines mean by readability. The first example uses type traits:

```
template<typename T>
void user(T& c) {
    // ...
    typename container_traits<T>::value_type x; // bad, verbose
    // ...
}
```

Here is the equivalent case with template aliases:

```
template<typename T>
using value_type = typename container_traits<T>::value_type;

void user2(T& c) {
    // ...
    value_type<T> x;
    // ...
}
```

Readability is also the reason for the next rule.

T.43	Prefer `using` over `typedef` for defining aliases

There are two arguments from the readability perspective for preferring `using` over `typedef`. First, `using` comes first when used. Second, `using` feels quite similar to `auto`. Additionally, `using` can easily be used for template aliases.

```
typedef int (*PFI)(int);      // OK, but convoluted

using PFI2 = int (*)(int);    // OK, preferred

template<typename T>
typedef int (*PFT)(T);        // error (1)

template<typename T>
using PFT2 = int (*)(T);      // OK
```

The first two lines define a pointer to a function (`PFI` and `PFI2`), which takes an `int` and returns an `int`. In the first case, `typedef` is used and, in the second case, `using`. The last two lines define a function template (`PFT2`), which takes a type parameter `T` and returns an `int`. Line (1) is not valid.

T.44	Use function templates to deduce class template argument types (where feasible)

The primary reason that we have factory functions such as `std::make_tuple` or `std::make_unique` is that a function template can deduce its template arguments from its function arguments. During this process, the compiler applies a few simple conversions such as removing the outermost `const`/`volatile` qualifier and decaying C-arrays and functions to a pointer to the first element of the C-array or a pointer to the function.

This automatic template argument deduction makes our lives as programmers much more comfortable.

Instead of typing

```
std::tuple<int, double, std::string> myTuple = {2011, 20.11, "C++11"};
```

you can use the factory function std::make_tuple.

```
auto myTuple = std::make_tuple(2011, 20.11, "C++11");
```

Since C++17, the compiler can in many situations deduce its template arguments not only from the function arguments but also from the constructor arguments. Here is the way to define myTuple in C++17:

```
std::tuple myTuple = {2017, 20.17, "C++17"};
```

An obvious effect of this C++17 feature is that most of the factory functions such as std::make_tuple become obsolete.

The following program templateArgumentDeduction.cpp, shows class and function argument deduction in action.

```
// templateArgumentDeduction.cpp; C++17

#include <iostream>

template <typename T>
void showMe(const T& t) {
    std::cout << t << '\n';
}

template <typename T>
struct ShowMe{
    ShowMe(const T& t) {
        std::cout << t << '\n';
    }
};

int main() {

    std::cout << '\n';

    showMe(5.5);         // not showMe<double>(5.5);
    showMe(5);           // not showMe<int>(5);

    ShowMe a(5.5);       // not ShowMe<double>(5.5);
    ShowMe b(5);         // not ShowMe<int>(5);

    std::cout << '\n';

}
```

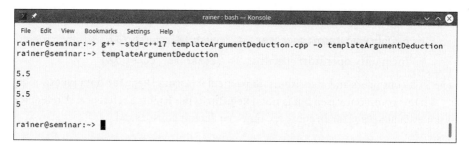

Figure 13.4 *Template argument deduction*

The comments display the explicit specification of the template arguments. With template argument deduction, the user invokes a function or a class. The fact that the function is a function template or that the class is a class template is an implementation detail. See Figure 13.4.

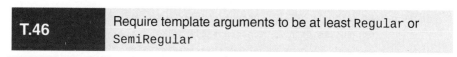

The concepts `Regular` and `SemiRegular` are quite important in C++. `Regular` types work well in the C++ ecosystem. A `Regular` type "behaves like an int." It can be copied, and the result of the copy operation is independent of the original one and has the same value.

Let's be more formal. All `Regular` types are also `SemiRegular`. Consequently, I start with defining a `SemiRegular` type.

- **SemiRegular:** A `SemiRegular` type has to support the rule of six and has to be swappable.

  - **Default constructor:** `X()`

  - **Copy constructor:** `X(const X&)`

  - **Copy assignment:** `X& operator = (const X&)`

  - **Move constructor:** `X(X&&)`

  - **Move assignment:** `X& operator = (X&&)`

  - **Destructor:** `~X()`

  - **Swappable:** `swap(X&, X&)`

- **Regular:** A SemiRegular type that supports equality comparable is Regular.
  - **Equality operator:** operator == (const X&, const X&)
  - **Inequality operator:** operator != (const X&, const X&)

The STL containers and algorithms, in particular, assume Regular data types.

What is commonly used but is not a Regular type? Right: a reference. A reference is not even SemiRegular because it cannot be default constructed.

```cpp
// semiRegular.cpp; C++17

#include <iostream>
#include <type_traits>

int main() {

    std::cout << std::boolalpha << '\n';

    std::cout << "std::is_default_constructible<int&>::value: "
              << std::is_default_constructible<int&>::value << '\n';
    std::cout << "std::is_copy_constructible<int&>::value: "
              << std::is_copy_constructible<int&>::value << '\n';
    std::cout << "std::is_copy_assignable<int&>::value: "
              << std::is_copy_assignable<int&>::value << '\n';
    std::cout << "std::is_move_constructible<int&>::value: "
              << std::is_move_constructible<int&>::value << '\n';
    std::cout << "std::is_move_assignable<int&>::value: "
              << std::is_move_assignable<int&>::value << '\n';
    std::cout << "std::is_destructible<int&>::value: "
              << std::is_destructible<int&>::value << '\n';
    std::cout << '\n';
    std::cout << "std::is_swappable<int&>::value: "
              << std::is_swappable<int&>::value << '\n';

    std::cout << '\n';

}
```

The type-traits library gives the authoritative answer. See Figure 13.5.

T.47	Avoid highly visible unconstrained templates with common names

To get the point of this rule, I have to make a short detour. This detour is about argument-dependent lookup (ADL), also known as Koenig lookup, after Andrew Koenig. First of all, what is argument-dependent lookup?

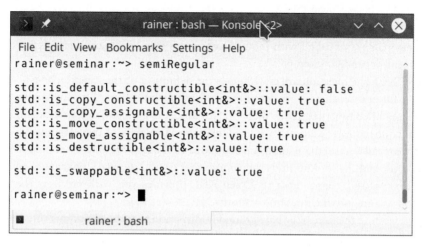

Figure 13.5 *A reference is not* SemiRegular

Argument-dependent lookup

- **Argument-dependent lookup (ADL)** is a set of rules for the lookup of unqualified function names. Unqualified function names are additionally looked up in the namespace of their arguments.

Unqualified function names means functions without the scope operator (::). Is argument-dependent lookup bad? Of course not—ADL makes our lives as programmers easier. Here is an example.

```
#include <iostream>

int main() {
    std::cout << "Argument-dependent lookup";
}
```

Fine. Let me remove the syntactic sugar of operator overloading and use the function call directly.

```
#include <iostream>

int main() {
    operator << (std::cout, "Argument-dependent lookup");
}
```

> This equivalent program shows what is happening under the hood. The function operator << is called with the two arguments std::cout and the C-string "Argument-dependent lookup."
>
> Fine? No? The question arises: Where is the definition of the function operator <<? Of course, there is no definition in the global namespace. operator << is an unqualified function name; therefore, argument-dependent lookup kicks in. The function name is additionally looked up in the namespace of their arguments. In this particular case, the namespace std is due to the first argument std::cout considered, and the lookup finds the appropriate candidate: std::operator << (std::ostream&, const char*). Often ADL provides you with precisely the function you are looking for, but sometimes . . .
>
> Now we have the necessary background information to write about this rule.

In the expression std::cout << "Argument-dependent lookup", the overloaded output operator << is the highly visible common name because it is defined in the namespace std. The following program, based on the program of the C++ Core Guidelines, shows the crucial point of this rule.

```cpp
// argumentDependentLookup.cpp

#include <iostream>
#include <vector>

namespace Bad {

    struct Number {
        int m;
    };

    template<typename T1, typename T2>      // generic equality  (5)
    bool operator == (T1, T2) {
        return false;
    }

}

namespace Util {

    bool operator == (int, Bad::Number) {       // equality to int (4)
        return true;
    }
```

```
void compareSize() {
    Bad::Number badNumber{5};                          // (1)
    std::vector<int> vec{1, 2, 3, 4, 5};

    std::cout << std::boolalpha << '\n';

    std::cout << "5 == badNumber: " <<
                 (5 == badNumber) << '\n';              // (2)
    std::cout << "vec.size() == badNumber: " <<
                 (vec.size() == badNumber) << '\n';     // (3)

    std::cout << '\n';
  }
}

int main() {

  Util::compareSize();

}
```

I expect that in both cases (2) and (3), the overloaded `Util::operator ==` (4) is called because it takes an argument of type `Bad::Number` (1); therefore, I should get true twice. See Figure 13.6.

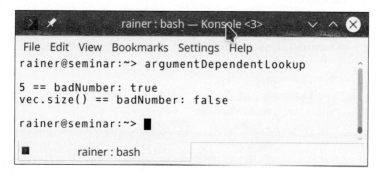

Figure 13.6 *Surprise with argument-dependent lookup*

What happened here? The call in (3) is resolved by the generic equality operator in (5)? The reason for the surprise is that `vec.size()` returns a value of type `std::size_type`, which is an unsigned integer type. This means that the equality operator requires in (4) a conversion to `int`. This conversion is not necessary for the generic equality (5) because this is an ideal fit. Thanks to argument-dependent lookup, the generic equality operator belongs to the set of possible overloads.

The rule states "Avoid highly visible unconstrained templates with common names." Let me see what would happen if I followed the rule and removed the generic equality operator. Here is the fixed code.

```cpp
// argumentDependentLookupResolved.cpp

#include <iostream>
#include <vector>

namespace Bad {

    struct Number {
        int m;
    };

}

namespace Util {

    bool operator == (int, Bad::Number) {      // compare to int (4)
        return true;
    }

    void compareSize() {
        Bad::Number badNumber{5};                          // (1)
        std::vector<int> vec{1, 2, 3, 4, 5};

        std::cout << std::boolalpha << '\n';

        std::cout << "5 == badNumber: " <<
                     (5 == badNumber) << '\n';             // (2)
        std::cout << "vec.size() == badNumber: " <<
                     (vec.size() == badNumber) << '\n';    // (3)

        std::cout << '\n';
    }
}

int main() {

    Util::compareSize();

}
```

Now, the result matches my expectations. See Figure 13.7.

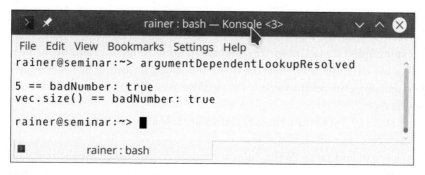

Figure 13.7 *Surprises with argument-dependent lookup solved*

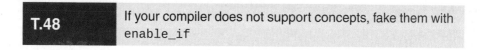

T.48   If your compiler does not support concepts, fake them with `enable_if`

When I present `std::enable_if` in my seminars, a few participants are scared. Here is the simplified version of a generic greatest-common-divisor algorithm.

```cpp
// enable_if.cpp

#include <iostream>
#include <type_traits>

template<typename T,                                      // (1)
    typename std::enable_if<std::is_integral<T>::value, T>::type = 0>
T gcd(T a, T b) {
    if( b == 0 ){ return a; }
    else{
        return gcd(b, a % b);                             // (2)
    }
}

int main() {

    std::cout << '\n';

    std::cout << "gcd(100, 10)= " <<  gcd(100, 10)  << '\n';
    std::cout << "gcd(3.5, 4)= " << gcd(3.5, 4.0) << '\n';

    std::cout << '\n';

}
```

The algorithm is too generic. It should only work for integral types. Now std::enable_if from the type-traits library (1) comes to my rescue. See Figure 13.8.

The expression std::is_integral (1) is critical for the understanding of the program. This line determines whether the type parameter T is integral. If T is not integral, and therefore the return value is false, there is no template instantiation for this specific type.

Only if std::is_integral returns true does std::enable_if have a public member typedef type. But this is not an error.

The C++ standard says, "When substituting the deduced type for the template parameter fails, the specialization is discarded from the overload set instead of causing a compile error." There is an acronym for this rule: SFINAE (Substitution Failure Is Not An Error).

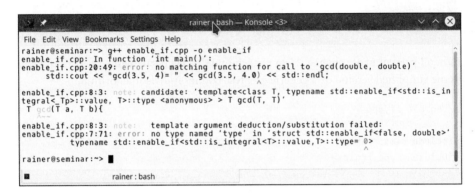

Figure 13.8 std::enable_if

The output of the compilation (enable_if.cpp: 20:49) shows it. There is no template specialization for the type double available.

Definition

When defining templates, you should minimize dependencies, avoid overparameterizing, and factor out code from the template that does not depend on its type parameters.

T.60	Minimize a template's context dependencies

To be honest, it took me a moment to get this rule. Let's look at the function templates sort and algo. Here is a simplified example from the C++ Core Guidelines.

```
template<typename C>
void sort(C& c) {
    std::sort(begin(c), end(c)); // necessary and useful dependency
}


template<typename Iter>
Iter algo(Iter first, Iter last) {
    for (; first != last; ++first) {
        auto x = sqrt(*first);    // potentially surprising dependency:
                                  // which sqrt()?

        helper(first, x);         // potentially surprising dependency:
                                  // helper is chosen based on first
                                  // and x
    }
}
```

It would be optimal but not always manageable if a template operated only on its arguments. This argument holds for the function template sort but not for algo. The function template algo has dependencies on sqrt and the function helper. Moreover, the implementation of algo introduces more dependencies than the interface shows. For example, the calls sqrt and helper are not qualified, and therefore, argument-dependent lookup kicks in. Using std::sqrt instead of sqrt reduces the dependencies.

T.61   Do not over-parameterize members

If a member of a template does not depend on a template parameter, remove it from the template. A member may be a type or a member function. By following this rule, you may decrease the code size because the nongeneric code is factored out.

The example from the guidelines is straightforward.

```
template<typename T, typename A = std::allocator{}>
    // requires Regular<T> && Allocator<A>
class List {
public:
    struct Link {   // does not depend on A
        T elem;
```

```
        T* pre;
        T* suc;
    };

    using iterator = Link*;

    iterator first() const { return head; }

    // ...
private:
    Link* head;
};


List<int> lst1;
List<int, My_allocator> lst2;
```

The type Link does not depend on the template parameter A. Consequently, you can extract it and use it in List2.

```
template<typename T>
struct Link {
    T elem;
    T* pre;
    T* suc;
};


template<typename T, typename A = std::allocator{}>
    // requires Regular<T> && Allocator<A>
class List2 {
public:
    using iterator = Link<T>*;

    iterator first() const { return head; }

    // ...
private:
    Link* head;
};


List2<int> lst1;
List2<int, My_allocator> lst2;
```

The next rule also helps to fight code bloat.

T.62	Place non-dependent class template members in a non-templated base class

Let's reformulate it more informally: Put the functionality of the template that does not depend on the template parameters in a nontemplated base class.

The C++ Core Guidelines present a quite obvious example.

```cpp
template<typename T>
class Foo {
public:
    enum { v1, v2 };
    // ...
};
```

The enumeration is independent of the type parameter T and should, therefore, be placed in a nontemplated base class.

```cpp
struct Foo_base {
    enum { v1, v2 };
    // ...
};


template<typename T>
class Foo : public Foo_base {
public:
    // ...
};
```

Now Foo_base can be used without template arguments and template instantiation.

This technique is quite interesting if you want to reduce your code size. Here is a simple class template Array.

```cpp
// genericArray.cpp

#include <cstddef>
#include <iostream>

template <typename T, std::size_t N>
class Array {
public:
    Array()= default;
    std::size_t getSize() const{
```

```
        return N;
    }
private:
  T elem[N];
};


int main(){

    Array<int, 100> arr1;
    std::cout << "arr1.getSize(): " << arr1.getSize() << '\n';

    Array<int, 200> arr2;
    std::cout << "arr2.getSize(): " << arr2.getSize() << '\n';


}
```

If you study the class template Array, you notice that the member function getSize is the same except for type parameter N. Let me refactor the code and declare a class template Array that depends on the type parameter T and the size n.

```
// genericArrayInheritance.cpp

#include <cstddef>
#include <iostream>

class ArrayBase {
protected:
    ArrayBase(std::size_t n): size(n) {}
    std::size_t getSize() const {
        return size;
    };
private:
    std::size_t size;
};

template<typename T, std::size_t N>
class Array: private ArrayBase {
public:
    Array(): ArrayBase(N){}
    std::size_t getSize() const {
        return  ArrayBase::getSize();
    }
```

```
private:
    T data[N];
};


int main() {

    Array<int, 100> arr1;
    std::cout << "arr1.getSize(): " << arr1.getSize() << '\n';

    Array<double, 200> arr2;
    std::cout << "arr2.getSize(): " << arr2.getSize() << '\n';

}
```

Array has two template parameters for the type T and the size N, but ArrayBase is no template. Array derives from ArrayBase. This means ArrayBase is shared between all instantiations of Array. In the concrete case, the getSize member function of Array uses the getSize method of ArrayBase. ArrayBase is shared between the instantiations Array<int, 100> and Array<double, 200>.

Alternative implementations with specializations

- T.64: Use specialization to provide alternative implementations of class templates
- T.67: Use specialization to provide alternative implementations for irregular types

The rules in this section address mainly one concern: using template specialization to provide alternative implementations.

Let's start simple. I have a class Account, and I want to know which account is smaller. Smaller means in this case that the balance is lower.

```
// isSmaller.cpp

#include <iostream>

class Account {
 public:
    Account() = default;
```

```
    Account(double b): balance(b) {}
 private:
    double balance{0.0};
};


template<typename T>                    // (1)
bool isSmaller(T fir, T sec) {
    return fir < sec;
}


int main() {

    std::cout << std::boolalpha << '\n';

    double firDoub{};
    double secDoub{2014.0};

    std::cout << "isSmaller(firDoub, secDoub): "
              << isSmaller(firDoub, secDoub) << '\n';

    Account firAcc{};
    Account secAcc{2014.0};

    std::cout << "isSmaller(firAcc, secAcc): "
              << isSmaller(firAcc, secAcc) << '\n';

    std::cout << '\n';

}
```

To make my job easier, I wrote a generic `isSmaller` function (1) for comparing two accounts. As you presumably expected, I cannot compare accounts because its oper-ator < is not overloaded. See Figure 13.9.

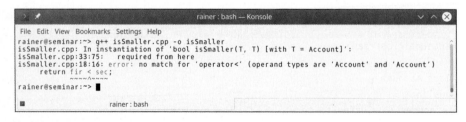

Figure 13.9 *Comparing two accounts*

Now to the interesting question. Which techniques are available to compare two accounts? For the sake of simplicity, I show only the essential part of the next programs. The complete programs are part of the source code to this book.

Overloading *operator < for the class*

Overloading operator < is probably the most obvious way. Even the error message of the program isSmaller.cpp showed it.

```
// accountIsSmaller1.cpp

class Account {
 public:
    Account() = default;
    Account(double b): balance(b) {}
    friend bool operator < (Account const& fir, Account const& sec) {
        return fir.getBalance() < sec.getBalance();
    }
    double getBalance() const {
        return balance;
    }
 private:
    double balance{0.0};
};

template<typename T>
bool isSmaller(T fir, T sec) {
    return fir < sec;
}
```

Full specialization of the comparison function

If you cannot change Account, you can at least fully specialize isSmaller for Account.

```
// accountIsSmaller2.cpp

class Account {
 public:
    Account() = default;
    Account(double b): balance(b) {}
    double getBalance() const {
        return balance;
    }
```

```
private:
    double balance{0.0};
};


template<typename T>
bool isSmaller(T fir, T sec){
    return fir < sec;
}


template<>
bool isSmaller<Account>(Account fir, Account sec){
    return fir.getBalance() < sec.getBalance();
}
```

By the way, a nongeneric function bool isSmaller(Account fir, Account sec) would also do the job.

Extending the comparison function

There is another way: Extend isSmaller. I extend the generic function with an additional type parameter Pred that can hold a binary predicate. This pattern is heavily used in the Standard Template Library.

```
// accountIsSmaller3.cpp

#include <functional>
#include <iostream>
#include <string>

class Account {
 public:
    Account() = default;
    Account(double b): balance(b){}
    double getBalance() const {
        return balance;
    }
 private:
    double balance{0.0};
};

template <typename T, typename Pred = std::less<T> >    // (1)
bool isSmaller(T fir, T sec, Pred pred = Pred() ) {     // (2)
    return pred(fir, sec);                             // (3)
}
```

```cpp
int main() {

    std::cout << std::boolalpha << '\n';

    double firDou{};
    double secDou{2014.0};

    std::cout << "isSmaller(firDou, secDou): "
              << isSmaller(firDou, secDou) << '\n';

    Account firAcc{};
    Account secAcc{2014.0};

    auto res = isSmaller(firAcc, secAcc,                      // (4)
                [](const Account& fir, const Account& sec){
                    return fir.getBalance() < sec.getBalance();
                }
    );

    std::cout << "isSmaller(firAcc, secAcc): " <<  res << '\n';

    std::cout << '\n';

    std::string firStr = "AAA";
    std::string secStr = "BB";

    std::cout << "isSmaller(firStr, secStr): "
              << isSmaller(firStr, secStr) << '\n';

     auto res2 = isSmaller(firStr, secStr,                    // (5)
                 [](const std::string& fir, const std::string& sec){
                     return fir.size() < sec.length();
                 }
    );

    std::cout << "isSmaller(firStr, secStr): " <<  res2 << '\n';

    std::cout << '\n';

}
```

The generic function uses the predefined function object `std::less<T>` as the default ordering (1). The binary predicate `Pred` is instantiated in (2) and used in (3). Additionally, you can provide your binary predicate such as in (4) or (5). A lambda expression is an ideal fit for this job.

Finally, Figure 13.10 shows the output of the program.

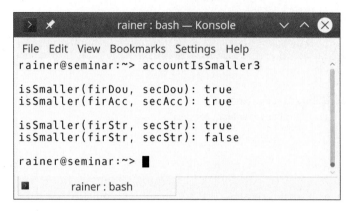

Figure 13.10 *Comparing two accounts with a binary predicate*

Comparing the three techniques

What are the differences between these three techniques (see Table 13.1)?

Table 13.1 *Comparing two accounts*

	General solution	Configuration time	Extension	Variability
`operator <`	Yes	Compile time	Type	No
Full specialization	No	Compile time	Function	No
Extension with predicate	Yes	Run time	Function	Yes

The full specialization is not a general solution. It works only for the function `isSmaller`. In contrast, the `operator <` is quite often applicable, and any type can use the extension with predicate. The `operator <` and the full specialization are static. This means the ordering is defined at compile time and is encoded in the type or the generic function. In contrast, the extension with the predicate can be invoked with different predicates. The decision happens at run time. The `operator <` extends the type, both of the other variants the function. The extension with predicate allows it to order your type in various ways. For example, you can compare strings lexicographically or by their length.

Based on this comparison, a good rule of thumb is to implement an `operator <` for your types and add an extension to your generic functions if necessary.

Hierarchies

Virtual functions used in templates are special. Here is why.

T.80   Do not naively templatize a class hierarchy

Here is the example of a naively templatized class hierarchy from the C++ Core Guidelines:

```
template<typename T>
struct Container {        // an interface
    virtual T* get(int i);
    virtual T* first();
    virtual T* next();
    virtual void sort();
};


template<typename T>
class Vector : public Container<T> {
public:
    // ...
};


Vector<int> vi;
Vector<std::string> vs;
```

This is naive because the base class `Container` has many virtual functions. The presented design introduces unnecessary code bloat. Virtual member functions must be instantiated for each type used in a class template. This observation applies to the `Container` and the `Vector<int>` and `Vector<std::string>`. In contrast, nonvirtual functions are instantiated only if they are used.

T.83   Do not declare a member function template virtual

Let me try to use a virtual member function template.

```
// virtualMemberFunction.cpp

class Shape {
    template<class T>
    virtual void intersect(T* p) {}
};
```

```
int main(){

    Shape shape;

}
```

The error message for the GCC is crystal clear: Templates may not be virtual. See Figure 13.11.

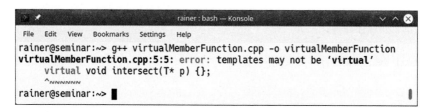

Figure 13.11 *Compiler error with a virtual member function*

Variadic templates

- T.100: Use variadic templates when you need a function that takes a variable number of arguments of a variety of types
- T.101: How to pass arguments to a variadic template
- T.102: How to process arguments to a variadic template

These three rules about variadic templates have little content. Consequently, I have to improvise. Let me use std::make_unique as an example. As a side note, the three lines of std::make_unique, which I'm going to develop in this section, are the most impressive three lines of code I know in modern C++.

std::make_unique is a function template that returns a dynamically allocated object, wrapped into a std::unique_ptr. Here are a few use cases.

```
// makeUnique.cpp

#include <memory>

struct MyType {
    MyType(int, double, bool){};
};
```

```
int main() {

    int lvalue{2020};

    std::unique_ptr<int> uniqZero = std::make_unique<int>();
    auto uniqEleven = std::make_unique<int>(2011);
    auto uniqTwenty = std::make_unique<int>(lvalue);
    auto uniqType = std::make_unique<MyType>(lvalue, 3.14, true);

}
```

Based on these use cases, what are the requirements for `std::make_unique`?

1. `std::make_unique` should deal with an arbitrary number of arguments. It gets 0, 1, and 3 arguments.

2. `std::make_unique` should accept lvalues and rvalues. It gets an rvalue (`2011`) and an lvalue (`lvalue`). The last call even gets both an rvalue and an lvalue.

3. `std::make_unique` should forward its arguments unchanged to the underlying constructor. This means that the constructor of `std::unique_ptr` should get an lvalue/rvalue if `std::make_unique` gets an lvalue/rvalue.

These requirements are typical for factory functions such as `std::make_unique`, `std::make_shared`, `std::make_tuple`, but also `std::thread`. Factory functions in modern C++ rely on two powerful features in C++11:

- Perfect forwarding
- Variadic templates

Now I want to create my factory function `createT`. Let's start the job with perfect forwarding.

Perfect forwarding

First of all: What is perfect forwarding?

Perfect forwarding allows you to preserve an argument's value category (lvalue/rvalue) and `const`/`volatile` type qualifiers.

Perfect forwarding follows a typical pattern, consisting of a universal reference (perfect forwarding reference) and std::forward.

```
template<typename T>       // (1)
void createT(T&& t) {      // (2)
    std::forward<T>(t);    // (3)
}
```

The three parts of the pattern to get perfect forwarding are as follows:

1. Start with a template parameter T: typename T,

2. Bind T by universal reference, also known as perfect forwarding reference: T&& t,

3. Invoke std::forward on the argument: std::forward<T>(t),

The key observation is that T&& (2) can bind an lvalue or an rvalue and that std::forward (3) does the perfect forwarding. std::forward is a conditional std::move. It moves an rvalue and copies an lvalue.

It's time to create the prototype of the createT factory function, which should behave at the end similarly to std::make_unique in the program makeUnique.cpp. I just replaced std::make_unique with the createT call, added the createT factory function, and commented the two lines (1) out. Additionally, I removed the header <memory> (std::make_unique) and added the header <utility> for std::forward.

```
// createT1.cpp

#include <utility>

struct MyType {
    MyType(int, double, bool) {};
};

template <typename T, typename Arg>
T createT(Arg&& arg) {
    return T(std::forward<Arg>(arg));
}

int main() {

    int lvalue{2020};
```

```
//std::unique_ptr<int> uniqZero = std::make_unique<int>();
auto uniqEleven = createT<int>(2011);
auto uniqTwenty = createT<int>(lvalue);
//auto uniqType = std::make_unique<MyType>(lvalue, 3.14, true);
```

```
}
```

Excellent! The rvalue (2011) and the lvalue (lvalue) pass my test.

Variadic templates

Sometimes dots are important. Insert exactly nine dots at the right place, and the two commented-out lines work.

```
// createT2.cpp

#include <utility>

struct MyType {
    MyType(int, double, bool) {};
};

template <typename T, typename ... Args>
T createT(Args&& ... args) {
    return T(std::forward<Args>(args) ... );
}

int main() {

    int lvalue{2020};

    int uniqZero = createT<int>();
    auto uniqEleven = createT<int>(2011);
    auto uniqTwenty = createT<int>(lvalue);
    auto uniqType = createT<MyType>(lvalue, 3.14, true);

}
```

How does the magic work? The three dots stand for an ellipsis. By using them, Args or args becomes a parameter pack. To be more precise, Args is a template parameter pack, and args is a function parameter pack. You can apply only two operations to a parameter pack: pack or unpack. If the ellipsis is left of Args, the parameter pack is packed; if the ellipsis is right of Args, the parameter pack is unpacked. In the case of the expression `std::forward<Args>(args)...`, this means the expression is unpacked until the parameter pack is consumed and a comma is just placed between the unpacked components. That's all.

C++ Insights helps you to visualize this unpacking process.

Now I'm nearly done. The two missing steps are as follows.

1. Create a `std::unique_ptr<T>` instead of a plain `T`.

2. Rename the function to `make_unique`.

Voila.

```
template <typename T, typename ... Args>
std::unique_ptr<T> make_unique(Args&& ... args) {
    return std::unique_ptr<T>(new T(std::forward<Args>(args) ... ));
}
```

Metaprogramming

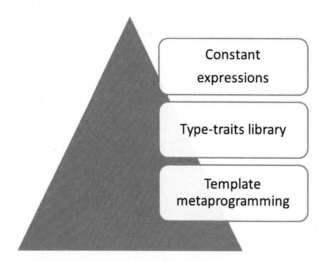

Metaprogramming is programming at compile time. It started in C++98 with template metaprogramming, was formalized in C++11 with the type-traits library, and since C++11, has steadily improved. The main driving force is constant expressions. The introduction to template metaprogramming in the C++ Core Guidelines ends uniquely: "The syntax and techniques needed are pretty horrendous."

My perception is that template metaprogramming is not so horrendous, the C++ Core Guidelines lack content, and a straightforward introduction to metaprogramming is missing. Consequently, this section provides a concise introduction to metaprogramming. As the various concepts are introduced, I refer to the four rules about metaprogramming.

Template metaprogramming

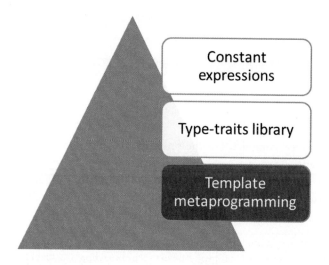

- T.120: Use template metaprogramming only when you really need to
- T.122: Use templates (usually template aliases) to compute types at compile time

How did it all start?

In 1994, Erwin Unruh presented at a C++ committee meeting a program that didn't compile. Here is probably the most famous program that never compiled.

```
// Prime number computation by Erwin Unruh
template <int i> struct D { D(void*); operator int(); };

template <int p, int i> struct is_prime {
   enum { prim = (p%i) && is_prime<(i > 2 ? p : 0), i -1> :: prim };
   };
```

```
template < int i > struct Prime_print {
    Prime_print<i-1> a;
    enum { prim = is_prime<i, i-1>::prim };
    void f() { D<i> d = prim; }
    };

struct is_prime<0,0> { enum {prim=1}; };
struct is_prime<0,1> { enum {prim=1}; };
struct Prime_print<2> { enum {prim = 1}; void f() {
    D<2> d = prim; }
};
#ifndef LAST
#define LAST 10
#endif
main () {
    Prime_print<LAST> a;
    }
```

Erwin Unruh used the Metaware compiler, but the program does not produce the presented error messages with a recent C++ compiler. A newer variant from the author can be found at http://www.erwin-unruh.de/prim.html. Why is this program so famous? Let's have a closer look at the original error messages (see Figure 13.12).

```
01 | Type `enum{}' can't be converted to txpe `D<2>' ("primes.cpp",L2/C25).
02 | Type `enum{}' can't be converted to txpe `D<3>' ("primes.cpp",L2/C25).
03 | Type `enum{}' can't be converted to txpe `D<5>' ("primes.cpp",L2/C25).
04 | Type `enum{}' can't be converted to txpe `D<7>' ("primes.cpp",L2/C25).
05 | Type `enum{}' can't be converted to txpe `D<11>' ("primes.cpp",L2/C25).
06 | Type `enum{}' can't be converted to txpe `D<13>' ("primes.cpp",L2/C25).
07 | Type `enum{}' can't be converted to txpe `D<17>' ("primes.cpp",L2/C25).
08 | Type `enum{}' can't be converted to txpe `D<19>' ("primes.cpp",L2/C25).
09 | Type `enum{}' can't be converted to txpe `D<23>' ("primes.cpp",L2/C25).
10 | Type `enum{}' can't be converted to txpe `D<29>' ("primes.cpp",L2/C25).
```

Figure 13.12 *Calculating primes at compile time*

I highlighted the important parts in red. I think you see the pattern. The program calculates at compile time the first 30 prime numbers. This means template instantiation empowers you to do math at compile time. It is even better. Template metaprogramming is Turing complete, and can, therefore, be used to solve any computational problem. (Of course, Turing completeness holds only in theory for template metaprogramming because the recursion depth (at least 1024 with C++11) and the length of the names that are generated during template instantiation provide some limitations.)

How does the magic work?

Let me decompose what is going on step by step.

Calculating at compile time

Calculating the factorial of a number is the "Hello World" of template metaprogramming.

```cpp
// factorial.cpp

#include <iostream>

template <int N>                                        // (2)
struct Factorial {
    static int const value = N * Factorial<N-1>::value;
};

template <>                                             // (3)
struct Factorial<1> {
    static int const value = 1;
};

int main() {

    std::cout << '\n';

    std::cout << "Factorial<5>::value: "
              << Factorial<5>::value << '\n';           // (1)
    std::cout << "Factorial<10>::value: "
              << Factorial<10>::value << '\n';

    std::cout << '\n';

}
```

The call `factorial<5>::value` (1) causes the instantiation of the primary or general template (2). This instantiation triggers the call of `Factorial<4>::value`. This recursion ends with the fully specialized class template `Factorial<1>` as a boundary condition (3). See Figure 13.13.

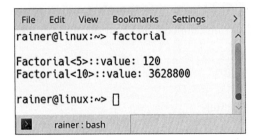

Figure 13.13 *Calculating the factorial of 5 at compile time*

Compiler Explorer allows you to visualize this compile-time calculation. The factorial program is nice but is not idiomatic for template metaprogramming.

Type manipulation at compile time
Manipulating types at compile time is typical in template metaprogramming. For example, here is what std::move is conceptionally doing:

```
static_cast<std::remove_reference<decltype(arg)>::type&&>(arg);
```

std::move takes its argument arg, deduces its type (decltype(arg)), removes its reference (remove_reference), and casts it to an rvalue reference (static_cast<...>::type&&>). Essentially, std::move is an rvalue reference cast. Now move semantics can kick in.

How can a function remove constness from its argument?

```
// removeConst.cpp

#include <iostream>
#include <type_traits>

template<typename T >
struct removeConst {
    using type = T;          // (1)
};

template<typename T >
struct removeConst<const T> {
    using type = T;          // (2)
};
```

```
using std::boolalpha;
using std::cout;
using std::is_same;

int main() {

  cout << boolalpha;

  cout << is_same<int, removeConst<int>::type>::value << '\n';
  cout << is_same<int, removeConst<const int>::type>::value << '\n';

}
```

Both function calls is_same in the main function return true.

I implemented removeConst the way std::remove_const is probably implemented in the type-traits library. std::is_same_v from the type-traits library helps me to decide at compile time if both types are the same. In case of removeConst<int>, the primary or general class template kicks in; in case of removeConst <const int>, the partial specialization for const T applies. The critical observation is that both class templates return the underlying type in (1) and (2) via the alias type. As promised, the constness of the argument is removed.

There are additional exciting observations:

- Template specialization (partial or full) is conditional execution at compile time. Let me be more specific: When I use removeConst with a non-constant int, the compiler chooses the primary or general template. When I use a constant int, the compiler chooses the partial specialization for const T.

- The expression using type = T serves as the return value, which is in this case a type.

More meta

At run time, we use data and functions. At compile time, we use metadata and metafunctions. Quite logically, it's called "meta" because we do metaprogramming.

Metadata   **Metadata**: values that metafunctions use at compile time

There are three types of values:

- Types such as int or double
- Nontypes such as integrals, enumerators, pointers, or references
- Templates such as std::vector or std::deque

Metafunctions   **Metafunction**: a function that is executed at compile time

Admittedly, this sounds strange. Types are used in template metaprogramming to simulate functions. Based on the definition of metafunctions, `constexpr` functions that can be executed at compile time, are also metafunctions.

Here are two metafunctions.

```cpp
template <int a , int b>
struct Product {
    static int const value = a * b;
};


template<typename T >
struct removeConst<const T> {
    using type = T;
};
```

The first metafunction `Product` returns a value, and the second one `removeConst` returns a type. The name value and type are just naming conventions for the return values. If a metafunction returns a value, it is called value; if it returns a type, it is called type. The type-traits library follows exactly this naming convention.

I think it is quite enlightening to compare functions with metafunctions.

Functions versus metafunctions

The following function `power` and the metafunction `Power` calculate `pow(2, 10)` at run time and compile time.

```cpp
// power.cpp

#include <iostream>

int power(int m, int n) {
  int r = 1;
  for(int k = 1; k <= n; ++k) r *= m;
  return r;
}

template<int m, int n>
struct Power {
  static int const value = m * Power<m, n-1>::value;
};
```

```
template<int m>
struct Power<m, 0> {
  static int const value = 1;
};

int main() {

  std::cout << '\n';

  std::cout << "power(2, 10)= " << power(2, 10) << '\n';
  std::cout << "Power<2,10>::value= " << Power<2, 10>::value << '\n';

  std::cout << '\n';
}
```

This is the main difference:

- **Arguments:** The function arguments go into the round brackets ((...)) and the metafunction arguments go into the sharp brackets (< ... >). This observation also holds for the definition of the function and the metafunction. The function uses round brackets, the metafunction sharp brackets. Each metafunction argument produces a new type.

- **Return value:** The function uses a return statement, and the metafunction uses a static integral constant value.

I elaborate more on this comparison in the section discussing constant expressions later in this chapter. Figure 13.14 shows the output of the program.

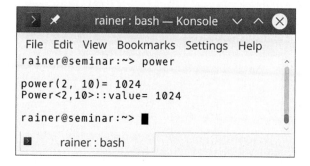

Figure 13.14 *Calculating at run time and compile time*

power is executed at run time and Power at compile time, but what is happening in the following example?

```cpp
// powerHybrid.cpp

#include <iostream>

template<int n>
int power(int m) {
    return m * power<n-1>(m);
}

template<>
int power<1>(int m) {
    return m;
}

template<>
int power<0>(int m) {
    return 1;
}

int main() {

    std::cout << '\n';

    std::cout << "power<10>(2): " << power<10>(2) << '\n'; // (1)

    std::cout << '\n';

    auto power2 = power<2>;                              // (2)

    for (int i = 0; i <= 10; ++i) {                     // (3)
        std::cout << "power2(" << i << ")= "
                  << power2(i) << '\n';
    }

    std::cout << '\n';

}
```

The call power<10>(2) (1) uses sharp and round brackets and calculates 2 to the power of 10. This means 10 is the compile-time argument and 2 the run-time argument. To say it differently: power is at the same time a function and a metafunction (see Figure 13.15). Now I can instantiate the class template for 2 and give it the name power2 (2).

The function argument is a run-time argument and can, therefore, be used in a for loop (3).

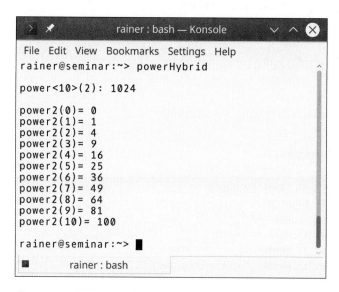

Figure 13.15 *power as function and metafunction*

Type-traits library

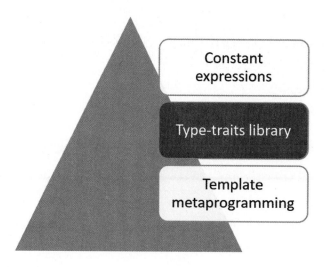

- T.124: Prefer to use standard-library TMP facilities

The type-traits library is part of C++11 and supports type checks, type comparisons, and type modifications at compile time. The library has more than 100 functions but grows with each new C++ standard release.

Type checks

Each type belongs precisely to one of the 14 primary type categories.

Primary type categories

Here they are:

```
template <class T> struct is_void;
template <class T> struct is_integral;
template <class T> struct is_floating_point;
template <class T> struct is_array;
template <class T> struct is_pointer;
template <class T> struct is_null_pointer;
template <class T> struct is_member_object_pointer;
template <class T> struct is_member_function_pointer;
template <class T> struct is_enum;
template <class T> struct is_union;
template <class T> struct is_class;
template <class T> struct is_function;
template <class T> struct is_lvalue_reference;
template <class T> struct is_rvalue_reference;
```

The following program gives an example of a type fulfilling the check for each one of these primary type categories.

```
// primaryTypeCategories.cpp

#include <iostream>
#include <type_traits>

struct A {
  int a;
  int f(int) { return 2011; }
};
```

```cpp
enum E {
  e= 1,
};

union U {
  int u;
};


int main() {

  using namespace std;

  cout <<  boolalpha <<  '\n';

  cout << is_void<void>::value << '\n';
  cout << is_integral<short>::value << '\n';
  cout << is_floating_point<double>::value << '\n';
  cout << is_array<int []>::value << '\n';
  cout << is_pointer<int*>::value << '\n';
  cout << is_null_pointer<nullptr_t>::value << '\n';
  cout << is_member_object_pointer<int A::*>::value <<  '\n';
  cout << is_member_function_pointer<int (A::*)(int)>::value << '\n';
  cout << is_enum<E>::value << '\n';
  cout << is_union<U>::value << '\n';
  cout << is_class<string>::value << '\n';
  cout << is_function<int * (double)>::value << '\n';
  cout << is_lvalue_reference<int&>::value << '\n';
  cout << is_rvalue_reference<int&&>::value << '\n';

  cout <<  '\n';

}
```

Each of the 14 calls of type-traits functions in the main program returns true. Composite type categories are then assembled from those primary type categories.

Composite type categories
Table 13.2 gives you the relation between the primary type categories and the composite type categories.

Table 13.2 *Composite type categories*

Composite type categories	Primary type categories
std::is_arithmetic	std::is_floating_point or std::is_integral
std::is_fundamental	std::is_arithmetic or std::is_void or std::is_null_pointer
std::is_object	std:::is_scalar or std::is_array or std::is_union or std::is_class
std::is_scalar	std::is_arithmetic or std::is_enum or std::is_pointer or std::is_member_pointer or std::is_null_pointer
std::is_compound	!std::is_fundamental
std::is_reference	std::is_lvalue_reference or std::is_rvalue_reference
std::is_member_pointer	std::is_member_object_pointer or std::is_member_function_pointer

Type properties

The type-traits library offers additional checks for type properties.

```
template <class T> struct is_const;
template <class T> struct is_volatile;
template <class T> struct is_trivial;
template <class T> struct is_trivially_copyable;
template <class T> struct is_standard_layout;
template <class T> struct is_pod;
template <class T> struct is_literal_type;
template <class T> struct is_empty;
template <class T> struct is_polymorphic;
template <class T> struct is_abstract;
template <class T> struct is_signed;
template <class T> struct is_unsigned;
template <class T, class... Args> struct is_constructible;
template <class T> struct is_default_constructible;
template <class T> struct is_copy_constructible;
template <class T> struct is_move_constructible;
template <class T, class U> struct is_assignable;
template <class T> struct is_copy_assignable;
template <class T> struct is_move_assignable;
template <class T> struct is_destructible;
template <class T, class... Args> struct is_trivially_constructible;
template <class T> struct is_trivially_default_constructible;
template <class T> struct is_trivially_copy_constructible;
template <class T> struct is_trivially_move_constructible;
```

```
template <class T, class U> struct is_trivially_assignable;
template <class T> struct is_trivially_copy_assignable;
template <class T> struct is_trivially_move_assignable;
template <class T> struct is_trivially_destructible;
template <class T, class... Args> struct is_nothrow_constructible;
template <class T> struct is_nothrow_default_constructible;
template <class T> struct is_nothrow_copy_constructible;
template <class T> struct is_nothrow_move_constructible;
template <class T, class U> struct is_nothrow_assignable;
template <class T> struct is_nothrow_copy_assignable;
template <class T> struct is_nothrow_move_assignable;
template <class T> struct is_nothrow_destructible;
template <class T> struct has_virtual_destructor;
```

Many of the metafunctions like std::is_trivially_copyable have "trivially" in their name. That means that the compiler provides this method. Requesting a method from the compiler with the keyword default is also trivial.

The type-traits library has more metafunctions to offer. Read the details on cppreference.com.

Type comparisons

The type-traits library supports three kinds of comparisons:

- std::is_base_of<Base, Derived>
- std::is_convertible<From, To>
- std::is_same<T, U>

The following example uses all three functions:

```
// compare.cpp

#include <cstdint>
#include <iostream>
#include <type_traits>

class Base{};
class Derived: public Base{};

int main() {

  std::cout << std::boolalpha << '\n';
```

```
std::cout << "std::is_base_of<Base, Derived>::value: "
          << std::is_base_of<Base, Derived>::value << '\n';
std::cout << "std::is_base_of<Derived, Base>::value: "
          << std::is_base_of<Derived, Base>::value << '\n';
std::cout << "std::is_base_of<Derived, Derived>::value: "
          << std::is_base_of<Derived, Derived>::value << '\n';
std::cout << '\n';
std::cout << "std::is_convertible<Base*, Derived*>::value: "
          << std::is_convertible<Base*, Derived*>::value << '\n';
std::cout << "std::is_convertible<Derived*, Base*>::value: "
          << std::is_convertible<Derived*, Base*>::value << '\n';
std::cout << "std::is_convertible<Derived*, Derived*>::value: "
          << std::is_convertible<Derived*, Derived*>::value << '\n';

std::cout << '\n';

std::cout << "std::is_same<int, int32_t>::value: "
          << std::is_same<int, int32_t>::value << '\n';
std::cout << "std::is_same<int, int64_t>::value: "
          << std::is_same<int, int64_t>::value << '\n';
std::cout << "std::is_same<long int, int64_t>::value: "
          << std::is_same<long int, int64_t>::value << '\n';

std::cout << '\n';

}
```

The program produces the expected outcome (see Figure 13.16).

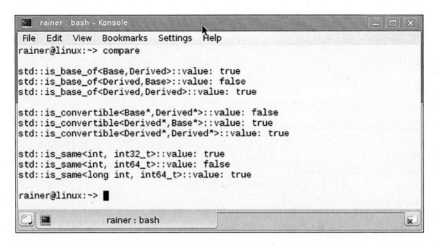

Figure 13.16 *Type comparisons*

Template metaprogramming with the type-traits functions

Okay, let's step back and think about the functions of the type-traits library. Here are a few observations.

- The functions from the type-traits library are metafunctions because they run at compile time. Metafunctions are class templates.

- The arguments of the metafunctions that go into the sharp brackets (<...>) are metadata. Metadata are, in this case, types.

- The return value of the functions is (::value). value is an alias. Since C++17, there is a simpler form for getting the result: Instead of std::is_void<void>::value, you just type std::is_void_v<void>.

If these three observations remind you of the previous section about template metaprogramming, it is no coincidence: These are precisely the conventions that were presented there.

Type modifications

Type modifications are the domain of template metaprogramming and, therefore, are supported by the type-traits library.

The type-traits library offers many metafunctions to manipulate types. Here are the most interesting ones.

```
// const-volatile modifications:
remove_const;
remove_volatile;
remove_cv;
add_const;
add_volatile;
add_cv;

// reference modifications:
remove_reference;
add_lvalue_reference;
add_rvalue_reference;

// sign modifications:
make_signed;
make_unsigned;
```

```
// pointer modifications:
remove_pointer;
add_pointer;

// other transformations:
decay;
enable_if;
conditional;
common_type;
underlying_type;
```

To get an int from an int or a const int, you have to ask for the type with ::type.

```
std::is_same<int, std::remove_const<int>::type>::value;          // true
std::is_same<int, std::remove_const<const int>::type>::value;    // true
```

Since C++14, you can just use _t to get the type such as with std:: remove_const_t:

```
std::is_same<int, std::remove_const_t<int>>::value;          // true
std::is_same<int, std::remove_const_t<const int>>::value;   // true
```

To get an idea of how useful these metafunctions from the type-traits library are, here are a few examples.

- **std::decay** is applied by std::thread to its arguments. std::thread gets as arguments the executed function f and its function arguments args. "Decay" means that implicit conversions from array to pointer and function to pointer are performed and const/volatile qualifiers and references are removed.
- **std::enable_if** is a convenient way to use SFINAE. SFINAE stands for Substitution Failure Is Not An Error and applies during overload resolution of a function template. It means that if substituting the template parameter fails, the specialization is discarded from the overload set but this failure causes no compiler error.
- **std::conditional** is the ternary operator at compile time.
- **std::common_type** determines the common type among all types to which all types can be converted.
- **std::underlying_type** determines the type of an enum.

Maybe you are not convinced about the benefit of the type-traits library. Let me end my short introduction to the type-traits library with its two main goals: correctness and optimization.

Correctness

Correctness means on one hand that you can use the type-traits library to implement concepts such as Integral, SignedIntegral, and UnsignedIntegral.

```
template <typename T>
concept Integral = std::is_integral<T>::value;

template <typename T>
concept SignedIntegral = Integral<T> && std::is_signed<T>::value;

template <typename T>
concept UnsignedIntegral = Integral<T> && !SignedIntegral<T>;
```

But it also means that you can use them to make your algorithm safer.

```
// gcd2.cpp

#include <iostream>
#include <type_traits>

template<typename T>
T gcd(T a, T b) {
    static_assert(std::is_integral<T>::value,
                  "T should be an integral type!");
    if( b == 0 ){ return a; }
    else{
        return gcd(b, a % b);
    }
}

int main() {

    std::cout << gcd(100, 33) << '\n';     // (1)
    std::cout << gcd(3.5,4.0) << '\n';     // (2)
    std::cout << gcd("100","10") << '\n'; // (3)

}
```

The error message is quite explicit. See Figure 13.17.

```
                              rainer : bash — Konsole                          ∨ ∧ ⊗
 File  Edit  View  Bookmarks  Settings  Help
 rainer@seminar:~> g++ gcd2.cpp -o gcd2
 gcd2.cpp: In instantiation of 'T gcd(T, T) [with T = double]':
 gcd2.cpp:18:29:   required from here
 gcd2.cpp:8:5: error: static assertion failed: T should be an integral type!
      static_assert(std::is_integral<T>::value, "T should be an integral type!");
      ^~~~~~~~~~~~~
 gcd2.cpp:11:25: error: invalid operands of types 'double' and 'double' to binary 'operator%'
      return gcd(b, a % b);
                   ~~^~~
 gcd2.cpp: In instantiation of 'T gcd(T, T) [with T = const char*]':
 gcd2.cpp:19:32:   required from here
 gcd2.cpp:8:5: error: static assertion failed: T should be an integral type!
      static_assert(std::is_integral<T>::value, "T should be an integral type!");
      ^~~~~~~~~~~~~
 gcd2.cpp:11:25: error: invalid operands of types 'const char*' and 'const char*' to binary 'operator%'
      return gcd(b, a % b);
                   ~~^~~
 rainer@seminar:~> ▌
```

Figure 13.17 *Correctness with the type-traits functions*

The compiler complains immediately that a `double` or a `const char*` is not an integral.

The added value of the type-traits library lies not only in the correctness it enables, but also in optimization.

Optimization

The key idea of the type-traits library is straightforward. The compiler analyzes the used types and makes decisions on the code that should be created. For the algorithms `std::copy`, `std::fill`, or `std::equal` of the Standard Template Library, this means that in one case the algorithm is applied to each element of the range one by one or on the entire memory. In the other case, C functions such as memcpy, memmove, memset, or memcmp are used, which makes the algorithm faster. The small difference between `memcpy` and `memmove` is that `memmove` can deal with overlapping memory areas.

The following three code snippets from the GCC 6 implementation (layout adjusted) make one point clear: The checks of the type traits help to generate better-optimized code.

```
// fill
// Specialization: for char types we can use memset.
template<typename _Tp>
  inline typename
  __gnu_cxx::__enable_if<__is_byte<_Tp>::__value, void>::__type   // (1)
  __fill_a(_Tp* __first, _Tp* __last, const _Tp& __c)
```

```
  {
    const _Tp __tmp = __c;
    if (const size_t __len = __last - __first)
      __builtin_memset(__first, static_cast<unsigned char>(__tmp), __len);
  }

// copy

template<bool _IsMove, typename _II, typename _OI>
  inline _OI
  __copy_move_a(_II __first, _II __last, _OI __result)
  {
    typedef typename iterator_traits<_II>::value_type _ValueTypeI;
    typedef typename iterator_traits<_OI>::value_type _ValueTypeO;
    typedef typename iterator_traits<_II>::iterator_category _Category;
    const bool __simple = (__is_trivial(_ValueTypeI)          // (2)
                        && __is_pointer<_II>::__value
                        && __is_pointer<_OI>::__value
                        && __are same< ValueTypeI,  ValueTypeO>::  value);

    return std::__copy_move<_IsMove, __simple,
  }

// lexicographical_compare

template<typename _II1, typename _II2>
  inline bool
  __lexicographical_compare_aux(_II1 __first1, _II1 __last1,
      _II2 __first2, _II2 __last2)
  {
    typedef typename iterator_traits<_II1>::value_type _ValueType1;
    typedef typename iterator_traits<_II2>::value_type _ValueType2;
    const bool __simple =                                     // (3)
      (__is_byte<_ValueType1>::__value
      && __is_byte<_ValueType2>::__value
      && !__gnu_cxx::__numeric_traits<_ValueType1>::__is_signed
      && !__gnu_cxx::__numeric_traits<_ValueType2>::__is_signed
      && __is_pointer<_II1>::__value
      && __is_pointer<_II2>::__value);

    return std::__lexicographical_compare<__simple>::__lc(__first1,
                                                          __last1,
                                                          __first2,
                                                          __last2);
  }
```

The markers (1) through (3) show that the type-traits library is used to generate better-optimized code. Internally, the GCC 6 compiler uses functions such as __enable_if or __is_pointer to provide the type-traits functions such as std::enable_if or std::is_pointer.

Constant expressions

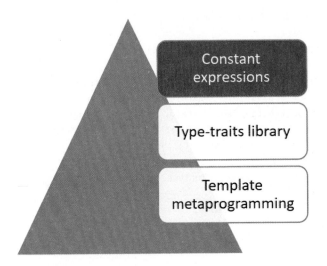

- T.123: Use constexpr functions to compute values at compile time

Finally, we are at the peak of the graphic.

constexpr allows you to program at compile time with the typical C++ syntax. The focus of this section is not to provide you with all details of constexpr but to compare template metaprogramming with constexpr functions. Before I compare both techniques, I will give you a short overview of constexpr. What are the advantages of constant expressions?

Constant expressions with constexpr can have three forms.

Variables

- Are implicit const
- Have to be initialized by a constant expression

Functions

- Can invoke other `constexpr` functions
- Can have variables that have to be initialized by a constant expression
- Can use conditional expressions or loops
- Are implicit inline
- Cannot have `static` or `thread_local` data
- Cannot use exception handling

User-defined types

- Must have a constructor, which is a constant expression
- Cannot have virtual functions
- Cannot have a virtual base class

Advantages

A constant expression

- Can be evaluated at compile time
- Gives the compiler deep insight into the code
- Is implicitly thread safe
- Can be constructed in the read-only memory (ROM-able)

`constexpr` functions can depend only on other constant expressions. Being a `const-expr` function does not mean that the function is executed at compile time. It means that the function has the potential to be executed at compile time. A `constexpr` function can also be executed at run time. The compiler and the optimization level determine if a `constexpr` function runs at compile time or run time.

There are two contexts in which a `constexpr` function `func` *has* to run at compile time.

1. The `constexpr` function is used in a context that is evaluated at compile time. This can be a `static_assert` expression, the instantiation of a template, or the initialization of a C-array.

2. The value of a `constexpr` function is explicitly requested during compile time:
   `constexpr auto res = func(5)`.

To see the theory in praxis, study the gcd.cpp program in the rule "Per.11: Move computation from run time to compile time."

Finally, I come to my main point.

Template metaprogramming versus `constexpr` functions

Table 13.3 shows the big picture.

Table 13.3 *Template metaprogramming versus `constexpr` functions*

Characteristic	Template metaprogramming	`constexpr` functions
Execution time	Compile time	Compile time and run time
Arguments	Types, nontypes, and templates	Values
Programming paradigm	Functional	Imperative
Modification	No	Yes
Control structure	Recursion	Conditions and loops
Conditional execution	Template specialization	Conditional statements

I want to add a few remarks about the table.

- A template metaprogram runs at compile time, but a `constexpr` function can run at compile time or run time.

- Arguments of a template metaprogram can be types, nontypes (for example, 5), and templates. `constexpr` functions are functions that have the potential to run at compile time.

- There is no state at compile time and, therefore, no modification. This means template metaprogramming is programming in a pure functional style. Here are the characteristics from the functional style perspective:

  - In template metaprogramming, instead of modifying a value you return a new value each time.

  - Controlling a for loop by incrementing a variable such as i is not possible at compile time: `for (int i; i <= 10; ++i)`. Template metaprogramming, therefore, replaces loops with recursion.

  - In template metaprogramming, conditional execution is replaced by template specialization.

Admittedly, this comparison was quite concise. A pictorial comparison of a metafunction and a constexpr function should answer the remaining open questions. Both functions calculate the factorial of a number.

- The function arguments of a constexpr function correspond to template arguments of a metafunction. See Figure 13.18.

```
constexpr int factorial(int n){
  auto res= 1;
  for ( auto i= n; i >= 1; --i ){
    res *= i;
  }
  return res;
}




                         template <int N>
                         struct Factorial{
                            static int const value= N * Factorial<N-1>::value;
                         };

                         template <>
                         struct Factorial<1>{
                            static int const value = 1;
                         };
```

Figure 13.18 *Function versus template arguments*

- A constexpr function can have variables and modify them. A metafunction generates new values. See Figure 13.19.

```
constexpr int factorial(int n){
  auto res= 1;
  for ( auto i= n; i >= 1; --i ){
    res *= i;
  }
  return res;
}




                         template <int N>
                         struct Factorial{
                            static int const value= N * Factorial<N-1>::value;
                         };

                         template <>
                         struct Factorial<1>{
                            static int const value = 1;
                         };
```

Figure 13.19 *Modification versus new value*

- A metafunction uses recursion to simulate a loop. See Figure 13.20.

```
constexpr int factorial(int n){
  auto res= 1;
  for ( auto i= n; i >= 1; --i ){
    res *= i;
  }
  return res;
}

                           template <int N>
                           struct Factorial{
                             static int const value= N * Factorial<N-1>::value;
                           };

                           template <>
                           struct Factorial<1>{
                             static int const value = 1;
                           };
```

Figure 13.20 *Recursion versus loop*

- Instead of an end condition, a metafunction uses a full specialization of a template to end a recursion. Additionally, a metafunction uses partial or full specialization to perform conditional execution such as an `if` statement. See Figure 13.21.

```
constexpr int factorial(int n){
  auto res= 1;
  for ( auto i= n; i >= 1; --i ){
    res *= i;
  }
  return res;
}

                           template <int N>
                           struct Factorial{
                             static int const value= N * Factorial<N-1>::value;
                           };

                           template <>
                           struct Factorial<1>{
                             static int const value = 1;
                           };
```

Figure 13.21 *Template specialization for conditional execution*

- Instead of an updated value `res`, the metafunction generates a new value in each iteration. See Figure 13.22.

```
constexpr int factorial(int n){
  auto res= 1;
  for ( auto i= n; i >= 1; --i ){
    res *= i;
  }
  return res;
}



                          template <int N>
                          struct Factorial{
                            static int const value= N * Factorial<N-1>::value;
                          };

                          template <>
                          struct Factorial<1>{
                            static int const value = 1;
                          };
```

Figure 13.22 *Update versus new value*

- A metafunction has no return statement but uses `value` as the return value. See Figure 13.23.

```
constexpr int factorial(int n){
  auto res= 1;
  for ( auto i= n; i >= 1; --i ){
    res *= i;
  }
  return res;
}

                          template <int N>
                          struct Factorial{
                            static int const value= N * Factorial<N-1>::value;
                          };

                          template <>
                          struct Factorial<1>{
                            static int const value = 1;
                          };
```

Figure 13.23 *Simulating a return value*

Advantages of `constexpr` functions

Besides the advantages that `constexpr` functions are easier to write and to maintain and can run at compile time and run time, they have an additional advantage.

```
constexpr double average(double fir , double sec) {
    return (fir + sec) / 2;
}
```

```
int main() {
    constexpr double res = average(2, 3);
}
```

`constexpr` functions can deal with floating-point numbers. Template metaprogramming accepts only integral numbers.

Other rules

There are a few rules on templates that don't fit in any of the previous sections. They mainly target code quality.

T.140	Name all operations with potential for reuse

Honestly, I'm not so sure why this rule belongs to the templates section. Maybe templates are about reuse? The example in the C++ Core Guidelines uses the `std::find_if` algorithm of the STL. Bearing that in mind, the rule is fundamental from a code-quality perspective.

Imagine that you have a vector of records. Each record consists of a name, an address, and an identifier. Quite often, you want to find a record with a specific name; but to make it more challenging, you ignore the case sensitivity of the names.

```
// records.cpp

#include <algorithm>
#include <cctype>
#include <iostream>
#include <string>
#include <vector>

struct Rec {                                          // (1)
    std::string name;
    std::string addr;
    int id;
};

int main() {

    std::cout << '\n';
```

```
std::vector<Rec> vr{ {"Grimm", "Munich", 1},                    // (2)
                     {"huber", "Stuttgart", 2},
                     {"Smith", "Rottenburg", 3},
                     {"black", "Hanover", 4} };

std::string name = "smith";

auto rec = std::find_if(vr.begin(), vr.end(), [&name](Rec& r) {    // (3)
  if (r.name.size() != name.size()) return false;
    for (std::string::size_type i = 0; i < r.name.size(); ++i) {
      {
      if (std::tolower(r.name[i]) != std::tolower(name[i]))
        return false;
      }
    }
  return true;
});

if (rec != vr.end()) {
  std::cout << rec->name << ",  "
            << rec->addr << ", " << rec->id << '\n';
}

std::cout << '\n';

}
```

The struct `Rec` (1) has only public members; therefore, I can use aggregate initialization and initialize all members directly (2). In line (3), I use a lambda expression to search for the record with the name "smith". I first check if both names have the same size and then if the characters are identical when compared in a case-insensitive manner. See Figure 13.24.

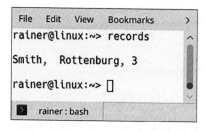

Figure 13.24 *Case-insensitive search in a* struct

What's the problem with this code? The requirement of the case-insensitive comparison of strings is very common, and we should, therefore, put the solution in its own entity and give it a name, which allows it to be reused.

```cpp
bool compare_insensitive(const std::string& a,
                         const std::string& b) {                    // (1)
    if (a.size() != b.size()) return false;
    for (std::string::size_type i = 0; i < a.size(); ++i) {
        if (std::tolower(a[i]) != std::tolower(b[i])) return false;
    }
    return true;
}


std::string name = "smith";

auto res = std::find_if(vr.begin(), vr.end(),
    [&name](Rec& r) { return compare_insensitive(r.name, name); }
);


std::vector<std::string> vs{"Grimm", "huber", "Smith", "black"};    // (2)

auto res2 = std::find_if(vs.begin(), vs.end(),
    [&name](std::string& r) { return compare_insensitive(r, name); }
);
```

The function `compare_insensitive` (1) gives a name to the general concept. Now, I can reuse it for a vector of strings (2).

T.141	Use an unnamed lambda if you need a simple function object in one place only

Admittedly, I often have this discussion in my classes: When should I use a named callable (function or a function object) or a lambda expression? Sorry, I have no easy answer. Here, two principles of code quality contradict:

1. Don't repeat yourself (DRY).

2. Explicit is better than implicit (The Zen of Python).

I borrowed the second point from Python. But what does that mean? Imagine that you have an old-fashioned Fortran programmer on your team, and they tell you:

"Each name must have three capital characters." So, you end up with the following code.

```
auto EUE = std::remove_if(USE.begin(), USE.end(), IGH);
```

What does the name IGH stand for? IGH stands for an id greater hundred. Now, you have to document the meaning of the predicate.

But if you use a lambda, the code documents itself.

```
auto earlyUsersEnd = std::remove_if(users.begin(), users.end(),
                [](const User &user) { return user.id > 100; });
```

The open question is now: When should you use a named entity (DRY) or a lambda expression (The Zen of Python)? My rule of thumb is that I use a named entity if I reuse a general concept at least three times.

T.143   Don't write unintentionally nongeneric code

A short example says more than a long explanation. In the following example, I iterate through a std::vector, a std::deque, and a std::list.

```
// notGeneric.cpp

#include <deque>
#include <list>
#include <vector>

template <typename Cont>
void justIterate(const Cont& cont) {
    const auto itEnd = cont.end();
    for (auto it = cont.begin(); it < itEnd; ++it) {  // (1)
        // do something
    }
}

int main() {

    std::vector<int> vecInt{1, 2, 3, 4, 5};
    justIterate(vecInt);                                // (2)

    std::deque<int> deqInt{1, 2, 3, 4, 5};
```

```
justIterate(deqInt);                              // (3)

std::list<int> listInt{1, 2, 3, 4, 5};
justIterate(listInt);                             // (4)

}
```

The code looks innocent, but when I compile the program, the compilation breaks. I get about one hundred lines of error messages. See Figure 13.25.

```
File   Edit   View   Bookmarks   Settings   Help
rainer@linux:~> g++-6 notGeneric.cpp -o notGeneric
notGeneric.cpp: In instantiation of 'void justIterate(const Cont&) [with Cont = std::list<int>]':
notGeneric.cpp:24:24:   required from here
notGeneric.cpp:10:37: error: no match for 'operator<' (operand types are 'std::_List_const_iterator<
int>' and 'const std::_List_const_iterator<int>')
     for (auto it = cont.begin(); it < itEnd; ++it) {   // (1)
                                  ^~~~~~~~~~
In file included from /usr/include/c++/6/vector:64:0,
                 from notGeneric.cpp:5:
/usr/include/c++/6/bits/stl_vector.h:1526:5: note: candidate: template<class _Tp, class _Alloc> bool
                              rainer : bash
```

Figure 13.25 *Iterating through a few containers*

The beginning of the error message shows the problem: "notGeneric.cpp:10:37: error: no match for 'operator<' (operand types are 'std::_List_const_iterator."

What is the issue? The issue lies in (1). The iterator comparison (1) works for the std::vector (2) and the std::deque (3) but breaks for the std::list (4). Each container returns an iterator representing its structure. This iterator in case of a std::vector and a std::deque is a random access iterator, and this iterator in case of the std::list is a bidirectional iterator. A look at the iterator categories helps a lot (see Table 13.4).

Table 13.4 *Iterator categories*

Iterator category	Properties	Containers
Forward iterator	++It, It++, *It	std::unordered_set
		std::unordered_map
	It == It2, It != It2	std::unordered_multiset
		std::unordered_multimap
		std::forwared_list

Iterator category	Properties	Containers
Bidirectional iterator	`--It, It--`	`std::set`
		`std::map`
		`std::multiset`
		`std::multimap`
		`std::list`
Random access iterator	`It[I]`	`std::array`
	`It += n, It -= n`	
	`It + n, It -n`	`std::vector`
	`n + It`	
	`It + It2`	`std::deque`
	`It < It2, It <= It2`	
	`It < It2, It >= It2`	`std::string`

The random access iterator category is a superset of the bidirectional iterator category, and the bidirectional iterator category is a superset of the forward iterator category. Now the issue is obvious. An iterator given by a `std::list` does not support the `<` comparison. Fixing the bug is straightforward. Iterators of each iterator category support the `!=` comparison.

Here is the improved `justIterate` function template.

```
template <typename Cont>
void justIterate(const Cont& cont) {
    const auto itEnd = cont.end();
    for (auto it = cont.begin(); it != itEnd; ++it) {
        // do something
    }
}
```

By the way, it is typically a bad idea to loop explicitly through a container. By explicitly, I mean that you manually increment the counter variable. This is a job for an algorithm of the Standard Template Library: Prefer an algorithm to a raw loop.

T.144   Don't specialize function templates

This rule is special. Consequently, I have been contemplating for a long time whether or not I should include it. I ended up including it for two reasons. First, it helps me to give an idea of partial template specialization, and second, the rule is easy to comprehend.

Template specialization

Templates define the behavior of families of classes and functions. Often, special arguments must be treated separately. To support this use case, you can fully specialize templates. Class templates can even be partially specialized.

The next code snippet presents the general idea.

```
template <typename T, int Line, int Column>        // (1)
class Matrix;

template <typename T>                              // (2)
class Matrix<T, 3, 3> {};

template <>                                         // (3)
class Matrix<int, 3, 3> {};
```

Line (1) is the primary or general template. This template must be declared at least and has to be declared before the partially or fully specialized templates. Line (2) follows with the partial specialization. Line (3) is the full specialization.

To better understand partial and full specialization, I want to present a visual explanation. Think about an n-dimensional space of template parameters. In the primary template (1), you can choose an arbitrary type and two arbitrary ints. In the case of the partial specialization in line (2), you can only choose the type. This partial specialization means the three-dimensional space is reduced to a line. In contrast, full specialization stands for a point in a three-dimensional space.

What is happening when you invoke the templates?

```
Matrix<int, 3, 3> m1;        // class Matrix<int, 3, 3>

Matrix<double, 3, 3> m2;     // class Matrix<T, 3, 3>

Matrix<std::string, 4, 3> m3;  // class Matrix<T, Line, Column> => ERROR
```

m1 uses the full specialization, m2 uses the partial specialization, and m3 uses the primary template. m3 causes an error because the definition of the primary template is missing.

Here are three rules that the compiler uses to determine which specialization to pick.

1. The compiler finds only one specialization. The compiler uses this specialization.

2. The compiler finds more than one specialization. The compiler uses the most specialized one. If this process ends in more than one specialization, the compiler throws an error.

3. The compiler finds no specialization. It uses the primary specialization.

Now, I have to explain what "A is a more specialized template than B" means. Here is the informal definition on cppreference.com: "A accepts a subset of the types that B accepts."

After this first overview, I can dig a little bit deeper into function templates.

Specialization and overloading of function templates

Function templates make the job of template specialization easier but also more difficult at the same time.

- Easier because a function template only supports full specialization
- More difficult because function overloading comes into play

From a design perspective, you can specialize a function template with template specialization or overloading.

```
// functionTemplateSpecialization.cpp

#include <iostream>
#include <string>

template <typename T>            // (1)
std::string getTypeName(T) {
    return "unknown type";
}

template <>                      // (2)
std::string getTypeName<int>(int) {
    return "int";
}

std::string getTypeName(double) { // (3)
    return "double";
}
```

```
int main() {

    std::cout << '\n';

    std::cout << "getTypeName(true): " << getTypeName(true) << '\n';
    std::cout << "getTypeName(4711): " << getTypeName(4711) << '\n';
    std::cout << "getTypeName(3.14): " << getTypeName(3.14) << '\n';

    std::cout << '\n';

}
```

(1) is the primary template, (2) the full specialization for int, and (3) the overload for double. The compiler deduces the types, and the correct function or function template is invoked. In the case of the function overloading, the compiler prefers the function overloading to the function template when the function overloading is a perfect fit. See Figure 13.26.

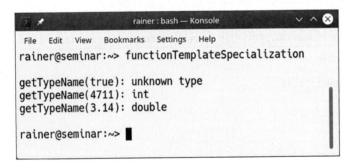

Figure 13.26 *Specialization and overloading of function templates*

Now comes the reason for this rule.

The surprise

The reason for the rule is quite brief: Function template specialization doesn't participate in overloading. Let's see what that means. My program is based on a code snippet from Dimov/Abrahams.

```
// dimovAbrahams.cpp

#include <iostream>
#include <string>
```

```cpp
// getTypeName

template<typename T>          // (1) primary template
std::string getTypeName(T) {
  return "unknown";
}

template<typename T>       // (2) primary template that overloads (1)
std::string getTypeName(T*) {
  return "pointer";
}

template<>               // (3) explicit specialization of (2)
std::string getTypeName(int*) {
  return "int pointer";
}

// getTypeName2

template<typename T>       // (4) primary template
std::string getTypeName2(T) {
  return "unknown";
}

template<>                 // (5) explicit specialization of (4)
std::string getTypeName2(int*) {
  return "int pointer";
}

template<typename T>       // (6) primary template that overloads (4)
std::string getTypeName2(T*) {
  return "pointer";
}

int main() {

  std::cout << '\n';

  int *p;

  std::cout << "getTypeName(p): " << getTypeName(p) << '\n';
  std::cout << "getTypeName2(p): " << getTypeName2(p) << '\n';

  std::cout << '\n';

}
```

Admittedly, the code looks quite boring, but bear with me. I defined the primary template getTypeName at (1). (2) is an overload for pointers, and (3) is a full specialization for an int pointer. In the case of TypeName2, I made a small variation. I put the explicit specialization (5) before the overload for pointers (6). See Figure 13.27.

This reordering has some surprising consequences.

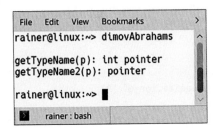

Figure 13.27 *Specialization of function templates*

In the first case, the full specialization for the int pointer is called, and in the second case, the overload for pointers is called. What? The reason for this nonintuitive behavior is that overload resolution ignores function template specialization. Overload resolution operates on primary templates and functions. In both cases, overload resolution finds both primary templates. In the first case (getTypeName), the pointer variant is the better fit, and therefore, the explicit specialization for the int pointer is chosen. In the second variant (getTypeName2), the pointer variant also is chosen, but the full specialization belongs to the primary template (4). Consequently, it is ignored. This is why this rule recommends that you do not specialize function templates.

Related rules

I already wrote about the rule "T.80: Do not naively templatize a class hierarchy" in the rule "ES.23: Prefer the {}-initializer syntax."

The rule "T.84: Use a non-template core implementation to provide an ABI-stable interface" was already the topic of the previous rule "T.62: Place non-dependent class template members in a non-templated base class."

The rule "T.141: Use an unnamed lambda if you need a simple function object in one place only" presents the use case for lambdas. The section about lambdas provides more information on the question of when to use lambdas.

Distilled

Important

- Concepts are predicates on templates that are evaluated at compile time. They should model semantic categories such as `Arithmetic` or `Iterator` but not syntactic restrictions such as `HasPlus` or `IsInvocable`.

- Use function objects to pass operations to algorithms. They provide a higher optimization potential and more expressiveness than a function. Additionally, they can have state.

- Let the compiler deduce the types of the template arguments.

- Template arguments should be at least `Regular` or `SemiRegular`.

- Place nondependent class template members in a nontemplated base class to reduce code size.

- When a user-defined type `MyType` should support a generic function such as `isSmaller`, there are various possibilities. Extend `MyType` with the required operations, implement a full specialization of `isSmaller` for `MyType`, or extend `isSmaller` with the possibility of providing a special predicate.

- Virtual member functions are instantiated for each type in a class template and can, therefore, cause code bloat. A member function template cannot be virtual.

- A factory function such as `std::make_unique` relies on two powerful features in C++11: perfect forwarding and variadic templates. Thanks to perfect forwarding and variadic templates, a factory function can accept an arbitrary number of arguments. The arguments can be lvalues or rvalues.

- The three typical ways of metaprogramming in C++ are template metaprogramming, the type-traits library, and the `constexpr` function. Prefer `constexpr` functions to the type-traits library; prefer the type-traits library to template metaprogramming.

- Use a lambda if you need a simple operation in place. Name operations with a potential for reuse.

Chapter 14

C-Style Programming

Cippi mixes C with C++ code.

Due to the shared history of C and C++, both languages are closely related. Because neither of them is a subset of the other, you have to know a few rules to mix them.

This section in the C++ Core Guidelines consists of three rules. These three rules cover the typical issues encountered when dealing with legacy code.

CPL.1	Prefer C++ to C

Without further ado, here is the reason the C++ Core Guidelines prefer C++: "C++ provides better type checking and more notational support [than C]. It provides better support for high-level programming and often generates faster code."

> **CPL.2**   If you must use C, use the common subset of C and C++, and compile the C code as C++

The first question that you have to answer when mixing C and C++ is, Can you compile the entire code base with a C++ compiler?

Entire source code available

If the entire source code is available, you are almost done. I say "almost" because C is not a subset of C++. Here is a small and bad C program that breaks with a C++ compiler.

```
// cStyle.c

#include <stdio.h>

int main() {

    double sq2 = sqrt(2);                        // (1)

    printf("\nsizeof(\'a\'): %d\n\n", sizeof('a')); // (2)

    char c;
    void* pv = &c;
    int* pi = pv;                                // (3)

    int class = 5;                               // (4)

}
```

First, let me compile the program and execute it with the C90 standard. The compilation succeeds with a few warnings (see Figure 14.1).

```
File  Edit  View  Bookmarks  Settings  Help
rainer@linux:~> gcc -std=c99 cStyle.c -o cStyle
cStyle.c: In function 'main':
cStyle.c:7:5: warning: implicit declaration of function 'sqrt' [-Wimplicit-function-declaration]
    double sq2 = sqrt(2);                // (1)
      ^
cStyle.c:7:18: warning: incompatible implicit declaration of built-in function 'sqrt' [enabled by default]
    double sq2 = sqrt(2);                // (1)
             ^
rainer@linux:~> cStyle

sizeof('a'): 4

rainer@linux:~> 
                    rainer : bash
```

Figure 14.1 *Warnings with a C compiler*

The program cStyle.c has a few issues. There is no declaration for the sqrt function (1), (3) performs an implicit conversion from a void pointer to an int pointer, and (4) uses the class keyword.

Let's see how the C++ compiler reacts to the same code. See Figure 14.2.

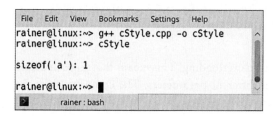

```
File   Edit   View   Bookmarks   Settings   Help
rainer@linux:~> g++ cStyle.cpp -o cStyle
cStyle.cpp: In function 'int main()':
cStyle.cpp:7:24: error: 'sqrt' was not declared in this scope
    double sq2 = sqrt(2);                      // (1)
                 ^
cStyle.cpp:13:15: error: invalid conversion from 'void*' to 'int*' [-fpermissive]
    int* pi = pv;                              // (3)
              ^
cStyle.cpp:15:5: error: expected primary-expression before 'int'
    int class = 5;                             // (4)
        ^
cStyle.cpp:15:5: error: expected ';' before 'int'
rainer@linux:~> █
                        rainer : bash
```

Figure 14.2 *Errors with a C++ compiler*

I get what I deserve: three compiler errors. The program cStyle.c shows more subtle differences between a C and a C++ compiler. Figure 14.3 shows the program reduced (2): printf("\nsizeof(\'a\'): %d\n\n", sizeof('a'));. Here is the output.

```
File   Edit   View   Bookmarks   Settings   Help
rainer@linux:~> g++ cStyle.cpp -o cStyle
rainer@linux:~> cStyle

sizeof('a'): 1

rainer@linux:~> █
          rainer : bash
```

Figure 14.3 *Different size of a char with a C++ compiler*

Instead of 4, such as for the C compiler, sizeof('a') is 1 with the C++ compiler. 'a' **is an** int **in** C.

Now, let's discuss the more challenging case where the entire source code is not available.

Entire source code not available

These are the essential points.

1. **Use your C++ compiler to compile your** main **function.** In contrast to a C compiler, a C++ compiler generates additional startup code that is executed before the main function. For example, the startup code calls constructors of global (static) objects.

2. **Use your C++ compiler to link your program.** The C++ compiler, when used for linking the program, automatically links in standard C++ libraries.

3. **Use a C and C++ compiler from the same vendor, which should have the same calling conventions.** A calling convention specifies the method that a compiler sets up to access a function. This includes in which order parameters are allocated, how parameters are passed, or whether the caller or the callee prepares the stack. Read the full details of x86's calling conventions on Wikipedia (https://en.wikipedia.org/wiki/X86_calling_conventions).

CPL.3	If you must use C for interfaces, use C++ in the calling code using such interfaces

In contrast to C, C++ supports function overloading. This means that you can define functions having the same name but different parameters. The compiler picks the right function when a function is invoked.

```cpp
// functionOverloading.cpp

#include <iostream>

void print(int) {
    std::cout << "int" << '\n';
}

void print(double) {
    std::cout << "double" << '\n';
}

void print(const char*) {
```

```
    std::cout << "const char* " << '\n';
}

void print(int, double, const char*) {
    std::cout << "int, double, const char* " << '\n';
}


int main() {

    std::cout << '\n';

    print(10);
    print(10.10);
    print("ten");
    print(10, 10.10, "ten");

    std::cout << '\n';

}
```

The output is as expected (see Figure 14.4).

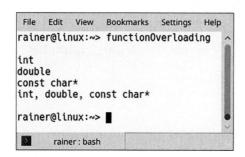

Figure 14.4 *Function overloading*

The interesting question is now: How can the C++ compiler distinguish the various functions? The C++ compiler additionally encodes the type and numbers of the parameters into the function name. This process is called "name mangling" and is specific for each C++ compiler. The process, which is not standardized, is often also called "name decoration."

With the help of the `functionOverloading.cpp` on Compiler Explorer, it is quite easy to see the mangled names. Just disable the button Demangle.

Table 14.1 shows the names that the GCC 8.3 and the MSVC 19.16 are producing.

Table 14.1 *Name mangling*

Function	GCC 8.3	MSVC 19.16
print(int)	_Z5printi	?print@@YAXH@Z
print(double)	_Z5printd	?print@@YAXN@Z
print(const char*)	_Z5printPKc	?print@@YAXPEBD@Z
print(int, double, const char*)	_Z5printidPKc	?print@@YAXHNPEBD@Z

By using the `extern "C"` linkage specifier, you can prevent the C++ compiler from mangling the names. The result is that you can call a C function from C++ or a C++ function from C.

You can use `extern "C"` for

- Each function.
  ```
  extern "C" void foo(int);
  ```

- Each function in a scope.
  ```
  extern "C" {
      void foo(int);
      double bar(double);
  }
  ```

- The entire header file by using include guards. The macro `__cplusplus` is defined when the C++ compiler is used.
  ```
  #ifdef __cplusplus
  extern "C" {
  #endif
      void foo(int);
      double bar(double);
      .
      .
      .

  #ifdef __cplusplus
  }
  #endif
  ```

Distilled

Important

- If you have to support C code, compile the C code with a C++ compiler. If that is not possible, compile your main function with a C++ compiler and link the program with a C++ linker. Use a C and C++ compiler from the same vendor.
- By using the extern "C" linkage specifier, you can prevent the C++ compiler from mangling the names. The result is that you can call a C function from C++ or a C++ function from C.

Chapter 15

Source Files

Cippi juggles with source files.

With C++20 we get modules, but until we have modules available, we should distinguish between the implementation and the interface of our code.

The guidelines make their point regarding source files quite clear: "Distinguish between declarations (used as interfaces) and definitions (used as implementations). Use header files to represent interfaces and to emphasize logical structure." Consequently, there are more than ten rules for source files. Most of the rules are quite concise. The first rules focus on interface and implementation files, and the remaining rules address namespaces.

Interface and implementation files

Declarations or interfaces are typically in *.h files and definitions or implementations in *.cpp files.

SF.1	Use a `.cpp` suffix for code files and `.h` for interface files if your project doesn't already follow another convention

When you have a C++ project, header files should be called *.h and implementation files *.cpp. Convention beats this rule if you already have another policy in your project.

I have often seen other conventions for header and implementation files. Here are a few I have in mind:

- Header files
  - *.h
  - *.hpp
  - *.hxx
  - *.inl
- Implementation files
  - *.cpp
  - *.c
  - *.cc
  - *.cxx

SF.2	A .h file may not contain object definitions or non-inline function definitions

If your header file contains an object definition or a definition of a noninline function, your linker may complain. This complaint is the reason for this rule. To be more specific, C++ has the One Definition Rule.

One Definition Rule
ODR stands for One Definition Rule. Here is what it says in the case of a function:

- A function cannot have more than one definition in any translation unit.

- A function cannot have more than one definition in the program.

- Inline functions with external linkage can be defined in more than one translation. The definitions have to satisfy the requirement that they are all the same.

In modern compilers, the keyword `inline` is quite misleading. Modern compilers almost completely ignore it. The typical use case for `inline` is to mark functions for ODR correctness.

Let's see what my linker has to say when I try to link a program breaking the ODR. The following code example has one header file `header.h` and two implementation files. Each implementation file includes this header file and, therefore, breaks the ODR, because two definitions of `func` exist.

```
// header.h

void func(){}
// impl.cpp

#include "header.h"
// main.cpp

#include "header.h"

int main() {}
```

The linker complains in this concrete case about the multiple definitions of the function `func`. See Figure 15.1.

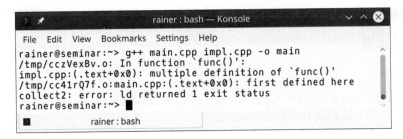

Figure 15.1 *Multiple definitions of a function*

SF.5	A .cpp file must include the .h file(s) that defines its interface

The interesting question is, What happens if you don't include the *.h file in the *.cpp file and there is a mismatch between the interface file *.h and the implementation file *.cpp?

Assume I am having a bad day. I define a function func that should get an int and return an int.

```
// impl.cpp

// #include "impl.h" (1)

int func(int) {
    return 5;
}
```

My mistake is that I declare this function in the header file impl.h, getting an int but returning a std::string.

```
// impl.h

#include <string>

std::string func(int);
```

I include the header in the main program because I want to invoke this function there.

```
// main.cpp

#include "impl.h"

int main() {

    auto res = func(5);

}
```

The issue is that the error may be delayed until link time when main.cpp is compiled. See Figure 15.2. This error is too late.

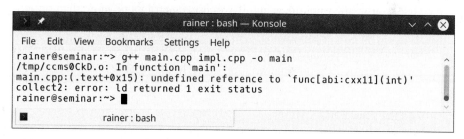

Figure 15.2 *Linker error because of mismatch between function declaration and definition*

When I include the header impl.h in my impl.cpp (1) file, I get a compile-time error. See Figure 15.3.

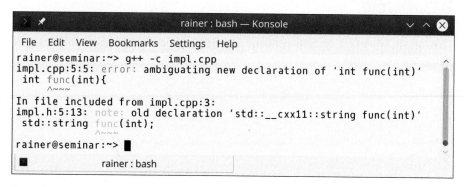

Figure 15.3 *Compiler error because of a mismatch between function declaration and definition*

SF.8   Use #include guards for all .h files

By putting an include guard around your header file, the header file is included only once. The following is the small example from the C++ Core Guidelines.

```
// file foobar.h:
#ifndef LIBRARYNAME_FOOBAR_H
#define LIBRARYNAME_FOOBAR_H
// ... declarations ...
#endif // LIBRARYNAME_FOOBAR_H
```

There are two points to keep in mind.

1. Give your guard a unique name. If you use a guard name more than once, it may exclude the inclusion of a header file.

2. #pragma is nonstandard but is a widely supported preprocessor directive. This pragma means the following variation of the header foobar.h is not portable.

```
// file foobar.h:
#pragma once

// ... declarations ...
```

SF.9   Avoid cyclic dependencies among source files

First of all, what is a cyclic dependency among source files? Imagine you have the following source files.

```
// a.h

#ifndef LIBRARY_A_H
#define LIBRARY_A_H
#include "b.h"

class A {
  B b;
};
```

```
#endif // LIBRARY_A_H
// b.h

#ifndef LIBRARY_B_H
#define LIBRARY_B_H
#include "a.h"

class B {
  A a;
};

#endif // LIBRARY_B_H
// main.cpp

#include "a.h"

int main() {
  A myA;
}
```

The compilation of the program fails (see Figure 15.4).

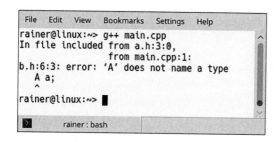

Figure 15.4 *Cyclic dependencies among source files*

The issue is that there is a circular dependency between the header files a.h and b.h. The problem manifests itself when myA is created in the main program. To create an object of type A, the compiler must figure out the size of an object of type B. To create an object of type B, the compiler must figure out the size of A. This is not possible if the respective members of type A and type B, a or b, are objects. The determination of the size would only be possible if a or b were pointers or references.

The straightforward fix is, therefore, to forward declare A in b.h or B in a.h. Depending on your platform, the size of the reference or pointer is 32 or 64 bits. Here is the modified header of a.h.

```
#ifndef LIBRARY_A_H
#define LIBRARY_A_H

class B;

class A {
  B* b;
  B& b2 = *b;
};


#endif // LIBRARY_A_H
```

The standard library header <iosfwd> holds forward declarations of the input/output library.

| SF.10 | Avoid dependencies on implicitly #included names |

For example, the following program will compile with GCC 5.4 but will break with the Microsoft compiler 19.00.23506.

```
#include <iostream>

int main() {

    std::string s = "Hello World";
    std::cout << s;

}
```

I forgot to include a necessary header <string>. GCC 5.4 includes <string> with the header <iostream>. This automatic inclusion does not happen with the Microsoft compiler.

SF.11   Header files should be self-contained

This rule is concise but important. A self-contained header file can be included *topmost* in a translation unit. Self-contained means that the header does not depend on other headers that were included before. If you don't follow this rule, a user of your header may be surprised by difficult-to-understand error messages. Sometimes the header seems to work, sometimes not. It just depends on which header was included before.

Namespaces

A namespace is a scope for identifiers. Identifiers can be names of types, functions, or variables.

SF.6   Use using namespace directives for transition, for foundation libraries (such as std), or within a local scope (only)

Honestly, I want to reformulate this rule: Don't use namespace directives such as in the following example.

```
#include <cmath>
using namespace std;

int g(int x) {
    int sqrt = 7;
    // ...
    return sqrt(x); // error
}
```

The program does not compile because there is a name clash. This is not my main argument against a using directive. My main argument is that the using directive hides the origin of the name and breaks the readability of the code.

```
// namespaceDirective.cpp

#include <iostream>
#include <chrono>
```

```
using namespace std;
using namespace std::chrono;
using namespace std::literals::chrono_literals;

int main() {

  cout << '\n';

  auto schoolHour = 45min;

  auto shortBreak = 300s;
  auto longBreak = 0.25h;

  auto schoolWay = 15min;
  auto homework = 2h;

  auto schoolDayInSec = 2 * schoolWay + 6 * schoolHour +
                        4 * shortBreak + longBreak + homework;

  cout << "School day in seconds: " << schoolDayInSec.count() << endl;

  duration<double, ratio<3600>> schoolDayInHours = schoolDayInSec;
  duration<double, ratio<60>> schoolDayInMin = schoolDayInSec;
  duration<double, ratio<1, 1000>> schoolDayInMilli = schoolDayInSec;

  cout << "School day in hours: " << schoolDayInHours.count() << endl;
  cout << "School day in minutes: " << schoolDayInMin.count() << endl;
  cout << "School day in milliseconds: "
       << schoolDayInMilli.count() << endl;

  cout << endl;

}
```

Do you know by heart which function or object was declared in which namespace? If not, looking for the definition may be a challenge. This is true in particular if you are a novice.

Only the built-in literals in this example, such as 45min or 300s, are self-explanatory. Here is the adequate program, which this time doesn't use the using directive for std and std::chrono.

```
// namespaceDirectiveRemoved.cpp
```

```cpp
#include <iostream>
#include <chrono>

using namespace std::literals::chrono_literals;

int main() {

  std::cout << std::endl;

  auto schoolHour = 45min;

  auto shortBreak = 300s;
  auto longBreak = 0.25h;

  auto schoolWay = 15min;
  auto homework = 2h;

  auto schoolDayInSec = 2 * schoolWay + 6 * schoolHour +
                        4 * shortBreak + longBreak + homework;

  std::cout << "School day in seconds: "
        << schoolDayInSec.count() << std::endl;

  std::chrono::duration<double, std::ratio<3600>> schoolDayInHours =
    schoolDayInSec;
  std::chrono::duration<double, std::ratio<60>> schoolDayInMin =
    schoolDayInSec;
  std::chrono::duration<double, std::ratio<1, 1000>> schoolDayInMilli =
    schoolDayInSec;

  std::cout << "School day in hours: "
        << schoolDayInHours.count() << std::endl;
  std::cout << "School day in minutes: "
        << schoolDayInMin.count() << std::endl;
  std::cout << "School day in milliseconds: "
        << schoolDayInMilli.count() << std::endl;

  std::cout << std::endl;

}
```

SF.7 Don't write using namespace at global scope in a header file

Here is the rationale for this important rule.

A using namespace at global scope in the header injects names into every file that includes that header. This injection has a few bad consequences:

- When you use the header, you cannot undo the using directive.

- The possibility of a name collision increases drastically.

- A change to the included namespace may break your compilation because a new name is introduced.

SF.20	Use namespaces to express logical structure

Obviously, we have namespaces in the C++ standard to express logical structure. Examples? Here are a few:

```
std
std::chrono
std::literals
std::literals::chrono_literals
std::filesystem
std::placeholders

std::view      // C++20
```

SF.21	Don't use an unnamed (anonymous) namespace in a header

and

SF.22	Use an unnamed (anonymous) namespace for all internal/nonexported entities

An unnamed namespace has internal linkage. Internal linkage means that names inside the unnamed namespace can be referred only from within the current translation unit and are not exported. The same applies to names, which are declared in the unnamed namespace. Okay, what does that mean?

```
namespace {
    int i;  // defines ::(unique_name)::i
}
void inc() {
    i++;  // increments ::(unique_name)::i
}
```

When you refer to i from within the translation unit, you do so by an implicit unique_name that is specific to the current compilation unit, and therefore, there is no name clash. For example, you can define an add addition function inside the unnamed namespace, and the linker does not complain. In this case, you would not break the One Definition Rule even if your header is included more than once.

When you use an unnamed namespace in the header, each translation unit defines its unique instance of the unnamed namespace. Unnamed namespaces in headers have a few consequences:

- The resulting executable size bloats.

- Any declaration in an unnamed namespace refers to a different entity in each translation unit. This may not be the expected behavior.

The usage of an unnamed namespace is similar to the static keyword used in C.

```
namespace { int i1; }
static int i2;
```

Distilled

Important

- Header files should not contain object definitions or noninline functions. They should be self-contained and have #include guards. Don't write using namespace in a header file.

- Source files should include the necessary header files and avoid cyclic dependencies.

- Namespaces should express the logical structure of the software. Avoid the using namespace directive for readability, if possible.

Chapter 16

The Standard Library

Cippi admires the ISO Standard.

Despite the standard library's crucial importance, this section is not exhaustive. Many rules are missing, the mentioned rules are often quite concise, other rules are already the topic of other parts of the C++ Core Guidelines. Consequently, I complement those rules with additional information when necessary.

Containers

Let me start with a significant rule.

SL.con.1	Prefer using STL `array` or `vector` instead of a C-array

I assume that you know about `std::vector`. Why should you prefer `std::vector` to a C-array?

std::vector

One of the big advantages of a `std::vector` compared to a C-array is that the `std::vector` automatically manages its memory. Of course, that holds true for all standard containers. The following program gives a closer look at the automatic memory management provided by `std::vector`.

```cpp
// vectorMemory.cpp

#include <iostream>
#include <string>
#include <vector>

template <typename T>
void showInfo(const T& t, const std::string& name) {

  std::cout << name << " t.size(): " << t.size() << '\n';
  std::cout << name << " t.capacity(): " << t.capacity() << '\n';

}

int main() {

  std::cout << '\n';

  std::vector<int> vec;                                    // (1)

  std::cout << "Maximal size: " << '\n';
  std::cout << "vec.max_size(): " << vec.max_size() << '\n'; // (2)
  std::cout << '\n';
```

```cpp
    std::cout << "Empty vector: " << '\n';
    showInfo(vec, "Vector");
    std::cout << '\n';

    std::cout << "Initialized with five values: " << '\n';
    vec = {1,2,3,4,5};
    showInfo(vec, "Vector");                              // (3)
    std::cout << '\n';

    std::cout << "Added four additional values: " << '\n';
    vec.insert(vec.end(),{6,7,8,9});
    showInfo(vec,"Vector");                               // (4)
    std::cout << '\n';

    std::cout << "Resized to 30 values: " << '\n';
    vec.resize(30);
    showInfo(vec,"Vector");                               // (5)
    std::cout << '\n';

    std::cout << "Reserved space for at least 1000 values: " << '\n';
    vec.reserve(1000);
    showInfo(vec,"Vector");                               // (6)
    std::cout << '\n';

    std::cout << "Shrinked to the current size: " << '\n';
    vec.shrink_to_fit();                                  // (7)
    showInfo(vec,"Vector");

}
```

To spare typing, I wrote the small function showInfo. showInfo prints out the size and the capacity of a vector. The size of a vector is its number of elements; the capacity of a container is the number of elements a vector can hold without an additional memory allocation. Therefore, the capacity of a vector has to be at least as big as its size. You can adjust the size of a vector with its method resize; you can adjust the capacity of a container with its member function reserve.

But back to the program from top to bottom. I create an empty vector (1). Afterward, the program displays number of elements a vector can have (2). After each operation, I output its size and capacity. That happens for the initialization of the vector (3), the addition of four new elements (4), the resizing of the containers to 30 elements (5), and the reserving of additional memory for at least 1,000 elements (6).

With C++11, you can shrink a vector with the member function `shrink_to_fit` (7). That sets the vector's capacity to its size.

Before I present the output of the program in Figure 16.1, I have a few remarks.

- The adjustment of the size and the capacity of the container is done automatically. I don't have to use any memory operations like `new` and `delete`.

- By using the member function `vec.resize(n)`, the vector `vec` gets default-initialized elements if n > `vec.size()`.

- By using the member function `vec.reserve(n)`, the container `vec` gets new memory for at least n elements if n > `vec.capacity()`.

- The call `shrink_to_fit` is nonbinding. That means the C++ run time doesn't have to adjust the capacity of a container to its size. But my usage so far of the member function `shrink_to_fit` with GCC, Clang, or cl.exe has always freed unnecessary memory.

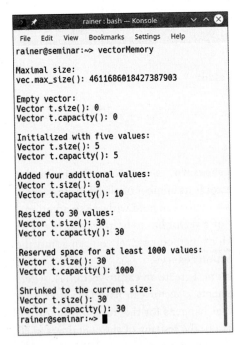

Figure 16.1 *Automatic management of memory*

std::array

Okay, but what is the difference between a C-array and a C++-array?

std::array combines the best of two worlds. On the one hand, std::array has the size and the efficiency of a C-array; on the other hand, std::array has the interface of a std::vector.

My small program compares the memory efficiency of a C-array, a C++-array (std::array), and a std::vector. See Figure 16.2.

```cpp
// sizeof.cpp

#include <iostream>
#include <array>
#include <vector>

int main() {

  std::cout << '\n';

  std::cout << "sizeof(int)= " << sizeof(int) << '\n';

  std::cout << '\n';

  int cArr[10] = {1, 2, 3, 4, 5, 6, 7, 8, 9, 10};

  std::array<int, 10> cppArr = {1, 2, 3, 4, 5, 6, 7, 8, 9, 10};

  std::vector<int> cppVec = {1, 2, 3, 4, 5, 6, 7, 8, 9, 10};

  std::cout << "sizeof(cArr)= " << sizeof(cArr) << '\n';      // (1)

  std::cout << "sizeof(cppArr)= " << sizeof(cppArr) << '\n'; // (2)

                                                    // (3)
  std::cout << "sizeof(cppVec) = " << sizeof(cppVec) + sizeof(int)
                                 * cppVec.capacity() << '\n';
  std::cout << "               = sizeof(cppVec): "
            << sizeof(cppVec) << '\n';
  std::cout << "               + sizeof(int)* cppVec.capacity(): "
            << sizeof(int)* cppVec.capacity() << '\n';

  std::cout << '\n';

}
```

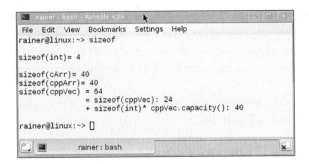

Figure 16.2 *sizeof a C-array, a C++-array, and a* `std::vector`

Both the C-array (1) and the C++-array (2) occupy 40 bytes. That is precisely `sizeof(int) * 10`. In contrast, the `std::vector` needs an additional 24 bytes (3) to manage its data on the heap.

This was the C part of a `std::array`, but the `std::array` supports to a large extent the interface of a `std::vector`. Supporting the interface of a `std::vector` means, in particular, that `std::array` knows its size.

SL.con.2   Prefer using STL `vector` by default unless you have a reason to use a different container

If you want to add elements to your container or remove elements from your container at run time, use a `std::vector`; if not, use a `std::array`. Additionally, a `std::vector` can be much larger than a `std::array` because its elements go to the heap. `std::array` uses a buffer that is local to the context in which it is being used.

`std::array` and `std::vector` offer the following advantages:

1. The fastest general-purpose access (random access, including being CPU vectorization friendly)

2. The fastest default access pattern (begin-to-end or end-to-begin is CPU cache prefetcher friendly)

3. The lowest space overhead (contiguous layout has zero per-element overhead, which is CPU cache friendly)

`std::array` and `std::vector` support the index operator, which boils down to pointer arithmetic. Consequently, advantage 1 is obvious. Advantage 2 was discussed in the section about performance. Read the details in the rule "Per.19: Access memory predictably." The last rule already covered advantage 3: "SL.con.1: Prefer using STL array or vector instead of a C array." `std::array` is comparable in size to a C-array, and `std::vector` adds 24 bytes.

SL.con.3	Avoid bounds errors

In the case of the C-array, there is no help: detecting a bounds error. Ignoring the bounds of a C-array can go unnoticed for too long. The rules "ES.103: Don't overflow," and "ES.104: Don't underflow" in Chapter 8, Expressions and Statements, clearly demonstrate the risks.

In the case of the C-array, there is no support to detect a bounds error. Many of the containers of the STL support an at member function that checks boundaries. In the case of accessing a nonexisting element, a `std::out_of_range` exception is thrown. The following containers have a boundary-checking at member function:

- Sequence container: `std::array`, `std::vector`, and `std::deque`
- Associative container: `std::map` and `std::unordered_map`
- `std::string`

The `std::string` in the next example shows the boundary check.

```
// stringBoundsCheck.cpp

#include <stdexcept>
#include <iostream>
#include <string>

int main() {

    std::cout << '\n';

    std::string str("1123456789");

    str.at(0) = '0';                          // (1)

    std::cout << str << '\n';
```

```
    std::cout << "str.size(): " << str.size() << '\n';
    std::cout << "str.capacity() = " << str.capacity() << '\n';

    try {
        str.at(12) = 'X';                              // (2)
    }
    catch (const std::out_of_range& exc) {
        std::cout << exc.what() << '\n';
    }

    std::cout << '\n';

}
```

Setting the first character of the string str to '0' (1) is fine, but accessing a character outside the size is an error. This even occurs if the access is within the capacity but outside the size of the std::string.

1. The size of a std::string str is the number of elements the str has.

2. The capacity of a str is the number of elements a str could have without allocating additional memory.

Compiling the program with GCC 8.2 and executing it produces a quite explicit error message. See Figure 16.3.

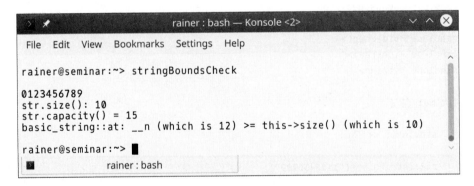

Figure 16.3 *Accessing a nonexisting element of a* std::string

Text

There are various kinds of text and various ways to present this text. Table 16.1 gives you a preview before I dive into the rules.

Table 16.1 *Various kinds of text*

Text	Semantic	Rule
std::string	Owns a character sequence	SL.str.1
std::string_view	Refers to a character sequence	SL.str.2
char*	Refers to a single character	SL.str.4
std::byte	Refers to byte values (not necessarily characters)	SL.str.5

To summarize, only std::string is an owner. All the others refer to existing text.

SL.str.1   Use std::string to own character sequences

Maybe you know another string that owns its character sequence: a C-string. Don't use a C-string! Why? Because you have to manually take care of the memory management, the string termination character, and the length of the string.

```c
// stringC.c

#include <stdio.h>
#include <string.h>

int main( void ) {

  char text[10];

  strcpy(text, "The Text is too long for text.");  // (1) too long
  printf("strlen(text): %u\n", strlen(text));     // (2) missing '\0'
  printf("%s\n", text);

  text[sizeof(text)-1] = '\0';
  printf("strlen(text): %u\n", strlen(text));

  return 0;

}
```

The simple program stringC.c has undefined behavior (1) and (2). Compiling it with a rusty GCC 4.8 seems to work. See Figure 16.4.

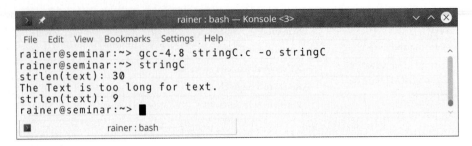

Figure 16.4 *Undefined behavior with a C-string*

The C++ equivalent does not have the same issues.

```cpp
// stringCpp.cpp

#include <iostream>
#include <string>

int main() {

    std::string text{"The Text is not too long."};

    std::cout << "text.size(): " << text.size() << '\n';
    std::cout << text << '\n';

    text +=" And can still grow!";

    std::cout << "text.size(): " << text.size() << '\n';
    std::cout << text << '\n';

}
```

In the case of a C++-string, you cannot make an error because the C++ run time takes care of the memory management and the termination character. Additionally, if you access the elements of the C++-string with the at operator instead of the index operator, bounds errors are automatically detected. You can read the details on the at operator in the rule "SL.con.3: Avoid bounds errors."

SL.str.2   Use `std::string_view` to refer to character sequences

A `std::string_view` refers to the character sequence. To say it more explicitly: A `std::string_view` does not own the character sequence. It represents a view of a sequence of characters. This sequence of characters can be a C++-string or C-string. A `std::string_view` needs two pieces of information: the pointer to the character sequence and the length. It supports the reading part of the interface of `std::string`. In addition to a `std::string`, `std::string_view` has two modifying operations: `remove_prefix` and `remove_suffix`.

    `std::string_view` shines brightly when it comes to memory allocation.

```cpp
// stringView.cpp; C++20

#include <cassert>
#include <iostream>
#include <string>

#include <string_view>

void* operator new(std::size_t count) {                    // (1)
  std::cout << "   " << count << " bytes" << '\n';
  return malloc(count);
}

void getString(const std::string& str) {}

void getStringView(std::string_view strView) {}

int main() {

  std::cout << '\n';

  std::cout << "std::string" << '\n';
                                                           // (2)
  std::string large = "0123456789-123456789-123456789-123456789";
  std::string substr = large.substr(10);                   // (2)

  std::cout << '\n';

  std::cout << "std::string_view" << '\n';
                                                           // (3)
```

```cpp
std::string_view largeStringView{large.c_str(), large.size()};
largeStringView.remove_prefix(10);                          // (3)

assert(substr == largeStringView);

std::cout << '\n';

std::cout << "getString" << '\n';

getString(large);
getString("0123456789-123456789-123456789-123456789"); // (2)
const char message []= "0123456789-123456789-123456789-123456789";
getString(message);                                     // (2)

std::cout << '\n';

std::cout << "getStringView" << '\n';

getStringView(large);                                       // (3)
getStringView("0123456789-123456789-123456789-123456789");
getStringView(message);                                     // (3)

std::cout << '\n';

}
```

I overloaded the global operator new (1) to trace each memory allocation. Memory allocations take place in (2) but not in (3). See Figure 16.5.

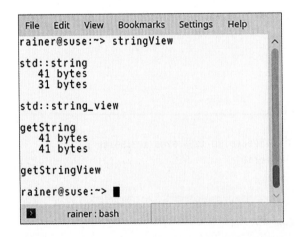

Figure 16.5 *No memory allocation with* std::string_view

SL.str.4	Use char* to refer to a single character

If you don't follow this rule and use const char* as a C-string, you may end up with a critical issue such as the following one.

```
char arr[] = {'a', 'b', 'c'};

void print(const char* p) {
    std::cout << p << '\n';
}

void use() {
    print(arr);   // undefined behavior
}
```

arr decays to a pointer when used as an argument of the function print. The issue is that arr is not zero terminated. The call print(arr) has undefined behavior.

SL.str.5	Use std::byte to refer to byte values that do not necessarily represent characters

std::byte (C++17) is a distinct type implementing the concept of a byte as specified in the C++ language definition. This means a byte is neither an integer nor a character. Its job is to access object storage. std::byte's interface consists of methods for bitwise logical operations.

```
template <class IntType>
    constexpr byte operator << (byte b, IntType shift);
template <class IntType>
    constexpr byte operator >> (byte b, IntType shift);
constexpr byte operator | (byte l, byte r);
constexpr byte operator & (byte l, byte r);
constexpr byte operator ~ (byte b);
constexpr byte operator ^ (byte l, byte r);
```

You can use the function `std::to_integer(std::byte b)` to convert a `std::byte` to an integer type and the call `std::byte{integer}` to do it the other way around. `integer` has to be a non-negative value smaller than `std::numeric_limits <unsigned_char>::max()`.

| **SL.str.12** | **Use the s suffix for string literals meant to be standard-library `strings`** |

Before C++14, there was no way to create a C++-string without a C-string. This is strange because we want to get rid of the C-string. With C++14, we got C++-string literals. They're C-string literals with the suffix s: `"cStringLiteral"s`.

Let me show you an example that makes my point: C-string literals and C++-string literals are different.

```
// stringLiteral.cpp

#include <iostream>
#include <string>
#include <utility>

int main() {

    std::string hello = "hello";
    auto firstPair = std::make_pair(hello, 5);

    auto secondPair = std::make_pair("hello", 15);      // (2)    ERROR

     using namespace std::string_literals;              // (1)
    // auto secondPair = std::make_pair("hello"s, 15);  // (3)    OK

    if (firstPair < secondPair) std::cout << "true\n";  // (4)

}
```

I have to include the namespace `std::string_literals` (1) to use the C++-string literals. Lines (2) and (3) are the critical lines in the example. I use the C-string literal `"hello"` to create a C++-string (2). This is the reason that the type of `firstPair` is of type (`std::string, int`), but the type of the `secondPair` is (`const char*, int`). In the end, the program does not compile when I use (2). The program compiles and the comparison works when I use (3).

Input and output

When you interact with the outside world, two input/output libraries come into play: the stream-based I/O library (short for iostream library) and the C-style I/O functions. Of course, you should prefer the iostream library. The C++ Core Guidelines give a good overview of iostreams: "**iostreams** is a type safe, extensible, formatted and unformatted I/O library for streaming I/O. It supports multiple (and user extensible) buffering strategies and multiple locales. It can be used for conventional I/O, reading and writing to memory (string streams), and user-defined extensions, such as streaming across networks (asio: not yet standardized)."

| SL.io.1 | Use character-level input only when you have to |

First, here is a bad example from the guidelines: using character-level input for more than one character.

```
char c;
char buf[128];
int i = 0;
while (cin.get(c) && !isspace(c) && i < 128)
    buf[i++] = c;
if (i == 128) {
    // ... handle too long string ....
}
```

Honestly, this is a terrible solution for a simple job. Here is the right way to do it:

```
std::string s;
std::cin >> s;
```

| SL.io.2 | When reading, always consider ill-formed input |

Each stream has a state associated with it, which is represented by flags. See Table 16.2.

Table 16.2 *State of the stream*

Flag	Query of the flag	Description	Examples
std::ios::goodbit	stream.good()	No bit set	
std::ios::eofbit	stream.eof()	End-of-file bit set	• Reading beyond the last valid character
std::ios::failbit	stream.fail()	Error	• False formatted reading • Reading beyond the last valid character • Opening a file failed
std::ios::badbit	stream.bad()	Undefined behavior	• Size of stream buffer cannot be adjusted • Code conversion of stream buffer failed • A part of the stream throws an exception

Operations on a stream have an effect only if the stream is in the std::ios:: goodbit state. If the stream is in the std::ios::badbit state, it cannot be reset to the std::ios::goodbit state.

```cpp
// streamState.cpp

#include <ios>
#include <iostream>

int main() {

    std::cout << std::boolalpha << '\n';

    std::cout <<  "In failbit-state: " << std::cin.fail() << '\n';

    std::cout << '\n';

    int myInt;
    while (std::cin >> myInt){
        std::cout << "Output: " << myInt << '\n';
        std::cout <<  "In failbit-state: " << std::cin.fail() << '\n';
        std::cout << '\n';
    }

    std::cout <<  "In failbit-state: " << std::cin.fail() << '\n';
    std::cin.clear();
```

```
    std::cout << "In failbit-state: " << std::cin.fail() << '\n';

    std::cout << '\n';

}
```

The input of the text `wrongInput` causes the stream `std::cin` to be in the `std::ios::failbit` state. Consequently, `wrongInput` and `std::cin.fail()` cannot be displayed. First, you have to set the stream `std::cin` to the `std::ios::goodbit` state.

SL.io.3   Prefer iostreams for I/O

Why should you prefer iostreams to `printf`? There is a subtle but critical difference between `printf` and iostreams. The format string with `printf` specifies the format, and the type of the displayed value, while the format manipulator with iostreams specifies only the format. To say it the other way around: *The compiler deduces the correct type automatically in case of iostreams.*

The following program makes my point clear. When you specify the wrong type in a format string, you get undefined behavior.

```
// printfIostreamsUndefinedBehavior.cpp

#include <cstdio>

#include <iostream>

int main() {

    printf("\n");

    printf("2011: %d\n",2011);
    printf("3.1416: %d\n",3.1416);
    printf("\"2011\": %d\n","2011");
    // printf("%s\n",2011);    // segmentation fault

    std::cout << '\n';
    std::cout << "2011: " <<  2011 << '\n';
    std::cout << "3.146: " << 3.1416 << '\n';
```

```
    std::cout << "\"2011\": " << "2011" << '\n';

    std::cout << '\n';

}
```

Figure 16.6 shows how this undefined behavior manifests itself on my computer.

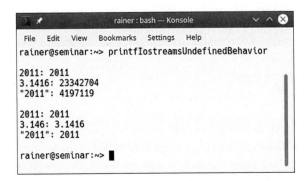

Figure 16.6 *Undefined behavior with* `printf`

You may assume that the compiler issues a warning in the case of a wrong format string, but you have no guarantee. Additionally, I know what often happens when the deadline has passed. You ignore the warnings and maybe decide to look into it later. Instead of facing the consequences of those errors later, avoid the errors in the first place.

SL.io.10	Unless you use `printf`-family functions call `ios_base::sync_with_stdio(false)`

Per default, operations on the C++ streams are synchronized with the C streams. This synchronization happens after each input or output operation.

- **C++ streams:** `std::cin`, `std::cout`, `std::cerr`, `std::clog`, `std::wcin`, `std::wcout`, `std::wcerr`, and `std::wclog`
- **C streams:** `stdin`, `stdout`, and `stderr`

This synchronization allows mixing C++ and C input or output operations because operations on the C++ streams go unbuffered to the C streams. What is also important to note from the concurrency perspective is that synchronized C++ streams are thread safe. All threads can write to the C++ streams without any need for synchronization. The effect may be an interleaving of characters but not a data race.

When you set the `std::ios_base::sync_with_stdio(false)`, the synchronization between C++ streams and C streams does not happen because the C++ streams may put their output into a buffer. Because of the buffering, the input and output operation may become faster. You have to invoke `std::ios_base::sync_with_stdio(false)` before any input or output operation. If not, the behavior is implementation defined.

SL.io.50   Avoid endl

Why should you avoid `std::endl`? Or to say it differently: What is the difference between the manipulators `std::endl` and `'\n'`?

- **`std::endl`:** writes a newline and flushes the output buffer
- **`'\n'`:** writes a newline

Flushing the buffer is an expensive operation and should, therefore, be avoided. If necessary, the buffer is automatically flushed. Honestly, I was curious to see the benchmarks. To simulate the worst case, here is my program, which puts a line break (1) after each character.

```
// syncWithStdioPerformanceEndl.cpp

#include <chrono>
#include <fstream>
#include <iostream>
#include <random>
#include <sstream>
#include <string>

constexpr int iterations = 500;                    // (2)
```

```cpp
std::ifstream openFile(const std::string& myFile){

  std::ifstream file(myFile, std::ios::in);
  if ( !file ){
    std::cerr << "Can't open file "+ myFile + "!" << '\n';
    exit(EXIT_FAILURE);
  }
  return file;

}

std::string readFile(std::ifstream file){

  std::stringstream buffer;
  buffer << file.rdbuf();

  return buffer.str();

}

template <typename End>
auto writeToConsole(const std::string& fileContent, End end){

  auto start = std::chrono::steady_clock::now();
  for (auto c: fileContent) std::cout << c << end;         // (1)
  std::chrono::duration<double> dur = std::chrono::steady_clock::now()
                                      - start;
  return dur;
}

template <typename Function>
auto measureTime(std::size_t iter, Function&& f){
  std::chrono::duration<double> dur{};
  for (int i = 0; i < iter; ++i){
    dur += f();
  }
  return dur / iter;
}

int main(int argc, char* argv[]){
```

```cpp
std::cout << '\n';

// get the filename
std::string myFile;
if ( argc == 2 ){
  myFile= argv[1];
}
else {
  std::cerr << "Filename missing !" << '\n';
  exit(EXIT_FAILURE);
}

std::ifstream file = openFile(myFile);

std::string fileContent = readFile(std::::move(file));

                                             // (3)
auto averageWithFlush = measureTime(iterations, [&fileContent] {
  return writeToConsole(fileContent,
        std::endl<char, std::char_traits<char>>);
});
                                             // (4)
auto averageWithoutFlush = measureTime(iterations, [&fileContent] {
  return writeToConsole(fileContent, '\n');
});

std::cout << '\n';
std::cout << "With flush(std::endl) " << averageWithFlush.count()
                                  << " seconds" << '\n';
std::cout << "Without flush(\\n): " << averageWithoutFlush.count()
                                  << " seconds" << '\n';
std::cout << "With Flush/Without Flush: "
        << averageWithFlush/averageWithoutFlush << '\n';

std::cout << '\n';

}
```

In the first case, I execute the program with std::endl (3); in the second case, I execute it with '\n' (4). When I perform the program with 500 iterations (2), I get the expected winner. `'\n'` is about 10% to 20% faster on Linux (GCC) and Windows (cl.exe) than `std::endl`.

Here are the concrete numbers.

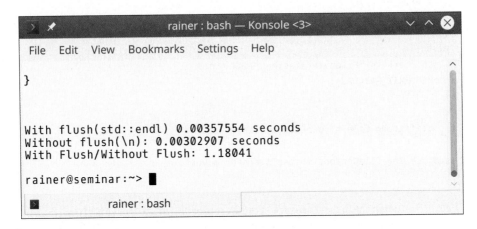

Figure 16.7 *Performance with/without flushing on Linux*

- GCC (see Figure 16.7).

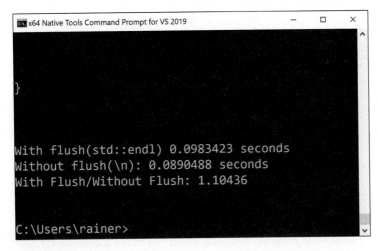

Figure 16.8 *Performance with/without flush on Windows*

- cl.exe (see Figure 16.8).

Related rules

The standard library is an important part of the C++ standard: "ES.1: Prefer the standard library to other libraries and to 'handcrafted code.'" This means that the rules in this book address various aspects of the library. Prominent examples are smart pointers in Chapter 7, Resource Management, or the threading components in Chapter 10, Concurrency.

Many rules present the pros of the STL containers over C-arrays. For completeness, here are a few of the rules:

- P.4: Ideally, a program should be statically type safe
- I.13: Do not pass an array as a single pointer
- ES.42: Keep use of pointers simple and straightforward
- ES.55: Avoid the need for range checking

Distilled

Important

- Use a `std::array` or a `std::vector` instead of a C-array. Prefer a `std::vector` to a `std::array` if the vector has to grow at run time or the number of elements is too big for a `std::array`. `std::vector` and `std::array` support the safe access to the element using the at operator.

- There are various kinds of text. `std::string` is the owner of the text. The other types, such as `std::string_view`, `const char*`, or `std::byte`, only refer to text.

- Prefer iostreams to C-style functions for input/output functionality. Always consider ill-formed input when reading text.

PART II

Supporting Sections

Chapter 17

Architectural Ideas

The first support section is quite short. It has only three rules, with a few sentences of content for each one. Their focus is programming-language agnostic, and they remind me of the philosophical chapter.

A.1   Separate stable code from less stable code

Here is the sentence from the C++ Core Guidelines: "Isolating less stable code facilitates its unit testing, interface improvement, refactoring, and eventual deprecation." What does that mean?

Putting an interface between stable and less stable code is a way to separate it. Due to the interface, your less stable code becomes a kind of subsystem, which you can test or refactor in isolation. You can now test not only the subsystem but also the integration of the subsystem into the system. The first kind of test is typically called the subsystem test, and the second is called the subsystem integration test. The subsystem has two channels into the system: the functional and the nonfunctional channels. Both have to be tested. The functional channel provides the functionality of the subsystem, and the nonfunctional channel propagates the exceptions that can happen and to which the system may react. Thanks to the interface, the concrete subsystem is an implementation of the interface and can, therefore, quite quickly be replaced by another, maybe more stable, implementation.

A.2   Express potentially reusable parts as a library

This is a straightforward idea. Immediately, a few questions arise:

1. When is a part of software potentially reusable?

2. When do the costs of implementing the library pay off?

3. What is the right kind of abstraction?

The three questions are quite blurry and are, therefore, difficult to answer in the general case. This is particularly true for the last question. Let me explain it.

First of all, don't put too much effort up front into your code to make it reusable as a library because "you aren't gonna need it" (YAGNI), but write your code so that it could be reusable. This means follow simple guidelines such as writing your code for understandability, maintainability, testability, and other quality attributes. It is highly probable that you or another programmer will have to work with your code in the future. Or to say it with the words of Philip Wadler: "Make your code readable. Pretend the next person who looks at your code is a psychopath, and he knows where you live."

The second principle that comes into play is "don't repeat yourself" (DRY) when you need the same or similar functionality more than once. Now you should think about abstraction. When I have two similar functions, I write a third function that provides the implementation, and the similar functions just become wrappers for using the implementation function. Here are my ideas put into code to make my point.

```cpp
std::vector<void*> myAlloc;

void* newImpl(std::size_t sz, char const* file, int line){  // (3)
    static int counter{};
    void* ptr = std::malloc(sz);
    std::cerr << file << ": " << line << " " << ptr << '\n';
    myAlloc.push_back(ptr);
    return ptr;
}

                                                    // (1)
void* operator new(std::size_t sz, char const* file, int line){
```

```
    return newImpl(sz, file, line);
}


                                                    // (2)
void* operator new[](std::size_t sz,char const* file, int line){
    return newImpl(sz, file, line);
}
```

The overloaded new operators in the simple form (1) and for arrays (2) invoke the common implementation in (3).

Third, I don't want to answer question 3 because it is very subjective and may be affected by many factors. The answer may depend on the domain of the software. Does the software, for example, run on a desktop, embedded device, or high-frequency server? It depends on factors such as maintainability, testability, scalability, to name a few traits, but also on performance. It may depend on the skill level of the users. Maybe your library is an infrastructure library or a library for your customers.

Writing reusable software in the form of a library is about three to four times more effort than doing a one-off implementation. Here's my rule of thumb: *You should think about a library when you know you reuse the functionality. You should write a library only when you will reuse the functionality at least twice.*

A.4	There should be no cycles among libraries

Cycles among libraries c1 and c2 make your software system more complicated. First, they make your libraries challenging to test and impossible to reuse independently. Second, your libraries become more difficult to understand, maintain, and extend. When you find such a dependency, you should break it. There are a few options, thanks to John Lakos (*Large Scale C++ Software Design*, p. 185):

1. Repackage c1 and c2 so they are no longer mutually dependent.

2. Physically combine c1 and c2 into a single component, c12.

3. Think of c1 and c2 as if they were a single component, c12.

Chapter 18

Nonrules and Myths

I assume that you already know many nonrules and myths about C++. Some of these nonrules and myths predate modern C++ and sometimes even contradict modern C++ techniques. Sometimes these nonrules and myths were *best practices* for writing good C++ code. The C++ Core Guidelines address the most resistant don'ts but also provide alternatives.

NR.1	Don't insist that all declarations should be at the top of a function

This rule is a relict of the C89 standard. C89 doesn't allow the declaration of a variable after a statement. This results in a significant distance between the variable declaration and its usage. Often the variable is not initialized. This is exactly what happens in the example provided by the C++ Core Guidelines:

```
int use(int x) {
    int i;
    char c;
    double d;
    // ... some stuff ...
    if (x < i) {
        // ...
        i = f(x, d);
    }
```

```
    if (i < x) {
        // ...
        i = g(x, c);
    }
    return ;
}
```

I assume that you have already found the issue in this code snippet. The variable i (the same holds true for c and d) is not initialized because it is a built-in variable used in a local scope, and therefore, the program has undefined behavior. If i was a user-defined type such as std::string, all would be fine. So, what should you do?

- Place the declaration of i directly before its first usage.

- Always initialize a variable such as in int i{}, or better, use auto. The compiler cannot guess from a declaration such as auto i; the type of i and, therefore, rejects the program. To put it the other way around: auto forces you to initialize variables.

NR.2	Don't insist to have only a single return-statement in a function

When you follow this rule, you implicitly apply the first nonrule.

```
template<class T>
std::string sign(T x) {
    std::string res;
    if (x < 0)
        res = "negative";
    else if (x > 0)
        res = "positive";
    else
        res = "zero";
    return res;
}
```

Using more than one return statement makes the code easier to read and also faster.

```
template<class T>
std::string sign(T x) {
```

```
    if (x < 0)
        return "negative";
    else if (x > 0)
        return "positive";
    return "zero";
}
```

What happens if automatic return-type deduction returns different types?

```
// differentReturnTypes.cpp

template <typename T>
auto getValue(T x) {
  if (x < 0)           // int
    return -1;
  else if (x > 0)
    return 1.0;        // double
  else return 0.0f;    // float
}

int main(){
    getValue(5.5);
}
```

As expected, the program is not valid. See Figure 18.1.

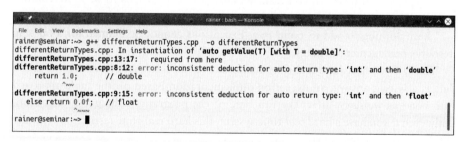

Figure 18.1 *Different return types in a function*

NR.3   Don't avoid exceptions

The rule starts by stating the four main reasons against exceptions:

1. Exceptions are inefficient.

2. Exceptions lead to leaks and errors.

3. Exception performance is not predictable.

4. Exception handling run-time support takes too much space.

The C++ Core Guidelines have profound responses to these statements.

First, the efficiency of exception handling is compared to a program that just terminates or displays the error code. Often the exception-handling implementation is poor. Of course, a comparison makes no sense in such cases. I want to explicitly mention the *Technical Report on C++ Performance* (TR18015.pdf), which presents two typical ways used by compilers to implement exceptions:

- The code approach, where code is associated with each try-block

- The table approach, which uses compiler-generated static tables

Simply said, the code approach has the downside that even when no exception is thrown, the bookkeeping of the exception-handling stack must be performed and, therefore, code unrelated to error handling slows down. This downside does not apply to the table approach, because it introduces no stack or run-time costs when no exception is thrown. In contrast, the table approach seems to be more complicated to implement, and the static table can get quite big.

I have nothing to add to point two. Exceptions cannot be blamed for a missing resource management strategy.

Third, if you have hard real-time guarantees to fulfill so that an answer that is too late is a wrong answer, an exception implementation based on the table approach will not—as we saw—affect the run time of the program in the good case. Honestly, even if you have a hard real-time system, this hard real-time restriction typically applies to only a small part of your system.

Instead of arguing against the nonrules, here are the reasons for using exceptions: Exceptions

- Clearly differentiate between erroneous return and ordinary return

- Cannot be forgotten or ignored

- Can be used systematically

Let me add an anecdote about a situation that I once faced in a legacy code base. The system used error codes to signal the success or failure of a function. They checked the error codes. This was fine. But due to the error codes, the functions didn't use return values. The consequence was that the functions operated on global variables and, consequently, had no parameters because they used the global variables anyway. The end of the story was that the system was not maintainable or testable, and my job was to refactor it.

To get more information about the correct handling of errors, read Chapter 11, Error Handling.

NR.4	**Don't insist on placing each class declaration in its own source file**

The adequate way to structure your code is not to use files; the correct way is to use namespaces. Using a file for each class declaration results in many files and can make your program, therefore, harder to manage and slower to compile.

NR.5	**Don't use two-phase initialization**

Obviously, the job of a constructor is straightforward: *After the constructor is executed, you should have a fully initialized object.* For that reason, the following code snippet from the C++ Core Guidelines is bad.

```
class Picture {
    int mx;
    int my;
    char * data;
public:
    Picture(int x, int y) {
        mx = x,
        my = y;
        data = nullptr;
    }

    ~Picture() {
        Cleanup();
    }
```

```
    bool Init() {
        // invariant checks
        if (mx <= 0 || my <= 0) {
            return false;
        }
        if (data) {
            return false;
        }
        data = (char*) malloc(x*y*sizeof(int));
        return data != nullptr;
    }

    void Cleanup() {                    // (2)
        if (data) free(data);
        data = nullptr;
    }
};

Picture picture(100, 0);
// this will fail..                     // (1)
if (!picture.Init()) {
    puts("Error, invalid picture");
}
```

picture(100, 0) is not initialized, and therefore, all operations on picture in (1) operate on an invalid picture. The solution to this problem is as simple as it is effective: Put all initialization into the constructor.

```
class Picture {
    std::size_t mx;
    std::size_t my;
    std::vector<char> data;

    static size_t check_size(size_t s) {
        Expects(s > 0);
        return s;
    }
public:
    Picture(size_t x, size_t y)
        : mx(check_size(x))
        , my(check_size(y))
        , data(mx * my * sizeof(int)) {
    }
};
```

Additionally, data is in the second example a std::vector instead of a raw pointer. This means the cleanup function (2) from the first example is not necessary anymore because the compiler automatically cleans up. Thanks to the static function check_ size, the constructor can validate its arguments. But this is not the end of the benefits modern C++ gives us.

Often you use a constructor to set the default behavior of an object. Don't do it. Directly set the default behavior of an object in the class body. Use constructors to vary the default behavior: "C.45: Don't define a default constructor that only initializes data members; use member initializers instead."

init member functions are often used to put common initialization or validation routines into one place. You invoke them immediately after the constructor call. Fine, you follow the essential DRY (don't repeat yourself) principle, but you automatically break another important principle: Objects should be fully initialized after the constructor call. How can you solve this riddle? Quite easily. Since C++11, we have had constructor delegation. This means that you put the common initialization and validation logic into one smart constructor and use the other constructors as a kind of wrapper constructor: "C.51: Use delegating constructors to represent common actions for all constructors of a class."

NR.6	Don't place all cleanup actions at the end of a function and goto exit

Okay, we can and should do better than the following code from the C++ Core Guidelines:

```cpp
void do_something(int n) {
    if (n < 100) goto exit;
    // ...
    int* p = (int*) malloc(n);
    // ...
exit:
    free(p);
}
```

By the way, do you spot the error? The jump goto exit bypasses the definition of the pointer p.

What I often saw in legacy C code was code structured like this.

```c
// lifecycle.c

#include <stdio.h>
```

```
void initDevice(const char* mess) {
    printf("\n\nINIT: %s\n",mess);
}

void work(const char* mess) {
    printf("WORKING: %s",mess);
}

void shutDownDevice(const char* mess) {
    printf("\nSHUT DOWN: %s\n\n",mess);
}

int main(void) {

    initDevice("DEVICE 1");
    work("DEVICE1");
    {
        initDevice("DEVICE 2");
        work("DEVICE2");
        shutDownDevice("DEVICE 2");
    }
    work("DEVICE 1");
    shutDownDevice("DEVICE 1");

    return 0;


}
```

This code is very error prone. Each usage of the device consists of three steps: initialization, usage, and release of the device. This is a job for RAII: "R.1: Manage resources automatically using resource handles and RAII (Resource Acquisition Is Initialization)."

```
// lifecycle.cpp

#include <iostream>
#include <string>

class Device {
 public:
    Device(const std::string& res):resource(res) {
        std::cout << "\nINIT: " << resource << ".\n";
    }
```

```
    void work() const {
        std::cout << "WORKING: " << resource << '\n';
    }
    ~Device() {
        std::cout << "SHUT DOWN: "<< resource << ".\n\n";
    }
 private:
    const std::string resource;
};

int main() {

    Device resGuard1{"DEVICE 1"};
    resGuard1.work();

    {
        Device resGuard2{"DEVICE 2"};
        resGuard2.work();
    }
    resGuard1.work();

}
```

Initialize the resource in the constructor and release it in the destructor. First, you cannot forget to initialize the object, and second, the compiler takes care of releasing the resource. The output of both programs is equivalent (see Figure 18.2).

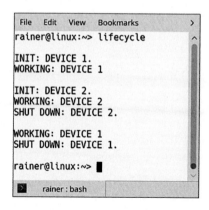

Figure 18.2. *Automatic managing of a device*

NR.7   Don't make all data members `protected`

Protected data makes your program complex and error prone. If you put protected data into a base class, you cannot reason about derived classes in isolation and, therefore, you break encapsulation. You always have to reason about the entire class hierarchy.

Protected data means you have to answer at least these three questions.

1. Do I have to implement a constructor in a derived class to initialize the protected data?

2. What is the actual value of the protected data if I use it?

3. Who is affected if I modify the protected data?

Answering these questions becomes more and more complicated the deeper your class hierarchy becomes.

Protected data is a kind of global data within the scope of the class hierarchy. And you know mutable, shared state is terrible. It makes testing and concurrency quite tricky, for example.

Chapter 19

Profiles

First of all: What is a profile according to the C++ Core Guidelines? Here is their definition: "A 'profile' is a set of deterministic and portably enforceable subset rules (i.e., restrictions) that are designed to achieve a specific guarantee."

Two terms in this definition are particularly interesting:

- **Deterministic:** The profiles require only local analysis that can be implemented by a compiler.

- **Portably enforceable:** Different tools on different platforms give you the same answer.

There are two main reasons for the profiles:

1. You have to deal with legacy code, and you cannot apply all rules of the C++ Core Guidelines in one step. You have to apply the rules step by step and, therefore, use some rules first and some rules later.

2. Some related rules may be more important to your code base than others. They aim for a specific goal such as the "avoidance of bounds errors" or the "correct usage of types." These related rules are called profiles.

The C++ Core Guidelines provide profiles for type safety, bounds safety, and lifetime safety, which can be automatically checked. Read more details about automatic checks in Appendix A, Enforcing the C++ Core Guidelines.

The following sections give a concise overview of the three profiles.

Pro.typeType safety

- **Type safety:** Use the types correctly, and therefore, avoid unsafe casts and unions.

  Type safety consists of eight rules, which are prefixed by type. The rules start with "Don't," "Always," or "Avoid" and refer to existing rules.

- Type.1: Avoid casts

  - Don't use `reinterpret_cast`: ES.48: Avoid casts and ES.49: If you must use a cast, use a named cast

  - Don't use `static_cast` for arithmetic types: ES.48: Avoid casts and ES.49: If you must use a cast, use a named cast

  - Don't cast between pointer types where the source type and the target type are the same: ES.48: Avoid casts

  - Don't cast between pointer types when the conversion could be implicit: ES.48: Avoid casts

- Type.2: Don't use `static_cast` to downcast: C.146: Use `dynamic_cast` where class hierarchy navigation is unavoidable

- Type.3: Don't use `const_cast` to cast away `const`: ES.50: Don't cast away const

- Type.4: Don't use C-style `(T)expression` or functional `T(expression)` casts: ES.34: Prefer the {}-initializer syntax and ES.49: If you must use a cast, use a named cast

- Type.5: Don't use a variable before it has been initialized: ES.20: Always initialize an object

- Type.6: Always initialize a member variable: ES.20: Always initialize an object, C.43: Ensure that a copyable (value type) class has a default constructor, and C.45: Don't define a default constructor that only initializes data members; use member initializers instead

- Type.7: Avoid naked union: C.181: Avoid "naked" unions

- Type.8: Avoid `va_args`: F.55: Don't use va_arg arguments

Pro.boundsBounds safety

- **Bounds safety**: Operate inside the bounds of allocated memory.

  The two enemies for bounds safety are pointer arithmetic and array indexing. Additionally, when you use a pointer, it should only address a single object but not an array. To make the profile bounds safety complete, you should combine it with the rules to type safety and lifetime safety.

Bounds safety consists of four rules:

- Bounds.1: Don't use pointer arithmetic: I.13: Do not pass an array as a single pointer and ES.42: Keep use of pointers simple and straightforward

- Bounds.2: Only index into arrays using constant expressions: I.13: Do not pass an array as a single pointer and ES.42: Keep use of pointers simple and straightforward

- Bounds.3: No array-to-pointer decay: I.13: Do not pass an array as a single pointer and ES.42: Keep use of pointers simple and straightforward

- Bounds.4: Don't use standard-library functions and types that are not bounds-checked: SL.con.3: Avoid bounds error

Pro.lifetimeLifetime safety

- **Lifetime safety:** Dereference only a valid pointer.

  A pointer is invalid if, for example, the pointer is uninitialized, is a `std::nullptr`, points outside the range of an array, or points to a deleted object. The profile lifetime safety consists of one rule:

- Lifetime.1: Don't dereference a possibly invalid pointer: ES.65: Don't dereference an invalid pointer

Chapter 20

Guidelines Support Library

The Guidelines Support Library (GSL) is a small library for supporting the rules of the C++ Core Guidelines. The GSL consists of components such as views, ownership pointers, assertions, utilities, and concepts.

The best-known implementation of the GSL is the one from Microsoft, hosted at GitHub: Microsoft/GSL (https://github.com/Microsoft/GSL). The Microsoft version requires C++14 support and runs on various platforms. But that is not all; more implementations are available on GitHub. I want to explicitly emphasize the GSL-lite implementation of Martin Moene. His implementation even works with C++98 and C++03.

This section does not present the GSL in detail but provides a first introduction. For your further investigation, use the concrete implementations such as Microsoft/GSL or GSL-lite.

The GSL consists of five components. I ignore the GSL concepts in this overview because they are already part of C++20. Appendix B, Concepts, gives you an introduction to concepts.

Views

A view is never an owner. In the case of a `gsl::span<T>`, it represents a nonowning range of continuous memory. This nonowning range can be an array, a pointer with a size, or a `std::vector`. The same applies to `gsl::string_span<T>` or zero-terminated C-strings: `gsl::czstring` or `gsl::wzstring`. The main reason for having a `gsl::span<T>` is to prevent a situation where a plain array is decayed to a pointer if passed to a function; therefore, the size information would be lost.

gsl::span<T> automatically deduces the size of the plain array or the std::vector. If you use a pointer, you have to provide the size.

```
template <typename T>
void copy_n(const T* p, T* q, int n){}

template <typename T>
void copy(gsl::span<const T> src, gsl::span<T> des){}

int main(){

    int arr1[] = {1, 2, 3};
    int arr2[] = {3, 4, 5};

    copy_n(arr1, arr2, 3);       // (1)
    copy(arr1, arr2);            // (2)

}
```

In contrast to the function copy_n (1), you do not have to provide the number of elements for the function copy (2). Hence, a common cause of errors is gone with gsl::span<T>. gsl::span<T> is similar to std::span<T>, which is part of C++20.

Ownership pointers

The GSL has various kinds of owners.

I assume that you know about std::unique_ptr and std::shared_ptr, and therefore, you know gsl::unique_ptr and gsl::shared_ptr. You may be wondering whether the GSL has its own smart pointers, because the C++11 standard has std::unique_ptr and std::shared_ptr. The answer is straightforward: You can use the GSL with a compiler that does not support C++11.

gsl::owner<T*> is a pointer that has ownership of the referenced object. You should use gsl::owner<T> if you cannot use resource handles such as smart pointers or containers. The crucial point is that you have to free the resource explicitly. Raw pointers that are not marked as gsl::owner<T*> are considered nonowning in the C++ Core Guidelines (see "R.3: A raw pointer (a T*) is non-owning" and "R.4: A raw reference (a T&) is non-owning"). Consequently, you don't have to free the resource.

gsl::dyn_array<T> and gsl::stack_array<T> are two new array types.

- **gsl::dyn_array<T>** is a heap-allocated array with a fixed number of elements that is specified at run time.

- **gsl::stack_array<T>** is a stack-allocated array with a fixed number of elements that is specified at run time.

Assertions

Thanks to `Expects()` and `Ensures()`, you can state preconditions and postconditions for your functions. Currently, you have to place them in the function body, but these will be moved in upcoming implementations to the function declaration. Both functions are part of contracts. Appendix C, Contracts, provides more details about contracts.

Here is an example using `Expects()` and `Ensures()` from the GSL.

```
int area(int height, int width) {
    Expects(height > 0);
    auto res = height * width;
    Ensures(res > 0);
    return res;
}
```

When the function invocation breaks the precondition `Expects(height > 0)` or the postcondition (`Ensures(res >0)`, the program terminates.

Utilities

`gsl::narrow_cast<T>` and `gsl::narrow` are two new casts.

- **gsl::narrow_cast<T>** is a `static_cast<T>` that expresses only its intent. A narrowing conversion may happen.

- **gsl::narrow** is a `static_cast<T>` that throws a narrowing_error exception if `static_cast<T>(x) != x`.

`gsl::not_null<T*>` models a pointer that never should be a null pointer. If you set a `gsl::not_null<T*>` pointer to a null pointer, you get a compiler error. You can even put a smart pointer such as `std::unique_ptr` or `std::shared_ptr` into a gsl::not_null<T*>. There is one main difference between gsl::not_null<T*> and a reference: You can rebind a gsl::not_null<T*> object but not a reference.

Typically, you use gsl::not_null<T*> for function parameters and their return type. Consequently, you do have to check to see if the pointer is a null pointer.

```
// p cannot be a null pointer
int getLength(gsl::not_null<const char*> p);

// p can be a null pointer
int getLength(const char* p);
```

finally allows you to register a callable that runs at the end of the scope.

```
void f(int n) {
    void* p = malloc(1, n);
    auto _ = finally([p] { free(p); });
    ...
} // the lambda is invoked
```

At the end of the function f, the lambda function [p] { free(p); } is invoked automatically.

According to the C++ Core Guidelines, you should consider finally as a last resort if you cannot use proper resource management such as smart pointers or STL containers.

PART III

Appendixes

Appendix A

Enforcing the C++ Core Guidelines

You can check to see if you are breaking the rules of the C++ Core Guidelines.

Let's start with a program that breaks type safety, bounds safety, and lifetime safety.

```cpp
1   // gslCheck.cpp
2
3   #include <iostream>
4
5   void f(int* p, int count) {
6   }
7
8   void f2(int* p) {
9       int x = *p;
10  }
11
12  int main() {
13
14      // Break of type safety
15      // use of a c-cast
16      double d = 2;
17      auto p = (long*)&d;
18      auto q = (long long*)&d;
19
20      // Break of bounds safety
21      // array-to-pointer decay
22      int myArray[100];
23      f(myArray, 100);
```

```
24
25      // Break of lifetime safety
26      // a is not valid
27      int* a = new int;
28      delete a;
29      f2(a);
30
31  }
```

The comments in the source code document the issues. Let me check the program with Visual Studio and clang-tidy.

Visual Studio

These are the steps to detect the issues with the program gslCheck.cpp.

1. Enable code analysis on build.

   You have to enable the checkbox. Per default, type-safety, bounds-safety, and lifetime-safety rules are not part of the Microsoft Native Recommended Rules. See Figure A.1.

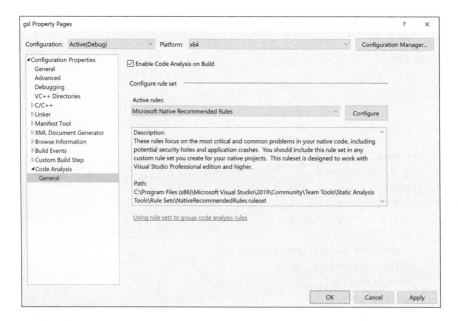

Figure A.1 *Enable code analysis*

2. Configure the active rules.

As you can see in Figure A.2, I create rule set CheckProfiles, which consists of the rules C++ Core Guidelines Bounds Rules, C++ Core Guidelines Type Rules, and C++ Core Guidelines Lifetime Rules.

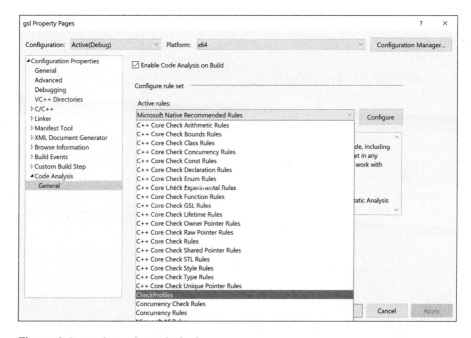

Figure A.2 *Configure the applied rules*

3. Run code analysis.

Applying the set of rules on the code example is quite promising. See Figure A.3.

```
1>gslCheck.cpp
1>gsl.vcxproj -> C:\Users\raine\source\repos\gsl\x64\Debug\gslCheck.exe
C:\Users\raine\source\repos\gsl\gsl\gslCheck.cpp(17): warning C26493: Don't use C-style casts (type.4).
C:\Users\raine\source\repos\gsl\gsl\gslCheck.cpp(18): warning C26493: Don't use C-style casts (type.4).
C:\Users\raine\source\repos\gsl\gsl\gslCheck.cpp(29): warning C26486: Don't pass a pointer that may be invalid to a function. Parameter 0 'a' in call to 'f2' may be invalid (lifetime.3).
C:\Users\raine\source\repos\gsl\gsl\gslCheck.cpp(23): warning C26485: Expression 'myArray': No array to pointer decay (bounds.3).
1>Done building project "gsl.vcxproj".
========== Rebuild All: 1 succeeded, 0 failed, 0 skipped ==========
```

Figure A.3 *Automatic managing of a device*

All issues are found. For each issue such as the first one, I get the line number (17) and the rule of the affected profile (Type.4).

4. Suppress warnings.

Sometimes you want to suppress specific warnings. You can achieve this with attributes. My next example, gslCheckSuppress.cpp, applies an array-to-pointer decay twice. Only the second call should give a warning.

```cpp
// gslCheckSuppress.cpp; C++20 with MSVC

#include <iostream>

void f(int* p, int count) {
}

int main() {

    int myArray[100];

    // Break of bounds safety
    [[gsl::suppress(bounds.3)]] {   // suppress warning
        f(myArray, 100);
    }

    f(myArray, 100);                // warning

}
```

The attribute gsl::suppress(bounds.3) behaves as expected. It's only valid in its scope. The second violation of bounds safety is displayed. See Figure A.4.

```
1>gslCheckSuppress.cpp
1>gsl.vcxproj -> C:\Users\raine\source\repos\gsl\x64\Debug\gslCheckSuppress.exe
C:\Users\raine\source\repos\gsl\gsl\gslCheckSuppress.cpp(17): warning C26485: Expression 'myArray': No array to pointer decay (bounds.3).
1>Done building project "gsl.vcxproj".
========== Build: 1 succeeded, 0 failed, 0 up-to-date, 0 skipped ==========
```

Figure A.4 *Suppress warnings*

clang-tidy

clang-tidy is a clang-based C++ "linter" tool. Its purpose is to provide an extensible framework for diagnosing and fixing typical programming errors, like style violations, interface misuse, or bugs that can be deduced via static analysis. clang-tidy is modular and provides a convenient interface for writing new checks—Extra Clang Tools 11 documentation (https://clang.llvm.org/extra/clang-tidy/).

clang-tidy supports more than 200 rules. About twenty of them are dedicated to the C++ Core Guidelines. Here are the steps to detect the issues with the program `gslCheck.cpp`.

1. Apply the C++ Core Guidelines checks.

   The command line

   ```
   clang-tidy –checks=-*,cppcoreguidelines-* gslCheck.cpp
   ```

   checks the C++ Core Guidelines exclusively (see Figure A.5). The option -checks expects comma-separated values of glob patterns and means the following in this case:

   - -*: Disable the default checks of clang-tidy.
   - **cppcoreguidelines-*:** Enable the C++ Core Guidelines checks.

   These checks detected only the type-safety issues in the program `gslCheck.cpp`.

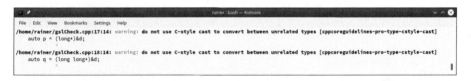

Figure A.5 *Check the C++ Core Guidelines exclusively*

2. Apply the clang-tidy checks and the C++ Core Guidelines checks.

   The slightly simplified command line

   ```
   clang-tidy –checks=cppcoreguidelines-* gslCheck.cpp
   ```

   also applies the clang-tidy checks (see Figure A.6). Now, the lifetime-safety issue is detected.

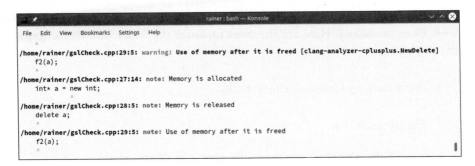

Figure A.6 *Check the C++ Core Guidelines with clang-tidy*

In contrast to Visual Studio, I could not detect the boundary-safety issue with clang-tidy.

Appendix B

Concepts

The C++20 feature "concepts" (also known as "named requirements") allows you to express the template parameter requirements as part of the interface. Before I dive deeper, here is the first example:

```
template<typename Cont>
    requires Sortable<Cont>   // Sortable is a user-defined concept
void sort(Cont& container);

template<typename Cont>
void sort(Cont& container) requires Sortable<Cont>;  // Trailing
                                                     // requires clause

template<Sortable Cont>        // Constrained template parameters
void sort(Cont& container);
```

The first version of the generic function sort requires that its argument supports the concept Sortable. The second and the third variants of the function sort are semantically identical. The second version uses the so-called trailing requires clause and just constrained the template parameter to the concept Sortable.

I assume you want to know the following: What are the benefits of concepts?

- Express the template parameter requirements as part of the interface.
- Support the overloading of functions and the specialization of class templates.
- Produce drastically improved error messages by comparing the requirements of the template parameter with the template arguments.

Essentially, you can use concepts in any template context. Besides the obvious use cases of class templates, function templates, and non-template members of class templates, you can use them for variadic templates. Variadic templates are templates that can accept an arbitrary number of arguments.

```
template<Arithmetic... Args>
bool all(Args... args) { return (... && args); }                // (1)

...

std::cout << all(true);                 // true                  // (2)
std::cout << all(5, true, 5.5, false);  // false                 // (3)
```

The function template `all` requires that the arguments are `Arithmetic`. `Arithmetic` means they have to be integrals or floating-point numbers. The *fold expression* (1) applies the logical AND operator to all arguments. In (2) and (3), the function is used. You can also overload on concepts, specialize templates with concepts, or use more than one concept. The following function template requires that the container is a `SequenceContainer` and that the elements of the container are `EqualityComparable`.

```
template <SequenceContainer S,
          EqualityComparable<value_type<S>> T>
Iterator_type<S> find(S&& seq, const T& val) {
    ...
}
```

With concepts, the usage of type deduction with `auto` and concepts is unified. `auto` is just an unconstrained placeholder, and a concept is a constrained placeholder. The rule to keep in mind is simple: Whenever you can use an unconstrained placeholder (auto) with C++11, you can use a constrained placeholder (concept) with C++20.

```
Integral auto getIntegral(int val) {                            // (1)
    return val;
}

...

std::vector<int> vec{1, 2, 3, 4, 5};
for (Integral auto i: vec) std::cout << i << " ";               // (2)
```

```
Integral auto b = true;                              // (3)

Integral auto integ = getIntegral(10);               // (4)
```

The code snippet shows a few usages of the concept `Integral`. Instead of the `auto` keyword, I use `Integral auto` for the return type of the function `getIntegral` (1), for the range-based for loop (2), for taking a `bool` value (3), and for taking an `int` value (4).

With concepts, C++20 supports a new and very convenient way to define function templates. Using a concept (constrained placeholder) or `auto` (unconstrained placeholder) in the function signature or as the return type creates a function template.

```
Integral auto gcd(Integral auto a, Integral auto b) {
    if( b == 0 ) return a;
    else return gcd(b, a % b);
}


auto gcd2(auto a, auto b) {
    if( b == 0 ) return a;
    else return gcd(b, a % b);
}
```

The function template `gcd` requires that each argument and the return type support the concept `Integral`. In contrast, the function template `gcd2` puts no requirements on its arguments.

Of course, you can define your own concepts. Most of the time it is not necessary to define your concepts because many *named requirements* are already available with C++20. This holds true for the following two concepts in particular: `Integral` and `Equal`. I defined them only for comprehensibility.

```
template<typename T>
concept Integral = std::is_integral<T>::value;

template<typename T>
concept Equal =
requires(T a, T b) {
    { a == b } -> std::convertible_to<bool>;
    { a != b } -> std::convertible_to<bool>;
};
```

The concept `Integral` requires that the call `std::is_integral<T>::value;` return true. `std::is_integral` is a function from the *type-traits* library, which evaluates its argument at compile time. The definition of the concept of `Equal` is more verbose. Both arguments must have the same type `T`, the type `T>` has to support the operators `==` and `!=`, and both operators have to return a `bool`.

Detailed information on concepts is available at https://en.cppreference.com/w/cpp/language/constraints. Additionally, you can read my blog post on www.ModernesCpp.com.

Appendix C

Contracts

First of all: What is a contract? A contract specifies, in a precise and checkable way, interfaces for software components. These software components are typically functions and member functions that have to fulfill preconditions, postconditions, and invariants. We may get contracts with C++23.

By default, a violation of a contract terminates the program.

Here are the simplified definitions from the C++ *proposal P0380r1*.

Preconditions, postconditions, and invariants

precondition A precondition is a predicate that is supposed to hold upon entry in a function.

postcondition A postcondition is a predicate that is supposed to hold upon exit from the function.

invariant An invariant is a predicate that is supposed to hold at its point in the computation.

The precondition and the postcondition are placed outside the function definition in C++, but the invariant is placed inside the function definition. A predicate is a function that returns a boolean.

The following code snippet applies all three types of conditions:

```
int push(queue& q, int val)
  [[ expects: !q.full() ]]
  [[ ensures: !q.empty() ]] {
  ...
  [[assert: q.is_ok() ]]
  ...
}
```

The attribute expects is a precondition, the attribute ensures is a postcondition, and the attribute assert is an invariant. The contract for the function push is that the queue is not full before adding an element, the queue is not empty after adding an element, and the queue is in a valid state: q.is_ok(). Preconditions and postconditions are part of the function interface. This means they can access only parameters of the function or public members of a class. In contrast, assertions are part of the implementation and can, therefore, access local members of a function of private or protected members of a class.

```
class X {
 public:
    void f(int n)
        [[ expects: n < m ]] { // error; m is private
        [[ assert: n < m ]];  // OK
        // ...
    }
 private:
    int m;
};
```

The variable m is private and cannot, therefore, be part of a precondition.

For the ensures attribute, there is an additional identifier available. The identifier lets you refer to the return value of the function.

```
int mul(int x, int y)
    [[expects: x > 0]]
    [[expects: y > 0]]
    [[ensures res: res > 0]] {
    return x * y;
}
```

The name res as the identifier is, in this case, an arbitrary name. As shown in the example, you can use more contracts of the same kind.

Until we get contracts, perhaps with C++23, you can use assertions from the Guidelines Support Library as a replacement for contracts.

Index

Symbols

( ) (parentheses), 187
{} (curly braces), 144, 166

A

ABI (application binary interface), 23–24
Abrahams, David, 280
abstract class, 101, 102
abstraction, 167, 302–304
access
    memory, 225–229
    nonexisting element of a std::string, 404
    objects, 114–117
    sequence containers, 229
accounts, comparing, 326
accumulate algorithm, 166
acquire-release semantics, singletons, 218
ADL (argument-dependent lookup), 126, 314, 315–316
algorithms, 8
    Euclidean, 223
    expressing, 304
    function objects, 305–307
    gcd, 223–225
    generic programming, 301, 302. *See also* generic programming
    parallel, 266
    preference over raw loops, 201
    std::accumulate, 166
    std::transform_exclusive_scan, 269
    STL (Standard Template Library), 12, 266
aliases
    defining, 311
    smart pointers, 162–164
    templates, 310, 311
ALL_CAPS, 134, 170–171
allocation
    memory, 147, 246
    resource management, 145–150

analysis, enabling code, 448
annotated graphs, 243
anonymous unions, 128–129
application binary interface. *See* ABI (application binary interface)
architecture, 423–425
    code stability, 423
    cycles among libraries, 425
    expressing reusable parts as libraries, 424–425
argument-dependent lookup. *See* ADL (argument-dependent lookup)
arguments
    binary callables, 21, 22
    defaults, 49, 113–114
    functions, 359
    metafunctions, 343
    order of evaluation, 195–196
    Regular type/SemiRegular type, 313–314
    template argument deduction, 313
    templates, 359
    va_arg, 49–52
arithmetic
    errors, 208–210
    rules, 204
    signed/unsigned integers, 204–208
array, 401–403
arrays, deleting, 194
artificial scope, 144
assembler instructions, 30
assertions, 443
assignments
    classes, 59–60, 78–80
    copy-assignment operator, 221, 222
    pointers, 117
auto, applying, 171–172
automatic management of devices, 435, 449
automatic memory management, 398. *See also* memory
automatic type deduction, 179
availability of source code, 376–377